The Political Economy of Oil-Exporting Countries

1. *Venezuela*
    Juan Carlos Boué

2. *Nigeria*
    Sarah Ahmad Khan

Nigeria
The Political Economy of Oil

Sarah Ahmad Khan

Published by the Oxford University Press
for the Oxford Institute for Energy Studies
1994

HD
9577
.N52
A334
1994

Oxford University Press, Walton Street, Oxford OX2 6DP
Oxford New York
Athens Auckland Bangkok Bombay
Calcutta Cape Town Dar es Salaam Delhi
Florence Hong Kong Istanbul Karachi
Kuala Lumpur Madras Madrid Melbourne
Mexico City Nairobi Paris Singapore
Taipei Tokyo Toronto
and associated companies in Berlin Ibadan

Oxford is a trade mark of Oxford University Press

© Oxford Institute for Energy Studies
1994

British Library Cataloguing in Publication Data
available

ISBN 0-19-730014-6

Cover design by Moss, Davies, Dandy, Turner Ltd.
Typeset by Philip Armstrong
Printed by Bookcraft, Avon

The Political Economy of Oil-Exporting Countries

Nigeria: The Political Economy of Oil is the second in a series of books on the major petroleum exporting nations, most of them part of the developing world. These countries occupy a central position in the global economy given that oil is the energy source most used in the world and the most important primary commodity in international trade. At the same time they find themselves inescapably dependent on a single source of income. Their own economic prospects are closely bound to the future of their oil.

Books in this series incorporate research work done at the Oxford Institute for Energy Studies. Their aim is to provide a broad description of the oil and gas sectors of the country concerned, highlighting those features which give each country a physiognomy of its own. The analysis is set in the context of history, economic policy and international relations. It also seeks to identify the specific challenges that the exporting country studies will face in developing its wealth to the best advantage of the economy.

CONTENTS

Abbreviations   xii

Maps   xiii

1   INTRODUCTION   1

2   THE POLITICAL AND INSTITUTIONAL
ENVIRONMENT   5
Politics and the Nigerian Oil Industry   5
The Legal Framework   15
Oil-Producing Companies and the Evolution of
the Concession Pattern   19
NNPC – Structure and Place in the Nigerian
Oil Industry   22
Nigeria and OPEC   28

3   THE NIGERIAN UPSTREAM SECTOR   39
Producing Areas and Oilfields   39
Reserves   40
Exploration and Development   43
Crude Oil Production   49
Types of Crude Oil   56
Appendix   60

4   NIGERIAN CONCESSIONS AND EQUITY
PRODUCERS   67
Oil Company Participation   67
Joint Ventures   68
Production-Sharing Contracts   74
Risk-Service Contracts   79
The Fiscal Regime   79
Production Costs   85
Producing Companies and Investment Plans   86
Problems of and Prospects for
Government–Oil Company Relations   92

5   THE INTERNATIONAL TRADE AND
     PRICING OF NIGERIAN CRUDES   101
     Introduction   101
     Nigerian Pricing Policies   101
     Price Formulae   109
     The Marketing of Nigerian Crude Oil   112
     International Trade in Nigerian Crude Oil   117
     Crude Oil Loading Terminals and Storage Facilities 121

6   THE NIGERIAN DOWNSTREAM   127
     Domestic Product Pricing   127
     The Domestic Supply and Demand Imbalance
     in Refined Products   130
     Nigerian Domestic Refineries   136
     The Distribution and Storage of Petroleum Products 143
     The Nigerian Petrochemicals Industry   147
     Outlook for the Nigerian Downstream Sector   149

7   THE NIGERIAN NATURAL GAS INDUSTRY   157
     Natural Gas Reserves, Exploration and Production   157
     Gas Flaring   159
     Domestic Gas Use and Supply Systems   164
     New Projects   167
     LNG Projects: Past and Present   169
     Issues and Future Prospects in Natural Gas Utilization 176

8   OIL AND THE ECONOMY   183
     Introduction   183
     Oil Revenues and Government Expenditure   185
     The Agriculture Sector   186
     The Introduction of the Structural Adjustment
     Programme (SAP)   189
     Nigerian External Accounts   193
     Policy Failure and the Lack of Public Accountability 195

9   CONCLUSION   201

     APPENDICES   209

     BIBLIOGRAPHY   225

     INDEX   231

TABLES

2.1 Nigerian Governments. 1960-93.

2.2 Oil Companies holding Nigerian Concessions in 1969, 1986 and 1993.

2.3 NNPC Subsidiaries.

3.1 Principal Oil Fields of Nigeria as of 31 December, 1990.

3.2 Nigerian Historical Oil Reserve Data and Reserves/Production Ratios. Billion Barrels of Oil and Remaining Years of Production at then Current Levels.

3.3 Historical Data on Wells Completed. 1962–92.

3.4 Nigerian Crude Oil Production, Historical Series. 1958–92. Thousand Barrels Daily.

3.5 Yield Structure of Nigerian Crude. Per Cent

3.6 Crude Oil Production, Refinery Allocation and Export by Type of Crude. February 1992. Barrels per Day.

A3.1 Crude Oil Pipelines in Nigeria, Current Status.

4.1 Evolution of Government Participation in the Nigerian Oil Industry.

4.2 Nigerian Crude Oil Producing Ventures as of 1992. Barrels per Day.

4.3 Comparison of Key Economic Parameters in Nigerian Production-Sharing Agreements.

4.4 Changes in the Pricing of Equity Crude Oil since 1982. Dollars per Barrel.

4.5 Crude Oil Production in Nigeria by Producing Venture. 1966–91. Thousand Barrels per Day.

5.1 Counter Trade Agreements Signed Between September 1984 and June 1985.

5.2 Nigerian Formula Pricing.

5.3 Equity Entitlement of Nigerian Joint Venture Producers. Average Barrels per Day. 1989–91.

5.4 Term Customers of NNPC Crude Oil and Destinations. Average Barrels/Day. 1991–4.

5.5 Share of Total Reported Trade of Nigerian Crude by Type of Crude. 1986–91. Per Cent.

5.6   Share of Total Reported Traded Deals by Seller.
      1986–91. Per Cent and Total Deals/Cargoes.
5.7   Share of Total Crude Oil Exports by Stream.
      1980–86, 1989. Per Cent.
5.8   Nigerian Crude Oil Exports by Destination.
      1980–85, 1987, 1989–92.
5.9   Distribution of Nigerian Crude Oil Exports
      to the USA in 1990 by Average API Gravity.
5.10 Crude Oil Loading Terminals in Nigeria.
6.1   Comparative Domestic Petroleum Product Prices
      in Exporting Countries. 1993.
6.2   Structure and Capacity of Nigerian Refineries.
      At 1 January, 1993. Barrels per Calendar Day.
6.3   Refining Operations of Nigerian Refineries in 1990.
6.4   Product Pipelines in Nigeria. Year end – 1992.
6.5   Share of Domestic Sales. By Company.
7.1   Historical Natural Gas Reserves.
      Billion Cubic Metres. 1971–92.
7.2   Main Gas Fields in Nigeria.
7.3   Production and Utilization of Natural Gas in
      Nigeria. Million Cubic Metres per Year. 1963–92.
7.4   Current Gas Supply Systems.
7.5   Proposed Gas Supply Systems.
7.6   LNG Sales Contracts.
8.1   Oil Export Revenues and as Share of
      Total Export Receipts. Various Years 1970–92.
      Million Dollars and Per Cent.
8.2   Projected and Actual Sectoral Allocation
      of Capital Expenditure 1975–80.
8.3   Historical Data on National Accounts. 1980,
      1985–92. Current Billion Naira and/or
      Dollars and Per Cent.
8.4   Nigerian Federal Budget. 1985–89. Per Cent.
8.5   Historical Balance of Payments Data.
      Million Dollars. 1980, 1985–91.
8.6   Historical Series of External Debt Statistics.
      1980, 1985–91. Billion Dollars and Per Cent.

FIGURES

2.1 Nigerian Crude Oil Production: Historical Series. Thousand Barrels per Day. 1958–92.

2.2 Organizational Structure of the Nigerian National Petroleum Corporation.

3.1 Historical Spot Prices of Nigerian Bonny Light. 1967–92. US Dollars per Barrel.

5.1 Forcardos–Brent Price Differentials.

6.1 Nigerian Production and Consumption of Refined Products. Thousand Barrels per Day. 1971–91.

6.2 Nigerian Production and Consumption of Gasoline. Thousand Barrels per Day. 1971–91.

6.3 Nigerian Production and Consumption of Kerosene. Thousand Barrels per Day. 1971–91.

6.4 Nigerian Production and Consumption of Gas Oil. Thousand Barrels per Day. 1971–91.

6.5 Nigerian Production and Consumption of Residual Fuels. Thousand Barrels per Day. 1971–91.

7.1 Associated and Non-Associated Gas Production and Utilization in Nigeria.

ABBREVIATIONS

APPA	African Petroleum Producers' Association
b	barrel
bcf	billion cubic feet
b/d	barrels per day
BNOC	British National Oil Corporation
Btu	British Thermal Unit
ECN	Electricity Corporation of Nigeria
ELP	Escravos–Lagos pipeline
ENDC	Eastern Nigeria Development Corporation
mb	million barrels
mb/d	million barrels per day
mcf	million cubic feet
MOU	Memorandum of Understanding
MTBE	Methyl-Tertiary-Buteylether
NAFCON	National Fertilizer Corporation of Nigeria
NAOC	Nigerian Agip Oil Company
NAPIMS	National Petroleum Investment Management Services
NEPA	Nigerian Electric Power Authority
NGC	National Gas Corporation
NNOC	Nigerian National Oil Corporation
NNPC	Nigerian National Petroleum Corporation
NPDC	Nigerian Petroleum Development Company
OEL	Oil exploration licence
OML	Oil mining lease
OPL	Oil prospecting licence
OSP	official selling price
PPT	Petroleum Profits Tax
PSC	production-sharing contract
RSC	risk-service contract
tcf	trillion cubic feet

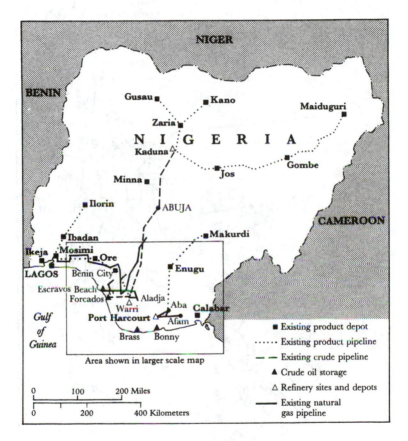

NIGER

BENIN

NIGERIA

Gusau •   • Kano

Maiduguri •

Zaria •

Kaduna △

Minna •

Jos •

Gombe •

Ilorin •

ABUJA

CAMEROON

Ibadan •

Makurdi •

Ikeja • Mosimi

LAGOS   Benin City

Ore •

Enugu •

Escravos Beach

Forcados △ Aladja △

Warri

Aba

Calabar •

Gulf

Port Harcourt △

Afam ▲

of

Brass ▲ Bonny ▲

Guinea

Area shown in larger scale map

■ Existing product depot

•••••• Existing product pipeline

— — Existing crude pipeline

▲ Crude oil storage

△ Refinery sites and depots

—— Existing natural
gas pipeline

0   100   200 Miles

0   200   400 Kilometers

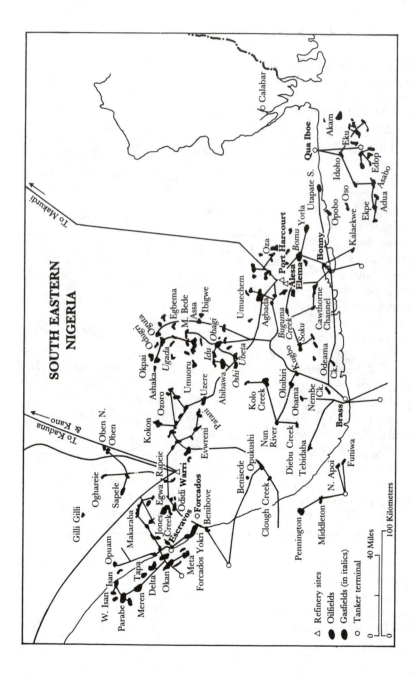

1 INTRODUCTION

Nigeria is the largest petroleum producer in Africa and the largest producer of sweet (almost sulphur free) crude oil among OPEC member countries. In addition, it is the most populated nation of the African continent, and its size together with its oil and gas wealth provides it with both political and economic clout.

The geographical location of the country provides it with substantial advantages. Situated in the Atlantic Basin, it is closer than the main Middle Eastern oil producers to two of the world's three largest markets for crude and petroleum products – Western Europe and the USA.[1] The advantages of location and the quality of Nigerian crudes usually yield price premia. Since Nigeria is at some distance from the Middle East, both geographically and politically, the wars and conflicts of this troubled region which have caused oil supply disruptions in the past decades have had no impact on its production. This was brought home most recently during the 1990 Gulf crisis when there were no political constraints on Nigerian oil production. The only limits to increased oil output were set by technical factors.

Consequently, Nigeria has played a critical role in the international petroleum market on more than one occasion. In the early 1980s, for instance, it found itself subjected to two powerful forces pulling in opposite directions: the market forces operating in the Atlantic Basin where the supply of sweet, light crudes was increasing rapidly in the North Sea, and those of the OPEC price administration system in which Nigeria participated. It was therefore on the boundary which separated two competing pricing systems, in the difficult interface between the rigid oil order prevailing in the Gulf and the dynamic emerging markets of North West Europe and the Eastern seaboard of North America.

For all these reasons, the study of Nigeria is relevant to the understanding of important aspects of the world petroleum market.

There are, however, two other sets of reasons which make the political economy of Nigerian oil a subject of interest. The first relates to foreign investment. As we shall see later in the study, one of the features that places Nigeria apart from most other OPEC oil producers is the presence of foreign oil companies

1

throughout the country's oil history. The dependence on foreign companies is to be found in all sectors of the oil industry but is most apparent, and indeed significant, in the upstream. This raises a host of interesting questions on the pattern of fiscal incentives offered by the Nigerian government for exploration and production (E&P), the crude oil pricing system and the attitude of foreign companies to political risk. In this study, the analysis of all important aspects of the upstream oil sector uses the explanatory framework of incentives, pricing, and politics.

Secondly, oil is central to the development of Nigeria and constitutes the backbone of the economy. In the early 1990s, petroleum production accounted for 25 per cent of its GDP, oil exports accounted for over 95 per cent of its total export earnings, and about 75 per cent of total government revenue. Petroleum operations in fact provide the only immediate hope for the development of the rest of the economy. And while the oil industry invariably received much attention from successive Nigerian governments, and foreign oil companies received the necessary incentives to ensure their continued presence, the story of oil in Nigeria is one of missed opportunities, administrative disorganization, and resource mismanagement. The performance of the economy has been disappointing despite the successes achieved from time to time on the oil investments or production fronts. The country has entered the 1990s with a weak economy burdened with foreign debt and beset by structural, particularly balance of payments problems.

This book is organized as follows. Chapter 1 is the Introduction. Chapter 2 provides the reader with a broad overview of the Nigerian oil industry and of the political, legal, institutional and international context. The purpose is to establish a basic context in which details and particular problems of the industry, discussed in subsequent chapters, will find their place and relative significance.[2] Chapter 3 discusses the salient characteristics of the Nigerian upstream sector and analyses exploration and production requirements given the particularities of the oil reservoirs. Chapter 4 presents the framework of government and oil company relations in the upstream sector by looking at the different forms of foreign participation in the industry, and the range of fiscal incentives offered by the government to ensure continued foreign interest. Chapter 5 considers the international trade, marketing and pricing of Nigerian crudes. Specifically considered are the markets for the country's crude, its marketing policy *vis à vis* term and spot sales, and the efficiency of its formula pricing. Chapter 6 on the Nigerian downstream sector discusses the three main problems in domestic refining: a production slate mismatched to consumption trends, product subsidies, and widespread product smuggling. Chapter 7 considers the natural gas industry in the country, in particular the prospects for the much delayed LNG project and the implications of this delay on Nigeria's credibility as a future LNG supplier. Chapter 8 places the oil industry in the context of the entire economy and discusses the significance of certain oil industry projects, such as the petrochemicals programme, in expediting the recovery of the economy as well as providing the much needed link between the oil and the non-oil economy. Finally, Chapter 9 concludes the study and suggests possible future development issues in the Nigerian oil industry.

I would like to thank Bernard Mommer (André Bello Fellow, St Antony's College, Oxford), John Mitchell (Independent Adviser to the Oxford Institute for Energy Studies) and Samu'ila Danko Makama (Ministry of Petroleum, Nigeria) for their helpful comments.

Notes

1. The third market consists of the industrialized and industrializing Far Eastern countries.
2. Appendix 1 provides a detailed chronology of Nigeria since 1953, as well as some significant dates relating to the oil industry before the mid-1950s.

2 THE POLITICAL AND INSTITUTIONAL ENVIRONMENT

Introduction

This chapter describes and analyses features of the political and legal environment in which Nigeria's oil industry has developed in the past four or five decades. Although the aspects studied here are sometimes unconnected, they all provide essential background and put our story in context. There are five main sections. The first looks at the nature of political instability in Nigeria and discusses the impact of frequent political upheaval on the oil industry.[1] The second section describes the legal framework for operations. It includes a description of the various laws and decrees regulating exploration and production, the evolution of petroleum ordinances such as those relating to the Petroleum Profits Tax and the Royalty Tax, and to participation agreements. The third section discusses the evolution of the concession pattern for the individual oil companies and briefly surveys the status of these producing ventures. In the fourth section we consider the structure of the Nigerian National Petroleum Company (NNPC) and its place in the Nigerian oil industry. Finally, we consider Nigeria's membership of OPEC, the latter's influence on production and pricing policies, and the development of the country's strategic importance in matters of pricing, particularly in the Atlantic basin.

Politics and the Nigerian Oil Industry

(a) *Background.* The particular nature of political instability in Nigeria sets it apart from other oil-producing countries, specifically those in the Middle East. Despite the frequency of political change, foreign investors continue to stay in Nigeria, perhaps because upheavals have not been as dramatic as they were in Iraq and Iran. Apart from the Biafran crisis, no change in government has been severe enough to interrupt oil production and/or cause a war. Perhaps the most important aspect of political instability in Nigeria has been the apparent lack of authority of its governments.

5

The stage for weak central government was set historically as a result of federal–state rivalry and the precedence given to regional concerns.[2] Presently, the system is one in which the states are politically autonomous and yet increasingly financially dependent on the federal government. This results in fiscal irresponsibility within the states along with increasing competition between them for access to federal funds. Furthermore, despite the increasing financial and administrative centralization, sources of opposition have not been incorporated formally or officially into the state apparatus (Forrest, 1993, pp. 3, 51). Political authority at the federal level remains weak and fragmented precisely because the most common means of incorporating this 'opposition' is through state patronage.[3] There now exists a vicious circle linking the lack of effective governance to the presence of regional, ethnic and parochial interest groups, and the very presence of these special interests to the lack of effective central political authority. It is no longer clear, therefore, whether the present lack of vision in policy formulation and the mismanagement of policy implementation is a cause or a result of special interest groups and lobbies wielding significant amounts of influence in decision making.

The lack of political authority and stability in Nigeria has largely been a consequence of its diverse ethnic social make-up, as well as the nature of central government–state relations. The federal system and the central government have to contend with Africa's largest populated state, currently at over 120 million inhabitants, of varying regional and religious loyalties.[4] All the different interest groups attempt to translate regional power into federal power in order to meet the revenue and resource needs of their particular states and constituents; and each federal government tends to plan its economic strategies and policies around ethnic and regional concerns in order to retain its own constituency. Until the government of General Murtala Mohammad took over in July 1975, ethnic and regional antagonisms had a clear part to play in the various political upheavals and changes in government. Murtala Mohammad, in fact, attempted to strengthen the central Federal government and weaken the regional powers by increasing the number of states from twelve to nineteen, and by officially decreeing the move of the capital from Lagos to the more neutral Abuja, in the middle-belt. Even during the Babingida regime (1985–93), increasing the number of states was seen as the way to diffuse regional tribal tensions – two were added in 1987, and a further nine in 1991, bringing the total number to thirty states. The only real effect of such additions was an increase in the federal government's financial responsibilities. Since the time of the civilian government of Shagari (which ended in 1983), while corruption and economic mismanagement have been the main reasons cited for military takeovers, federal and state government tensions and therefore regional rivalries have seldom been far from the surface.

The scale of the diversity in Nigeria is apparent from the fact that there are over 250 ethnic groups. Of these, the three large ethno-linguistic groups are the Hausa–Fulani in the North, the Yoruba in the West, and the Ibo in the East. Making this distribution even more complex are the religious affiliations which may or may not cut across even ethnic loyalties. More than half the country's population professes to be Muslim, 35 per cent call themselves Christian and the remaining 10–15 per cent is thought to be animist. The northern population is largely Muslim, cutting across and/or integrating Hausa–Fulani and some Yoruba loyalties, while the southern population is largely Christian, mainly in the Ibo, and partially in the Yoruba areas (Nelson, 1982, pp. 75–80). Political and religious alliances across ethnic groups are also significant. While political issues have tended to make allies of the Hausa–Fulani and Yoruba, religious issues tend to make allies of the Yoruba and the inhabitants of the Middle-belt. At times of electoral politics, however, ethnic loyalties take precedence over any other (Forrest, 1993, p. 6).

The other potentially conflictual relationship, mentioned earlier, is that between the central government and the states. The constant tension between federal and state politics has given rise to what can only be described as the parochial and short-term objectives of each government. Strategies are mainly political and are planned around regional and ethnic issues rather than national economic and general welfare issues. Effective economic management, the productive use of resources, policy making and implementation have all been sacrificed and exposed to the political 'distributive concerns' of successive governments (Ibid., pp. 40, 69, 89).

On the one hand, therefore, there are ethno-religious loyalties as a result of which the various 'tribes' look after and reward their own. Clearly, there is considerable scope for the inequitable and inefficient 'allocation' of favours therein. On the other hand, there is the government, which must ensure that it remains in power. This demands that it looks after its 'own' as well as other strong interest groups, whether on the state or tribal level.[5] The very nature of social ties in Nigeria, therefore, allows for an extensive and complex web of and avenue for patronage.

Oil has proved to be both the most convenient and the easiest available of 'lubricants'. It is the most convenient, because oil revenues accrue directly to government coffers, in general to be disbursed at will. It is the most available because of the Nigerian economy's initial response to unexpected oil earnings. In Nigeria, the size of the windfall in the 1970s was very large, and the limited absorptive capacity of its infrastructure, i.e. the lack of investment institutions, allowed the country's 'consumer' identity to take over.[6] This was helped by the very nature of oil revenues, which did not require any taxation of incomes or of property, thereby reducing 'the economic and political significance of taxpayers,' and removing another set of political pressures which might have checked the uncontrolled increase in federal and or state expenditure (Forrest, 1993, pp. 68–9). What ensued was waste through large, inefficient show-piece projects, waste through federal disbursements to the states which in turn were irresponsibly handled, waste through mismanagement and through corruption. For every palm greased, for every contract awarded and kick-back received, there has been that much less in the federal government's finances.[7]

In a paradoxical sense, it may have been the very promise of actual or even future access to oil wealth which has, to a large extent, kept the various separatist, conflictual and destructive influences in Nigeria at bay. In other words, while the promise of the piece of the 'oil' pie keeps Nigeria together as a nation, the very nature of its distribution has destroyed the social, economic and political fabric within. Thirty years of oil money rewarding and encouraging the lack of efficiency and the lack of productivity has taken its toll on the Nigerian economy. It is a matter of debate whether, if oil had not been discovered, tribal rivalries would have broken the Nigerian nation apart; but it is incontestable that Nigeria in the 1990s is in more dire straits, economically and perhaps even politically, than the Nigeria of the years when oil was not the mainstay of the economy.

(b) Politics and Biafra. The one domestic political factor which had a negative impact on the oil industry was the Biafran civil war, which started in July 1967 and ended in January 1970. Not only was crude oil production affected, government–oil company relations were also put under a certain amount of pressure. Crude oil production fell to a low of 140,000 b/d in 1968, from 420,000 b/d in 1966 and 320,000 b/d in 1967 (see Figure 2.1), with Shell–BP and Safrap concerns being the most affected given their large presence in the Eastern region. Safrap stopped producing for the period of the war, and Shell–BP production decreased from 367,000 b/d in 1966 to 43,000 b/d in 1968. Gulf, with its mostly offshore concessions, not only continued to produce during the war, it even increased its production from 51,000 b/d in 1966 to 98,000 b/d in 1968 and 186,000 b/d in 1969.[8]

Ethnic, economic and political factors all contributed to the Biafran civil war. In January 1966, a military coup removed the

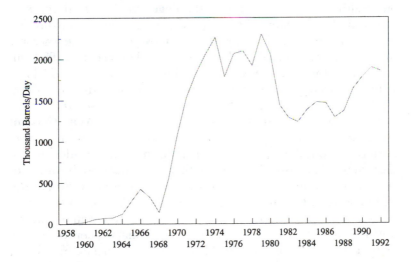

Source: BP Statistical Review of the World Oil Industry, various issues.

Figure 2.1: Nigerian Crude Oil Production: Historical Series. Thousand Barrels per Day. 1958–92.

civilian regime of Balewa. General Ironsi, who had not been involved in the coup, took over from the acting president of the federation. Soon after this, the coup began to assume a tribal and ethnic significance. There was an increasing perception that an Ibo conspiracy had been behind the coup – based on the fact that during the military takeover in January, mostly Northern and Western politicians had been killed, and that General Ironsi, himself, was an Ibo from the Eastern region. Massacres of Ibos living in the North followed, and by the summer the army was unable to control the riots. A counter coup in July 1966 brought a Christian Northerner, Colonel Gowon to power. Further killings of Ibos forced Colonel Ojukwu, the Governor of the Eastern region, to recall home Ibos resident elsewhere and declare that the Biafran people demanded the creation of a loose confederation in Nigeria. This was agreed to in the Aburi agreement negotiated in Ghana, but reneged on by Colonel Gowon on his return home from the negotiations. The renunciation of the agreement was related mainly to the issue of oil revenue distribution. The fear that the Eastern region would, in fact, benefit greatly from partial autonomy and therefore greater control over its substantial oil wealth, gave momentum to the degeneration of affairs into civil war. In February 1967, Ojukwu threatened to implement the Aburi agreement by himself if the Gowon regime did not do so by 31 March. In fact, on this date, instead of seceding, Ojukwu announced the Revenue Collection Edict No. 11 of 1967. This stated that as of 1 April, 1967, all revenues collected on behalf of the Federal government from the Eastern region would be paid to the treasury of the Eastern government. On 27 May, Gowon replaced the four states with twelve (including three states in the Eastern region alone), thus giving the non-Ibo minorities in the Eastern region a taste of autonomy that they would not be allowed in a Biafran state. Since most of the oil discovered in this region had been found in these minority non-Ibo areas, the possibility existed that some proportion of the oil revenues would find its way to state coffers. Gowon's propaganda managed, consequently, to find an audience. On 30 May, Ojukwu proclaimed Biafra independent, and full-scale war was declared on 6 July, 1967 by the Federal regime (Onoh, 1983, pp. 112–16; Olayiwola, 1987, pp. 86–9).

The oil factor in the civil war essentially meant that oil

companies with a strong presence in the Eastern region of Biafra found themselves in a very sensitive position *vis à vis* the Nigerian government. Safrap, for instance, was accused by the government of supporting the Biafran cause and of securing the military and political help of the French government to this end (Onoh, 1983, p. 114). Shell–BP in the meantime were concerned for the future of their concessions in the Eastern region and hoped that the support of the British government against Biafra would ensure that the secession would not be successful and the company would not lose its concessions. After the end of the war in 1970, the Nigerian government began to develop a nationalistic approach involving a desire to acquire greater control of the oil industry. Certainly, this development was strongly influenced by the role played by western powers during the civil war. The acquisition of 35 per cent equity in Safrap, the condition under which the company was allowed to resume production in Nigeria after the war, therefore involved both a nationalistic and a punitive element.[9]

(c) Political Change and Oil Operations. In addition to this major political upheaval, there have been numerous changes of government in Nigeria in the past three decades – including seven military governments, two elected civilian regimes, and one civilian interim government. The seven military coups, both violent and non-violent, have toppled two civilian governments, removed an interim government and four military regimes. These frequent, and mostly abrupt, political changes have had little if any significant impact on production operations, and have caused few if any changes in overall production or pricing policies.

Crude oil production, specifically, has remained largely insulated from political and economic instability. While Nigerian crude oil exports have benefited from specific political events elsewhere in the world (for instance the 1979 Iranian revolution and the 1990 Gulf war), no internal political development, other than the Biafran civil war, has been significant enough to either interrupt production or cause an important surge in the growth rate of Nigerian crude oil production. Production growth in the 1960s and the 1970s was largely due to exploration successes and the proximity and quality advantages of Nigerian relative to Middle Eastern crudes in the Atlantic Basin. The 1980s saw declining world oil demand, the introduction of OPEC production quotas, increasing production from the North Sea, and a scaling down of company operations in Nigeria. Consequently Nigerian production followed a decreasing trend (particularly in the first half of the decade) alongside a decline in productive capacity. The market for Nigerian crudes began to recover along with world oil demand after the price collapse of 1986. From an all time low production rate of 1.2 mb/d in 1983, crude oil production in 1992 averaged 1.85 mb/d.[10] These developments will be discussed in more detail in the next chapter.

As regards oil policies and the pattern of incentives provided to oil companies, there is a similar lack of evidence that changes in government were very significant. Nationalization in Nigeria, for instance, which was only partial, occurred mostly in the 1970s during which period the country was governed by three different military regimes, and was about to enter the period of the civilian regime of Shagari in 1979. In this frequently changing political landscape, relations with the oil companies provided the only element of continuity. Government incentives to oil company operations have evolved along with the changing conditions of the world oil market, regardless of the regime in power and specific ideologies. For example, the military regime of Obasanjo provided incentives for exploration; the civilian government of Shagari passed more restrictive laws on oil company equity offtake in 1981, and increased production cost allowances and official profit margins for the oil companies in 1982 and 1983; Buhari's military government reverted to pre-1981 equity offtake rules; and Babingida's military regime, between 1985 and 1993, issued two official Memoranda Of Understanding (MOUs) improving tax and production cost allowances, and revised and improved fiscal terms for oil companies in new production-sharing contracts.

This does not imply, of course, that no new regime has introduced new policies. A distinction must be made between oil policy changes consequent to changing economic conditions and oil policy changes consequent to changing political regimes. The former has of course occurred. Two examples which will be discussed in detail later illustrate this point. Firstly, counter-trade was discontinued when the Babingida regime came to power in 1986 because the economic need to continue to discount Nigerian crude was now being met by the use of netbacks with the added advantage that regular customers of Nigerian crude were also being satisfied. Secondly, the policy regarding the access given to traders for lifting Nigerian crudes changed under different oil ministers during the Babingida regime. This was due in large part to changing economic circumstances which at one point demanded that traders be encouraged as they lifted out-of-season crudes in periods when the market was soft; and/or that traders be discouraged, given that the foreign investment need of the oil industry required incentives to be geared toward potential sources of investment, such as joint-venture partners.

Nevertheless, it must be emphasized that the only element of continuity in oil policy despite successive government changes

Table 2.1: Nigerian Governments, 1960–93.

Period	Head of State	Ethnicity	Type of Government	How Ended
1960–66	Balewa	Hausa	Civilian	Attempted coup/ assassination
1966	Ironsi	Ibo	Military	Coup/assassination
1966–75	Gowon	Angas/ Middle Belt	Military	Coup
1975–76	Mohammad	Hausa	Military	Attempted coup/ assassination
1976–79	Obasanjo	Yoruba	Military	Elections
1979–83	Shagari	Fulani	Civilian	Coup
1984–85	Buhari	Fulani	Military	Coup
1985–93	Babingida	Minority Group in Niger State/ Middle Belt	Military	1992 elections cancelled (fraud cited); June '93 election results nullified; agreed to step down in August '93
1993 Jan–Nov	Shonekan		Civilian	Initially installed in Jan.'93 as head of Transitional Council; in Aug.'93 became President of Interim Government. Removed by coup in Nov.
1993 Nov.	Abacha		Military	Election date yet to be set.

Sources: Okeke, 1992, p. 133; EIU, 1986, p. 7; *FT*, various issues.

was that incentives to production and exploration have been enhanced from time to time. Because of their equity interests, oil companies have tended to cope with the political instability and generally preferred to continue their Nigerian operations rather than leave.[11] There is a view that the more unpredictable is the domestic political situation in Nigeria, the greater is the need to stabilize or periodically give new incentives to the development of the one dependable source of revenue, the oil industry. Despite this, however, the present crisis in the macro-economy has put at risk the government's continuing capacity to invest in the oil industry – thus threatening the growth of the oil sector itself and with it the stability of the entire economy.

There is a further problem. While the state has a continuing vested interest in the well-being of the oil industry, there has been and continues to be much to be desired in the management and formulation of petroleum policy. It is clear, for instance, that Nigeria remains a very political state and whatever the regime in power, political wrangling and lobbying is the norm. This has invariably caused delays in the implementation of legislation and in the launching and completion of various projects. Two examples will illustrate some of the problems caused by this incessant politicking and note that whereas changes in government may not have strong repercussions on oil policies and/or production rates, the political nature of government, itself, does influence the efficiency of the oil industry in terms of both policy formulation and implementation, and may even impact on the domestic supply of products.

The most important example concerns Nigeria's LNG project. The first LNG scheme collapsed in 1981 after five years of negotiations, mainly because of financing difficulties. Plans proposing a second much smaller project were presented in 1983. In 1987, the date for first deliveries to customers was set at 1995, with maximum capacity envisaged for 1997. The current status of the project suggests that completion cannot be expected before 1999 at the very earliest. The delays in the second project have stemmed largely from problems in selecting both the construction team and the actual process to be used in the liquefaction process. And this indecision on the part of the political regime is in turn linked to the strengths of the conflicting US and European financial lobbies in the country.

Our second example illustrates the way in which continued political wrangling may influence the domestic supply of petroleum products. The delay in the 1992 elections and the annulment of the June 1993 elections resulted in a strike by the oil workers' union in September 1993. This was directed mainly towards pressurizing the interim government to recognize the outcome of the 1993 elections. While neither crude oil production nor crude oil exports were interrupted, domestic fuel supply, at least in the south, was significantly affected. In the past, domestic fuel shortages have seldom been caused by strikes and protests against arbitrary political decisions and this is therefore an important indictment against the incessant vacillation and arbitrariness of decision making in the government.[12]

The Legal Framework

A discussion of the legal framework under which the Nigerian oil industry operates involves a consideration first of fiscal and regulatory petroleum legislation, and secondly of the operational and production arrangements between oil companies and the state, which are largely concerned with participation and equity. Both the legal and the contractual systems have evolved historically alongside changing government perceptions of the role of the oil sector in the economy and that of the state in the oil sector. These changing attitudes have been influenced significantly by the precedents set by OPEC on ameliorating fiscal and participation terms for the host countries.

During the exclusively Shell–BP concession era until 1955, and later in the period of the new concession holders, the oil companies more or less determined both the production and price levels of Nigerian crude oil. The government's interest in the oil industry, consequently, up until the mid-1960s, was limited to the collection of tax and rent or royalty. Legislation passed at this time reflected the dominance of the foreign oil company in the Nigerian oil industry in that significant incentives were given to exploration and production, sometimes at the expense of Nigerian interests (see description and analysis of the 1959 Petroleum Profits Tax Ordinance and further decrees in the next section). As production grew and the oil sector became significant for the Nigerian economy, petroleum legislation evolved to take into greater account the interests of the state in terms of oil revenues and profits and to reflect this changing balance of power. The 1970s saw increasing and more active government involvement in the oil industry. Wholly owned oil company concessions evolved into joint-venture participation agreements where the state held equity interest in the concession, as well as into at least one production-sharing contract and one risk-service contract, where the government retained exclusive title to oil in the ground and contracted out production operations to the oil companies. Both fiscal legislation and participation terms continue to evolve today to reflect the changing needs for exploration and production.[13]

(a)   Evolution of Fiscal Petroleum Ordinances. The 1914 Colonial Mineral Ordinance was the first oil related legislation in the newly amalgamated state of Nigeria and restricted the granting of leases and licences to British subjects and/or British companies.[14] Thus the Nigerian oil industry was made into a British monopoly, with complete ownership rights vested in the Crown. In 1937, the Colonial Mineral Ordinance granted the Shell D'Arcy company exclusive exploration and prospecting rights covering all of Nigeria. This ordinance was annulled by the Petroleum Act of 1969.

Prior to 1969, however, the stage had been set for greater state involvement in the Nigerian oil industry, in both fiscal and equity terms. In 1959, the Petroleum Profits Tax Ordinance established 'the assessment of the oil companies' taxable profits and the distribution of these profits between the government and the companies'.[15] A 50–50 profit-sharing arrangement with foreign producing concerns was agreed to with assessment based on the application of the companies' *realized prices* to the volume of crude oil produced and exported. This 50–50 profit-sharing formula had initially been introduced in Venezuela in 1948 when the government raised its tax rate, and by the early 1950s had been extended to some countries in the Middle East.[16]

By the mid-1960s, there was a growing awareness on the part of the Nigerian government that it should, as other oil-producing countries, profit from the enormous crude oil production increases. In 1964, Nigeria attended the OPEC Conference as an official observer for the first time and in 1967, OPEC terms for tax assessment were adopted with the promulgation of the Petroleum Profits Tax (Amendment) Decree, 1967.[17] This allowed taxes and profits to be assessed on posted prices and royalty to be assessed as current operational expenditure rather than included in the state's 50 per cent share of profits.[18] The concept of royalty expensing had been agreed at the fourth OPEC Conference in June 1962. One of the side-effects of this agreement was to encourage OPEC producers (Libya, Saudi Arabia and Venezuela at this time) to replace realized prices with posted prices as the basis for tax and profit assessment. This 'gap in OPEC's front' was fully closed by September 1966 (Seymour, 1980, p. 52).

Further important amendments were made to the original 1959 PPT Ordinance in 1973, 1974 and again in 1975. Until 1969, the royalty rate had been pegged at 12.5 per cent and the Petroleum Profits Tax at 50 per cent. In April 1973, as an amendment to the 1959 Mineral Oil Ordinance, PPT was raised to 55 per cent and royalty rates stayed at 12.5 per cent. OPEC Resolution XXI.120 of December 1970 had stated as one of its objectives a minimum tax rate of 55 per cent, which was later confirmed in the Tehran Agreement of February 1971. In 1974, PPT and royalty rates were increased to 67.75 per cent and 16.67 per cent, respectively. In 1975, there was a further increase to 85 per cent PPT and 20 per cent royalty. These changes were based on increases in tax and royalty rates agreed in various OPEC Conferences in 1974: royalty had been increased to 14.5 per cent as of 1 July, 1974; to 16.67 per cent as of 1 October, 1974; and to 20 per cent as of 1 November, 1974; the tax rate had been increased to 65.75 per cent as of 1 October, 1974 and to 85 per cent as of 1 November, 1974 (Skeet, 1988).

The 1980s and the early 1990s have seen a variety of negotiated settlements on fiscal incentives to the oil companies. The main ones have been the 1986 Memorandum of Understanding (MOU), a revision of this in 1991 which included additional incentives, and improved terms in new Production-Sharing Contracts (PSC) in 1992 and again in 1993 for deep water acreage. These various memoranda, in some form or the other, have given incentives to exploration and production to either/or joint-venture partners and partners in production-sharing ventures. Generally these incentives have taken the form of improved production cost allowances and profit margins, as well as reductions in taxes

(PPT and royalty) linked to capital and/or development expenditure by the oil companies.

(b)   Participation and Equity Decrees. The 'participation' issue in oil industry operations was officially introduced during the 16th OPEC Conference in June 1968 through Resolution XVI.90, also known as the 'Declaratory Statement of Petroleum Policy in Member Countries'. This resolution essentially advised member countries to acquire 'participation in and control over all aspects of oil operations'; it included a participation clause allowing host governments to acquire 'a reasonable level of participation in concessions' and it called for an acceleration in the relinquishment of acreage, the choice of which should be influenced by the government (Ibid., p. 49). During the same year, the Companies' Decree of October 1968 forced all companies operating in Nigeria to become Nigerian corporations, giving the state greater access to their accounts. Although Nigeria was to take a gradual and partial approach to nationalization when she finally became a member of OPEC in 1971, the new OPEC resolution seemed in some ways to encourage a more aggressive stance *vis à vis* oil companies and to heighten tensions between the various governments and foreign oil-producing concerns.

The 1969 Petroleum Act vested further control of the industry in the state. Firstly, it ensured the continued recruitment and training of Nigerians. Holders of oil mining leases, for instance, were obliged to ensure that within ten years of the lease being granted a certain proportion of the employees in the various grades were Nigerian citizens. Secondly, the Petroleum Act of 1969 also specified the form, rights, powers and restrictions on the different exploration and production licences. These included the oil exploration licence (OEL), the oil prospecting licence (OPL), and the oil mining lease (OML).[19] Licences or leases, under this decree, could only be granted to Nigerian citizens or companies incorporated in Nigeria.

Participation legislation in the 1970s was primarily related to the gradual and partial process of nationalization undertaken by the state through its intermediary Nigerian National Oil Corporation (NNOC) and then Nigerian National Petroleum Corporation (NNPC). The Nigerian government increased its equity stake in various ventures to 35 per cent in 1971, to 55 per cent in 1974 and finally to 60 per cent in 1979 (see section on the NNPC below for details). As in the case of fiscal legislation, the 1980s was a period of 'reconsideration' of the value of foreign oil companies and foreign capital. In the early 1990s, Nigeria took the first step in the direction of partial divestment of its share in certain ventures as a result of acute financial constraints.

Oil-Producing Companies and the Evolution of the Concession Pattern

In 1951, Shell–BP limited their original Oil Exploration Licence, granted in 1938 and covering all of Nigeria (924,871 km^2), to an OEL one-sixth of this area in southern Nigeria. By 1957, they had further reduced their concession area by one-third into Oil Prospecting Licences, and by 1962, they had converted about 38,860 km^2 of these OPLs into Oil Mining Leases, and relinquished the remaining acreage to the government (Schatzl, 1969, p. 1).

During the initial stages of the formation of a concession pattern in Nigeria, Shell–BP remained the sole holders in the country – until 1955 when their prospecting and exploration activities raised the interest of other companies. All the newcomers then obtained concessions in the areas that Shell–BP had abandoned for lack of viable prospects. For instance, in 1955, Mobil was granted an OEL covering 730,005 km^2 of northern Nigeria acreage relinquished by Shell–BP. Further OELs were granted to Mobil in the next couple of years, but all of these expired and were returned to the government for lack of any successful results. By 1962, however, with Shell–BP having converted a significant part of their OPLs into OMLs, newcomers had greater OPL options. Thus, during the early 1960s, Gulf, Agip and Safrap were granted OPLs.

Bidding for concessions on the continental shelf, however, was more competitive because Shell–BP's comparative advantage in exploration and production had been developed only on the mainland and did not extend to offshore acreage (Ibid., p. 5). In 1961, therefore, the Nigerian government gave four OELs to Shell–BP, while Mobil, Texaco and Gulf were granted two each. The licences were for the Nigerian continental shelf and each covered 2,560 km^2.[20] Five of these ten offshore concessions were relinquished at the end of 1968, and in 1970 the government accepted bids for new concessions in this continental shelf acreage (Pearson, 1970, p. 18), thus repeating the concession-granting process. This pattern of exploration and production continued over the years with the similar process of granting OELs, relinquishing OELs and/or converting the licences into OMLs, further open bidding rounds, and so on.

More recently, open bidding rounds have been held in 1991 and 1992. In 1991, the government's aim was to diversify foreign interests and to increase indigenous involvement in exploration. The acreage available was on the margins of the Niger delta and in the Benin and Benue basins in the north. Sixty-one blocks were offered to seventeen indigenous companies and eleven foreign companies. Of the latter, most of the licences went to existing foreign producers in Nigeria. The most recent acreage up for offer was in the deep offshore (from 200 m water depth to 2000–3000 m), thirteen blocks to the west and south west of the delta.[21] Blocks awarded in this licensing round have recently been finalized on production-sharing terms. Given the location of the acreage, the government was obviously aiming for offers from major foreign companies with the requisite financial and technological capacity to drill in such difficult areas.[22]

Table 2.2 shows the concession situation (Oil Prospecting Licences and Oil Mining Leases) in 1969, 1986 and in 1993. It does not indicate, however, the large influx of indigenous companies onto the concession scene in the early 1990s.[23] At least nineteen new companies were accounted for with concession acreage totalling about 33,000 km². These indigenous companies, however, have yet to produce.

It is clear that there have not been any large changes in foreign concession holders in Nigeria. British Petroleum was fully nationalized in 1979, and has recently returned as a partner of Statoil in an exploration venture. British Gas and Sun both acquired interest from a former Mobil venture in 1989. And NPDC and Dubri are local Nigerian concerns, one state owned, and the latter a private company, which have acquired equity interest in former NNPC and Phillips concerns, respectively.

As a result of the nationalization process of the 1970s and 1980s, the Nigerian state, through its intermediary NNPC, has a participating interest in all foreign mining leases. Currently, this

Table 2.2: Oil Companies holding Nigerian Concessions in 1969, 1986 and 1993. Square Kilometres.

1969		1986		1993 Total Concession Area	
Company	*Area(Km²)*	*Company*	*Area(Km²)*	*Company*	*Area(Km²)*
Shell-BP Petroleum Development Company	48,959	Shell	31,309	Shell	43,243
Safrap (Nigeria)	24,187	Elf	8,256	Elf	11,113
Gulf Oil Company	17,759	Gulf Oil	14,138	Gulf	14,138
Nigeria Agip Oil Company	5,262	Nigerian Agip Oil Company / Phillips	5,259	NAOC	9,966
Mobil Producing Nigeria Ltd.	5,246	Mobil	2,562	Mobil	4,928
Texas Overseas (Nigeria) Petroleum	5,003	Texaco	2,570	Texaco	2,570
Phillips Oil Company	3,630	Phillips	232	Dubri	232
Tenneco Oil Company	3,575	Mobil/Tenneco	2,259		n.a
Union Oil Nigeria	2,591	Agip Energy & Natural Resources (AENR)	360	AENR	360
		NNPC	40,440	NNPC	40,440
		Pan Ocean	1,005	Pan Ocean	1,005
		Nigus	1,025	Nigus	1,025
				Exxon	2,200
				Du Pont	2,422
				Statoil	5,698
				Ashland	2,346

Sources and Notes: Barrows *IPI Data Service, Africa*, No. 47, *Nigeria*, 1986, p. 26; Planning Department, Ministry of Petroleum and Mineral Resources; Pearson, 1970, pp. 16–17.
Concessions refer to acreage for oil prospecting licences and oil mining leases. See also Table 4.1 in Chapter 4. The difference in concession acreage between 1986 and 1993 refers mainly to that added through new PSCs in 1992–3.

participation takes the form of a 60 per cent equity interest in foreign producing ventures. The Shell venture, as indicated by its concession acreage (second after NNPC's), remains the largest producer in Nigeria, accounting for 51 per cent of total Nigerian crude oil production in 1990.

NNPC – Structure and Place in the Nigerian Oil Industry

The Nigerian National Oil Corporation was established in May 1971 by Decree No. 18. This preceded Nigeria's membership of OPEC in July 1971 and was mainly a consequence of OPEC Resolution No. XVI.90 of 1968 which called for member countries to acquire 51 per cent of foreign equity interests and to participate more 'actively in all aspects of oil operations', and of Nigerian Petroleum Decree No. 51 of 1969 which vested entire ownership and control of all petroleum in Nigeria with the state and/or its agencies (Onoh, 1983, pp. 19, 30). The other influential factor was that after the Biafra War ended in January 1970, the Nigerian government increasingly felt that it should secure greater control over its petroleum industry. Until the 1970s, foreign oil companies (particularly the largest joint venture, Shell–BP), operated in Nigeria with very few constraints. The creation of NNOC was the first important step towards the 'indigenization' of Nigerian interests since it served as the main agent of the state in the partial nationalization of the oil industry.

Equity participation by the government had started well before the creation of a national oil company. In 1962, the government signed a concession agreement with Nigerian Agip Oil Company (NAOC). The agreement included a provision for a government option to have one-third of the equity of the company, once a commercial discovery of oil had been made. The Nigerian government exercised this option in April 1971. This acquisition and the 35 per cent stake acquired in Safrap on the same date secured for the new state oil company its first participation in the oil industry. The strategic role of the state company in the country's oil industry was further emphasized by the declaration in February 1972 that henceforth no new concessions would be sold wholly to foreign concerns and that all unallocated and/or abandoned oil acreage (abandoned by Shell) would become the property of the state, and therefore could only be allocated by the government (Iwayemi, 1988, p. 28). By 1974, NNOC had increased its participation in the oil-producing companies to 55 per cent and in 1976 it drilled its first exploratory well offshore, discovering commercial quantities of oil and gas. It was then established as an oil and gas producing company in its own right (Jimoh, 1987, p. 5).

It was as the Nigerian National Petroleum Company, that the state oil company established itself firmly as a major participant in the oil industry, both in terms of greater equity participation and as an exploring and producing company in its own right. The NNPC was established by Decree No. 33 of 1 April 1977, and the main motive behind its creation, under Colonel Buhari's term as Federal Commissioner, was to make the best use of the government's limited petroleum expertise.[24] The new company combined some functions of the NNOC and the Ministry of Petroleum, thus creating an organization responsible for production, transportation, refining, and marketing of crude oil and petroleum products with extended regulatory powers. These regulatory functions, formerly of the ministry, were transferred to the Petroleum Inspectorate, created at the time of NNPC by Decree No. 33 in 1977. The main difference between the roles of NNOC and NNPC was that the latter had greater flexibility in both borrowing and in awarding contracts.[25]

Another step forward for a greater involvement of the Nigerian state oil company in the oil industry came in 1978 when NNPC had established its own seismic crew (Party X). The government hailed this as a great event in that the state exploration company not only broke the monopoly of foreign companies in crude oil exploration, but by undertaking third-party contracts, it also brought the NNPC onto a commercial footing at par with other companies. It is unlikely that the indigenous exploration company in fact functioned at par with foreign companies. By 1983, a seismic data processing centre had been set up in Benin City and by 1984, NNPC had established a second seismic crew (Party Y) (Jimoh, 1987, p. 5). And by 1986, at least ten offshore commercial discoveries had been made by NNPC.[26]

By 1979, NNPC had acquired a 60 per cent participation interest in most of the oil-producing ventures, with an 80 per cent interest in the former Shell–BP venture, following the nationalization of BP in 1979. In 1990, joint-venture production accounted for 96 per cent of total Nigerian crude oil production; and of this, NNPC's equity share was about 1.7 mb/d. Although the state oil company has also started producing crude of its own accord – through its subsidiary the Nigerian Petroleum Development Company (NPDC) – its more significant role remains that of marketing Nigerian crude oil.

The first important reorganization of the NNPC was initiated in 1981 under the civilian administration of the Shagari government. This followed the Irikefe Commission's Report in June 1980 which had found various irregularities in the awarding of third party oil-purchase contracts and inefficient accounting procedures. NNPC, as it was then structured, was thought to be much too large to run efficiently. Recommendations were made to decentralize the corporation and re-organize the administration.[27] The main changes implemented at this stage were the re-creation of a Ministry of Petroleum and Energy and the creation of nine subsidiaries. Since the Minister for Petroleum and Energy would also be the Chairman of the Board of NNPC, policy decisions and recommendations would be more speedily and efficiently conveyed to the President. This particular change was thought to be essential if NNPC was to respond promptly to changing issues in the international oil industry, in particular to changes in OPEC oil policies. The 'independent' regulatory arm of NNPC was to be called the Petroleum Inspectorate and was expected to regulate the Nigerian oil industry, including NNPC itself. Essentially this meant that NNPC would both operate as an oil company and regulate the industry, and given the inherent conflicts in carrying out both sets of functions it is clear that the issue of regulation of the industry had not been dealt with very seriously. The nine subsidiaries created at this time were intended to be independent, in the sense of taking their own policy decisions and being self-accountable. The decentralization of the three refineries, in particular, was an attempt to enhance competition between them, and to limit the area of responsibility of each and hence make the entire system more efficient.[28] It is evident with hindsight and with knowledge of the problems of bureaucracy and inefficiency plaguing the country and the oil industry in the 1980s, that few of these aims would be realized.

The most recent structural changes of NNPC were initiated in

1986 and finalized about two years later in 1988. At this time, the Petroleum Inspectorate was separated from the NNPC structure and merged with the new Ministry of Petroleum which had been re-established, after some delay, in 1986. The Department of Petroleum Resources, as it is now named, is responsible for policy formulation and regulation of the industry. This includes resource management i.e. the allocation of concessions and/or licences, technical control, and inspections in the downstream sector. While the final regulatory powers rest with the Minister who is still closely associated with NNPC, this structural change is nevertheless preferable, from a regulatory point of view, to a system in which NNPC was responsible for issuing licences to its so-called competitors. However if re-structuring of the industry is to be anything more than cosmetic, the issue of regulation will have to be given closer and more serious attention. Even if the Department is ascribed the role of the oil industry regulator, as it seems to have been in the latest changes, there remains an inherent regulatory problem because the Department is still in a similar position to the NNPC. To be efficient, a regulatory institution must be quasi-independent, answerable to an authority other than the Minister and/or Chairman of the NNPC, and professionally run.

An additional part of the re-structuring was the decision to give the state oil company a more stream-lined and commercial orientation as well as autonomy within the federal government structure. The following changes were to take effect as of 1 April, 1989, but in fact they were not implemented until a few years later. Product prices were to be deregulated and the federal government support and subsidy to NNPC was to be removed – in fact, NNPC was expected to render dividend to the Federal Government periodically. NNPC was officially allowed to set product prices as of 1 January, 1991 and NNPC became a 'commercial and autonomous' entity only as of 1 January, 1992.

The company can now operate without undue interference from the government and the Department. It has a responsibility towards its shareholders, and is expected to finance itself either through the capital markets or through its equity share in crude oil production. The NNPC budget, in other words, is no longer the responsibility of the state. While the re-structured NNPC now functions more like a private company, it retains some 'unwritten privileges'.[29] These include the fact that the regulation of NNPC as a state oil company will necessarily be different from that of other, mainly foreign, oil companies; that NNPC has shares in the other oil-producing concerns which ensures that its influence is spread throughout the industry and finally, that NNPC, since the official deregulation of product prices will be responsible for setting these prices.[30]

The company is comprised of six main groupings: Finance and Accounts takes care of the company's accounts, budgets, and treasury; Corporate Services is responsible for legal issues and insurance, administration and personnel and engineering and technology; Commercial and Investments oversees investments, as well as pipelines and products marketing; Refineries and Petrochemicals is responsible for the efficient functioning of the three refineries and the Eleme Petrochemical plant; the Upstream group oversees the Nigerian Petroleum Development Company (which is engaged in exploration and manages its own seismic crew), the Nigerian Gas Corporation, and the Integrated Data Service Company; the National Petroleum Investment Management Services (NAPIMS) deals with matters pertaining to federal investments in exploration and production particularly in frontier areas (it also explores and manages its own seismic crew), markets Nigerian crude oil and monitors joint venture activities (NNPC; Ikeh, 1991, p. 141). The twelve subsidiaries (see Table 2.3) are limited liability companies, and are expected to raise capital internationally and pay the dividends to the government. Figure 2.2 outlines the organizational structure of NNPC.

The NNPC is an essentially weak organization. In the words of one of its general managers, 'waste abounds in NNPC'.[31] With excessive red tape and bureaucratic delays in the organization, mechanical and management problems, it is unlikely that the company and the Nigerian oil industry can do without the investment and participation of foreign oil companies. The latter, therefore, have little to fear from the particular clause in the joint operating agreements which allows NNPC to take over exclusive operatorship of a concession when desired. Besides problems within it, one of the reasons for NNPC's inherent weakness is its relationship with the Nigerian state. The state oil company is involved in a number of joint ventures in which it

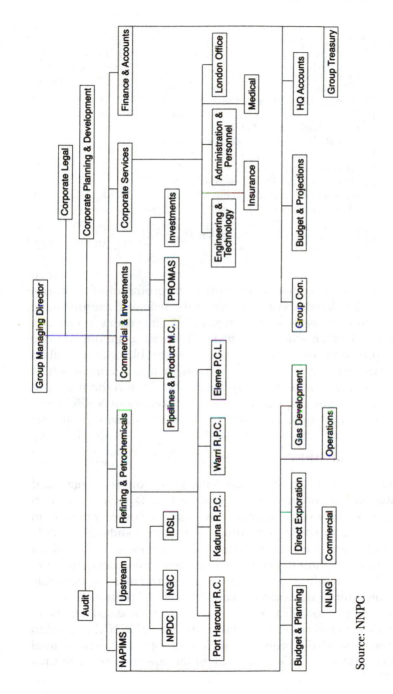

Source: NNPC

Figure 2.2 Organizational Structure of the Nigerian National Petroleum Corporation

Table 2.3: NNPC Subsidiaries.

> Eleme Petrochemical Co. Ltd.
> Warri Refining and Petrochemicals Co. Ltd.
> Engineering Co. of Nigeria Ltd.
> Hydrocarbon Services of Nigeria Co. Ltd.
> Integrated Data Service Co. Ltd.
> Kaduna Refining and Petrochemicals Co. Ltd.
> Liquified Natural Gas Co. Ltd.
> Nigerian Gas Development Co. Ltd.
> Nigerian Petroleum Development Co. Ltd.
> Pipelines and Products Marketing Co. Ltd.
> Port Harcourt Refining Co. Ltd.

Sources: *FT International Yearbooks, Oil & Gas 1992,* 1991

must contribute its share of the costs. The profits, or oil revenues, on the other hand accrue directly to the federal government. In the distribution of these revenues, NNPC is treated as one of a number of other state companies. There are consequently two main problems. First there are the issues, problems and conflicts associated with such a state of quasi-independence, one of which concerns that of accountability. Secondly, there is the perennial problem of an inadequate allocation of revenues to NNPC given its investment commitments in the oil industry (see Chapter 4).

Nigeria and OPEC

OPEC has had an important influence on the legal and institutional framework of the oil industry. As we have seen, a number of OPEC resolutions and decrees caused changes in fiscal and participation regulations in Nigeria. In addition OPEC played a role in determining the production and pricing policies of member countries. The latter is the most interesting aspect of the relationship between OPEC and Nigeria, and has probably had the most significant implications for both parties.

Nigeria joined OPEC in 1971 aware of two basic facts. First, its crude oil production had increased from 5,000 b/d in 1958 to 1.5 mb/d in 1971. From a contribution of 1 per cent to total export earnings in 1958, the share of oil export revenues in total exports increased to nearly 75 per cent in 1971.[32] The economy had become heavily dependent on its oil production. Secondly, this dependence meant that Nigeria was finding itself in 'an economic environment influenced significantly by circumstances beyond her control. She became dependent on international supply and demand conditions that determined her export revenues, limited her ability to attract investment in sectors other than her growth sectors, set the terms of foreign exchange, and as a result determined her trade losses or gains' (Olayiwola, 1987, p. 151). Nigeria felt that membership of OPEC and consensus on production and pricing policies, would act as a buffer between the country and the world oil market.

The early 1980s was a period of increasing competition from North Sea crude oil grades in the Atlantic Basin. In fact, while Nigerian crude oil prices 'had served as the main reference point for North Sea pricing, North Sea prices became the dominant influence on Nigerian prices after 1981' (Brown, 1990, p. 318). One of the reasons why Nigeria was seen as the 'weak link' in the OPEC price chain was precisely because the country found itself belonging to one pricing system in the Atlantic Basin where its crudes were competing with growing North Sea production, and to another pricing system administered by OPEC.

The tension between Nigeria and OPEC was highest, and the country's reputation as a 'maverick' in pricing issues greatest in the years 1983–4. In February 1983, and again in October 1984, Nigeria unilaterally cut its crude oil ceiling price, first by $5.50/b to $30.00/b, then by $2.00/b to $28.00/b. On both occasions, Nigeria was responding to cuts in both the British National Oil Corporation (BNOC) and Norwegian prices. Unilateral actions by Nigeria were eventually accepted by OPEC and on one occasion at least, OPEC had no option but to follow suit in cutting the price of its marker crude. It became evident that Nigeria, at that time, was effectively the linchpin of the world crude oil pricing system. Its reputation as a maverick in OPEC was mainly due to these pricing issues, in particular the price cutting of 1983–4, and had little to do with production over prescribed quota levels, given that Nigerian quotas were not generally lower than the country's production capacity.[33]

The other area of potential friction between OPEC and Nigeria was related to counter-trade dealings, particularly in 1984 and

1985, and the possibility therein for concealed discounting. An estimated 175,000 b/d of Nigerian crude was involved in counter-trade when General Buhari was in office (from December 1983 to August 1985). Crude oil was exchanged for trucks, automobile components and assembly parts, chemical products, food and planes. The main trading partners were Brazil, Austria, Italy and France, and approximately $1.75 billion worth of goods were exchanged (Iwayemi, 1988, p. 36). If these estimates are close to reality, then the Nigerians were substantially discounting the price of their oil, to the extent that some regular buyers were giving notice that they were pulling out of their normal contracts.[34] Although OPEC decided to keep quiet on this matter in view of the severe financial difficulties facing Nigeria, internal criticism of these counter-trade deals, most significantly on the part of the then Petroleum Resources Minister, David Tam-West, resulted in most of the arrangements being discontinued at the beginning of the Babingida regime in August 1985. The main argument against the deals was that Nigeria was in fact paying inflated prices for the goods imported in exchange for crude oil, and the heavy discounting was turning away regular lifters of Nigerian crude. Further details of counter-trade deals are given in Chapter 5.

Political and public criticisms of Nigeria's membership of OPEC were at their height in the early 1980s, largely due to OPEC quota restrictions, falling Nigerian production levels, and consequently, the significant decline in oil revenues. The installation of the new military government of Babingida, and the appointment of Dr. R. Lukman to the Presidency of the Conference of OPEC Oil Ministers in June 1986, ushered in a more accommodating period in terms of the Nigerian attitude to OPEC.[35] There appeared to be a greater degree of responsibility *vis à vis* the organization, a significant toning down of the 'Nigeria first' policies of the previous military government, and a reduction and/or discontinuation of a number of the old counter-trade deals. The policy outlook was now one in which the emphasis was on moderate prices, long-term price agreements, and the restoration of confidence between buyers and sellers.[36]

In early 1987, Nigeria became one of the founding members of the African Petroleum Producers' Association (APPA). The association also includes the following members: Algeria, Angola,

Benin, Cameroon, Gabon, Libya, Ivory Coast and Egypt. The aim of the regional grouping is essentially to co-ordinate marketing policies, and to encourage technical and informational co-operation between member countries. Since half the member countries do not belong to OPEC, the extent to which the former aim is realized is unclear. Despite this however, Lukman who was elected its first head (and who concurrently held the posts of the Nigerian oil minister and OPEC president) had to reassure OPEC, and Saudi Arabia in particular, that this new grouping was not in fact a bloc within the larger organization (Brown, 1990, p. 187).

In the last few years, as during Lukman's tenure, there has been little evidence of difficulties in the Nigeria–OPEC relationship. A few problems, involving alleged Nigerian over-production and the brief re-introduction of netbacks in 1992, have arisen but none have been as significant as those during the tenure of David Tam-West in the early 1980s.

Notes

1. An analysis of the evolution of production from an economic perspective is contained in Chapter 3.
2. Two factors contributing to weak-centred federalism in Nigeria, especially in the earlier pre-oil years, were the size and resources of the regions. At independence, there were three regions, with the North disproportionately large and dominant. The fact that this system was unworkable has been illustrated by the fact that in the late 1950s, political delegates remained in their regions, and sent their representatives to the centre. This symbolic subordination of the centre to the regions was removed in the late 1960s by Gowon, who created twelve states and attempted to restore both North–South parity and power at the centre at the expense of that in the states (Ayoade, 1988).
3. There is, however, a view that the military reacts to pressure from various interest groups differently from civilian regimes. The centralized power of the military machine, itself; the potential for coercion; and the limited constituency of the military (extending mainly to potential coup plotters), are assumed to make it relatively easier for these regimes to insulate executive authority from demands for party patronage and competition for a piece of the pie. It is generally accepted, for instance, that during the civilian regime of Shagari, a government characterized by 'a weak presidency, a weak party, and a form of clientelist politics that sapped the authority of the state,' corruption levels did intensify. This is not to say, however, that on the whole the scale of corruption has been significantly lower in times of military power, nor that the military regime has shown

itself to be significantly more authoritarian (Forrest, 1993, pp. 89–90, 126).

4. The World Bank estimated a 1988 mid-year population of 110 million. At an average annual growth rate of 3 per cent, the population currently stands at about 128 million. The government estimated a 1987 mid-year population of 112 million. If this grew at a rate of 3 per cent per annum, the total population of Nigeria should be about 135 million. The issue of actual figures has always been politically sensitive in Nigeria since it affects the level of federal disbursements to the states (EIU, 1990, p. 142).

5. As we shall see in Chapter 8, the notion of 'looking after one's own' has taken on ludicrous proportions in Nigeria. The federal states have to a large extent abandoned all real desire to have a 'productive' identity of their own. They rely on hand-outs from the federal government, and the 'result has been to give them power untempered by responsibility. The delighted states have managed to become miniature versions of their free-spending federal pay-masters' ('Nigeria', *Economist Survey*, 21 August, 1993, p. 12.)

6. High oil revenues in the 1970s led to major investments in Nigeria's basic infrastructure. After a point, increasing levels of investment were less easily absorbed and became less efficient and effective due to the lack of trained labour, infrastructural failures, and bottlenecks in crucial areas. Exceeding the absorptive capacity of the economy could lead to problems of surpluses on current account, inflation, and unemployment. Nigerian deficits in its current account during this period were due to increasing imports, and decreasing non-oil exports, rather than an indication that the economy was efficiently absorbing incremental investments from oil revenues (Cochrane and Struthers, 1983).

7. In 1990–91, when oil prices jumped as a result of the Gulf crisis, there was no corresponding increase in the government's recorded income. While a *Financial Times* journalist was expelled from the country at that time for questioning this inconsistency, the issue of understating earnings during the Gulf war price increase has been raised again by the World Bank in recent years. More significantly, the Bank has also made an estimate of the possible average annual loss from government coffers. In 1992, the gap between official earnings and estimated earnings (based on production and price levels) was $2.7 billion – approximately 10 per cent of GDP. *PE*, April 1992, p. 38; 'Nigeria', *Economist Survey*, 21 August, 1993, p. 8.)

8. Prospecting for oil in Nigeria began in 1908 when the German owned 'Nigerian Bitumen Corporation' drilled along the coast. At the end of the war in 1918, German commercial interests were expelled, including the Nigerian Bitumen Corporation. The first oil exploration licences were granted by the British in 1921 to the D'Arcy Exploration Company and the Whitehall Petroleum Company Ltd. However, there was little interest in oil exploration in Nigeria until 1937, when Shell/D'Arcy Exploration Parties was established (the company was known by 1946 as the Shell–BP Development Company of Nigeria, Ltd.) In 1938, the company received an oil exploration licence (OEL) covering all of Nigeria. However,

prospecting was interrupted by the Second World War, and it was not until 1951 that the first wildcat was drilled and the first non-commercial oil find was made in 1953. The first commercial oil find was made at Oloibiri in 1956 and in 1958 the first oil was exported (see Figure 1). Following first strikes, other companies entered into exploration and prospecting concessions. However, until 1965 Shell–BP were the sole producers of Nigerian crude oil. Gulf started producing in 1965, Safrap (later Elf) in 1966, Mobil in 1969, and Texaco and Agip in 1970. Production levels peaked in 1979.

9. The same year, NNOC exercised a previously agreed option of acquiring 33.33 per cent equity in Agip. The equity acquisition in Safrap was however without prior warning.

10. *BP Statistical Review of the World Oil Industry*, June 1993.

11. BP is the only main oil company to have left Nigeria, and even this exit was not voluntary. Its interests were nationalized in 1979, and in 1993 the company returned as a partner of Statoil in an exploration venture.

12. Fuel shortages have been a chronic problem in the economy, stemming mainly from the high subsidies on products which have made cross-border (where product prices are much higher) smuggling a lucrative option. For the seven years of the Babingida government, no substantial steps were taken to remove these subsidies. On the eve of his departure, his government introduced a two-tiered pricing system which essentially increased the price of 'premium' petrol ten-fold. While some union workers were protesting against this decree (the timing and objective of which remains unclear), the oil workers maintain their protest was entirely political.

13. The role of fiscal and regulatory petroleum legislation as well as concessions and equity producers in the Nigerian upstream sector will be discussed in some detail in Chapter 4.

14. Mineral Oil Ordinance, 31 December, 1914 in Barrows, *Basic Oil Laws & Concession Contracts, South and Central Africa*, vol. I (no. 1) / Page H-I.

15. When the 1959 Petroleum Profits Tax (PPT) Ordinance was implemented, Nigeria's crude oil reserves were only 21 million barrels and the reserve/production ratio was just twelve years. While there was a growing ambition to have more state involvement in the oil industry, there was also the continuing awareness that new legislation had to encourage further investment by oil companies in exploration and production. The 1959 PPT Ordinance was considered to be a fairly favourable piece of legislation for the oil companies. Schatzl has given the following four reasons for this:

(i)   Royalties varying between 8 and 12.5 per cent are assessed from the value of the crude oil at the place of extraction.

(ii) Royalties and other duties due to the government are included in the 50% share of profits due to the government.

(iii) Profits are assessed on the basis of realised proceeds.

(iv) The depreciation rates conceded to the oil companies are higher than justified by economic principles.

Depreciation rates were high to stimulate investment in exploration and royalty rates in Nigeria at this time were lower than in other oil-producing countries largely because these, as profits as a whole, were assessed on realized prices rather than posted prices. Realized prices tended to be lower than posted prices as these were set exclusively by the relevant oil company rather than after negotiation with the government. The government in 1959, therefore, was getting a lower share of profits from oil operations relative to other oil producing and exporting countries (Schatzl, 1969, pp.84, 94).

16. While this new formula greatly enhanced the host government's revenue earnings, previously limited to the collection of royalty, there was 'no corresponding fall in the production profits of the oil companies', which at least in the Middle East was about $0.80–0.90/bbl (Seymour, 1980, p. 14).

17. In addition to the concessionary agreements signed with the oil companies, the Nigerian government also agreed to certain 'Deeds of Covenant.' These essentially stipulated that the 1959 PPT Ordinance was valid for the entire period of the licence, until 1991–2 in the case of Shell–BP. However the 'Letters of Agreement' between the state and the oil companies allowed for an exception to this ruling in the case where 'the shareholders of an oil company operating in Nigeria or any company which they may directly or indirectly control concludes a contract or recognizes a law in any other African state under which the other country's share in profits is higher than Nigeria's'. This essentially introduced the 'most favoured nation' clause into Nigerian contracts on the basis of which previous regulations could be amended given the status of fiscal reform in the Libyan oil industry, for instance (Schatzl, 1969, pp. 94–6).

18. Barrows, *Basic Oil Laws and Concession Contracts, South and Central Africa*, Supplement No. XI, page A-0. This essentially meant that under the new OPEC terms, royalties to the government were treated as expenses rather than tax offsets. Under the 1959 PPT Ordinance, oil companies were able to use the royalties to the government as a '100 per cent offset against petroleum profits tax liabilities'. This change in the 1967 amendment significantly increased the tax revenues received by the government by an additional 50 per cent of the value of royalties (Pearson, 1970, p. 25).

19. It is worthwhile to note the basic differences between OELs, OPLs and OMLs after the promulgation of the 1969 Petroleum Act. Oil Exploration Licences entitle the holder to prospect but not drill for oil. This is not an exclusive right, and the duration of the licence generally lasts a year but can be extended/renewed for one further year depending on negotiations between the government and the oil company. The Oil Prospecting Licence entitles the holder to an exclusive right to prospect and drill for oil, to produce and to export oil, and to refine the crude in Nigeria. The duration of the licence is for a maximum of five years, including renewals. (Before the 1969 act, the maximum duration of the OPL was five years for mainland areas and seven years for the continental shelf area.) Expired OPLs must either be relinquished to the government or converted to OMLs. Half the OPL acreage can theoretically be converted into OMLs. The Oil Mining Lease entitles the holder to basically the same rights as

those for OPLs, with the exception of the duration: the maximum term for an oil mining lease was valid for a maximum of twenty years. (Before the 1969 Act, the OML was valid for thirty years for onshore acreage, with an extension possible for another thirty; and valid for forty years for offshore acreage, with an extension possible for another forty.) (Barrows, *Basic Oil Laws and Concession Contracts, South and Central Africa*, Supplement No. XXII, page A-0, B-0; and Schatzl, 1969, pp. 77–80).

20. Barrows, *IPI Data Service, Africa*, No. 47, *Nigeria*, 1986, p.17.
21. *PE*, March 1992, p. 23; February 1993, p. 34.
22. These licences were not finalized till end-1992 precisely because the companies wanted greater fiscal incentives in their contracts to explore in this high-cost acreage. An amended model contract offered in 1992/93 included improved tax, royalty and production-sharing terms (*PE*, June 1993).
23.

Name	Concession Date	Acreage (km2)
Alfred James	1991	1800
Allied Energy	1992	2500
Amalagamated Oil	1991	668
Atlas Petroleum	1991	772
Cavendish Petroleum	1990	920
Consolidated Oil Ltd.	1991	2560
Express Petroleum & Gas Company	1990	1027
Oriental Petroleum	1990	320
IPEC	1991	3576
Optmum	1992	2500
Moncrief Oil	1991	1191
OPIC	1991	1920
Paclantic	1990	1748
Queen Petroleum	1990	930
Solgas Nigeria	1991	1640
Summit Oil	1990	4011
Ultramar	1990	1036
Union Petrobras	1991	2362
Yinka Folawiyo	1991	1840

(Planning Department, Ministry of Petroleum and Mineral Resources, Lagos).

24. *PE*, February 1984, p. 55.
25. NNOC could only award contracts of up to Naira 100,000 and was not allowed to borrow without the permission of the Federal Executive Council. NNPC, on the other hand, was allowed to award contracts of up to Naira 5 million, and could borrow to a limited extent in local currency (Onoh, 1983, p. 35).
26. Barrows, *IPI Data Service, Africa*, No. 47, *Nigeria*, 1986, p. 25.
27. *Punch*, a Nigerian oil daily, in September 1979 alleged that Naira 2.841 billion were missing from NNPC's account with the Midland Bank in London. The money was said to be in the private account of a particular third-party oil purchaser of the NNPC. A judicial inquiry, headed by

Justice Irikefe, was set up to look into these allegations and other aspects of NNPC operations. The Commission's Report, published in June 1980, found irregularities in the awarding of third-party contracts; lax, almost non-existent, accounting procedures within NNPC; the inefficient marketing of crude oil and keeping of production records by NNPC; and the indolence of NNPC workers regarding the cross-checking of oil exports and loading forms. The report also uncovered that NNPC had been paying its share of operational costs for the production of oil which had never been lifted. Oil companies claimed that the crude remained unlifted because the state was not able to market it during this period. Compensation/repayment worth about 182 million barrels of oil was demanded from Shell, Mobil and Gulf (Barrows, *IPI Data Service, Africa*, No. 47, *Nigeria*, 1986, p. 33; Onoh, 1983, p. 37)

28. At the time these changes were made, the refining sector accounted for about 60 per cent of the Nigerian oil industry manpower (Onoh, 1983, p. 40).

29. *OPEC Bulletin*, March 1990, p. 10.

30. In early 1991, the government gave NNPC full permission to deregulate product prices in the country, essentially allowing market forces to determine prices of the various products to marketing companies. It was expected that NNPC would only gradually remove the subsidies on products. This has yet to be accomplished, and it is quite evident that this change is basically a cosmetic one, in keeping with NNPC's new commercial structure. On a sensitive political issue such as the removal of product subsidies, the federal government will invariably, if unofficially, always make the final decision (*Platts*, 12 February, 1991).

31. *PE*, February 1991, p. 23.

32. IMF, *International Financial Statistics*, various issues.

33. Over-production in Nigeria has never been a serious cause for concern for OPEC. In one analysis of production patterns and quotas in OPEC, three criteria are used for assessing over- and under-production during the periods April 1982–March 1983; April 1983–September 1984; October 1984–December 1986; January 1987–December 1988. The first criterion bases itself on a legal interpretation of the production agreement and compares production quotas with actual production levels for a given period. Under this criterion, although Nigeria over-produced for the latter three periods, the volume of over-production was either about the same as other countries such as Indonesia and Ecuador in the second period, or much lower than other countries, such as the UAE and Kuwait during the third and fourth periods. The second criterion takes a political perspective on the production agreement and compares quotas implicit in actual OPEC aggregate production with actual production in the various periods (see source for details on 'adjusted, implicit quotas'). Under this criterion, Nigeria over-produced in the middle two periods. Over-production as a share of its quota was significantly lower than that for Qatar and Ecuador in the second period, and significantly lower than that for the UAE and Ecuador for the third period. The third and final criterion interprets the production agreement from an economic perspective

and compares a notional output level, that required to fulfil the price objective of $18.00/b, with the actual output level during these periods. Results show that under this criterion, over-production, for OPEC as a whole, was only significant in 1988. And during this year, Nigeria's share of over-production at 3.7 per cent was significantly lower than that of the UAE, Saudi Arabia, Kuwait, Iraq, and Ecuador (Mabro, 1989, pp. 11–24). If, as this analysis shows, Nigeria's over-production has not been as significant as for other countries on an annual average basis, then it can be said that the crude output behaviour of foreign producing companies/concessions has not, on average, caused undue problems for NNPC in its setting of production allowables.

34. Barrows, *IPI Data Service, Africa,* No. 50, *Nigeria,* 1987, p.26.
35. Apart from the conventional justifications for retaining links with OPEC (the advantages of a cartel and the strength of individual countries within a cartel), two other reasons, one political and one psychological, have also been put forth. First, the close political, religious and economic relationships between Nigeria and Saudi Arabia work against the former renouncing OPEC. Secondly and more intangibly, Nigeria's relationship with Britain as a former colony is not an entirely flawless, smooth and tension-free one. The perception that Britain would be more than satisfied to see the break-up of OPEC suggests that this may in fact militate against the anti-OPEC tendency in Nigeria (Wright, 1986, p. 77).
36. *PE,* March 1987, p. 88.

3   THE NIGERIAN UPSTREAM SECTOR

Producing Areas and Oilfields

The structure of Nigeria's producing areas is interesting because – with the exception of sixteen giant oilfields and a few others – the country's oilfields tend to be small, with most producing under 10,000 b/d on average. Fifteen of the sixteen giants[1] (excluding Edop for which reliable production figures are not available) have been responsible for only 37.9 per cent of the country's historical production and only 30.4 per cent of the average production in 1990. The very numerous smaller fields, therefore, are significant both in terms of their share of total cumulative production up to 1990, and of average daily production in 1990. Despite the fact that only 57 per cent of total wells were actually producing in 1990, the small size of most of the oilfields resulted in fairly low average production rates of about 1,151 b/d per well.[2] An important implication of this is that there is a continuing need to explore in order to supplement and augment proven oil reserves. Furthermore, the small size of the fields necessitates a well-developed pipeline network between the fields in order that the gathering and blending of the crudes can be carried out without much difficulty.

The first Nigerian oilfield was found in 1956 in tertiary sediments in the Niger Delta Basin. Although it was small, the Oloibiri field, about 90 km. west of Port Harcourt, pointed to the existence of a commercially exploitable accumulation of oil in the area. Less than a year later Afam was discovered, 30 kilometres east of Port Harcourt. Larger, more prolific discoveries, including Imo River, Bomu, Umuechem and Koro Koro, were also discovered in the porous tertiary sandstones of the Delta area. The first offshore oilfield was discovered on the Okan structure in 1964, ten kilometres from the coast off the Bendel state, in the Delta Basin area.[3]

Other less explored yet promising oil-producing areas lie to the north and include the Chad Basin in Borno state in the north east and the Sokoto basin in the north west of the country. Oil-producing potential in the Chad and Sokoto basins is premised on the existence of a sedimentary geological structure similar to that in the Niger Delta (Oremade, 1986, p. 5).

Of the 176 oilfields in Nigeria, forty-five are offshore fields (or 26 per cent); sixteen are known 'giants', of which five are offshore fields (Okan, Meren, Ekpe, Edop and DeltaSouth). The first giant oilfield, Bomu, was discovered in 1958 about 40 km. east of Port Harcourt in Cross River state. Thirteen more were discovered between 1958 and 1969, all in the southern coastal states of Cross River, Imo, Rivers and Bendel. The last two giants to be discovered were Nembe Creek in 1973 and Edop in 1981. Nembe Creek is about 15 km. off the coast in the state of Rivers, and Edop is an offshore field, about 30 km. from Qua Iboe in the state of Cross Rivers.

Since oil was first discovered at Oloibiri, the Niger Delta Basin has proved to be the most prolific producing area in Nigeria, containing seventy-eight oilfields, including the largest, Forcados Yorki.[4] The Basin covers the Nigerian states of Rivers, Bendel, Imo, Cross River and Ondo, an area of about 75,000 sq. km. or about 8 per cent of the country. It lies to the south of the older Cretaceous Anambra Basin, and is separated by the Okitipupa High from the Benin Basin in the west, and by a line of Cameroon volcanics in the east (Tiratsoo, 1984, p. 228). Much of the inland area is covered by tropical rainforest while mangrove forest dissected by numerous creeks and rivers characterizes the coastal area. The terrain, therefore, is difficult to explore not only because of the inaccessibility of river and swamp areas onshore, but also because the reservoirs are generally small and numerous, at times stacked one above the other holding trapped gas or water in between.[5]

Table 3.1 lists the principal oilfields of Nigeria (See Appendix 2 for the complete list).

Reserves

In 1992, Nigerian proved crude oil reserves were estimated at 17.9 billion barrels. Recent government goals for the oil industry have included increasing recoverable reserves to 20 billion barrels by the year 2000, a level last reached in 1975, when reserves were estimated at 20.2 billion barrels.[6] Table 3.2 shows the historical series of Nigerian oil reserves as well as the evolution of

Table 3.1: Principal Oil Fields of Nigeria as of 31 December, 1990.

Name of Field Discovery Date	Production 1990 Average Barrels per day	Cumulative Production (31 December, 1990) Barrels
Afisere, 1966	11,844	125,204,182
Agbada, 1960	19,694	196,223,121
*Asabo, 1966	16,492	173,832,194
Benisede, 1973	34,325	127,045,999
Bomu, 1958	6,146	359,457,322
Cawthorne Chan, 1963	47,581	314,445,240
*Delta, 1965	18,348	183,849,519
***Delta South**, 1965	33,748	294,165,950
Diebu Creek, 1966	9,753	112,470,475
Ebocha, 1965	8,838	116,662,592
***Edop**, 1981	40,000	n.a.
Egwa, 1967	16,944	146,784,895
Ekulama, 1958	44,882	231,433,712
***Ekpe**, 1966	14,222	198,798,729
*Enang, 1968	17,261	144,339,212
Etelebou, 1971	14,529	132,206,501
*Etim, 1968	17,972	125,688,898
Forcados Yorki, 1968	53,562	590,642,984
Imo River, 1959	47,017	498,674,807
*Inim, 1966	13,432	154,868,705
Jones Creek, 1967	37,541	423,977,565
Kokori, 1961	19,387	322,186,233
Kolo Creek, 1971	20,691	144,265,152
Makaraba, 1973	24,294	109,307,897
*Malu, 1969	15,595	114,239,427
Mbede, 1966	12,589	172,997,990
*Meji, 1965	18,317	164,923,785
***Meren**, 1965	58,427	536,009,957
Nembe Creek, 1973	96,778	285,191,169
*North Apoi, 1973	34,706	189,057,507
Obagi, 1964	55,384	386,600,000
Obama, 1973	14,877	108,476,448
Oben, 1972	16,533	134,469,258
Obigbo North, 1963	12,142	183,246,416
Odidi, 1967	46,405	239,265,369
Oguta, 1965	10,622	136,391,060
***Okan**, 1964	42,108	471,062,427
Olomoro, 1963	16,609	292,362,402
Opukushi	25,222	133,578,606
Otumara, 1969	46,204	188,341,053
*Parebe/Eko, 1968	10,115	110,709,677

Table 3.1 Continued.

Name of Field Discovery Date	Production 1990 Average Barrels per day	Cumulative Production (31 December, 1990) Barrels
Sapele, 1969	10,725	122,119,031
Soku, 1958	9,563	118,849,660
Tebidaba, 1972	15,901	130,095,927
*Ubit, 1968	39,586	210,098,065
Umuchem, 1959	4,510	151,464,846
Utorogu, 1964	8,454	136,284,367
Uzere West, 1963	5,803	103,685,793

Sources and Notes: *IPE*, 1992; Tiratsoo, 1984.
* refers to offshore fields; fields in boldface are those estimated to be 'giants' (with at least 500 million barrels of oil reserves) at time of discovery. The Edop field was commissioned in 1991 at 250,000 b/d; according to the Economist Intelligence Unit, *Nigeria, Country Profile 1991–2*, it was producing an average 40,000 b/d in this period. The Olomoro field includes Afisiere, Eriemu, and Oweh. Obagi includes Erema, and Mbede includes Ebocha. Sapele, in the Niger Delta, is reported to contain 700,000,000 barrels of heavy viscous crude (*O&GJ*, 26 February, 1990). 1991 data contains aggregated cumulative production and has therefore not been taken.

Table 3.2: Nigerian Historical Oil Reserve Data and Reserves/Production Ratios. Billion Barrels of Oil and Remaining Years of Production at then Current Levels.

Year	Reserves	R/P Ratio
1958	0.02	12.0
1960	0.15	20.5
1965	3.0	29.9
1970	9.3	23.5
1975	20.2	31.0
1980	16.7	22.3
1985	16.7	31.0
1988	16.0	32.2
1989	16.0	27.5
1990	16.0	27.1
1991	17.1	26.0
1992	17.9	26.5

Sources: *IPE*, 1992; *Oil Data Sheet, Institute of Petroleum* for 1960 reserves; Schatzl, 1969: *Esso Magazine*, No.1, 1962 for reserves in 1958; *BP Statistical Review of World Energy* for R/P Ratios, various issues.

the reserves/production ratio over the period 1958–92.

In a country where most oil accumulations are small, a continual programme of exploration and exploratory drilling is necessary if the reserves/production ratios are to be kept high.[7] This has not been the case in Nigeria. The main addition to reserves took place in the period 1965–75 when they increased from 3 to 20 billion barrels and high exploratory and development activity coincided with a high finding rate. The period 1975–80 conversely saw the steepest decline in reserves, a result mainly of low exploratory and development activity. Oil reserves in the decade of the 1980s declined in the first half and stayed stable at 16 billion barrels in the second half.[8] The last few years have seen a pick-up in reserves, presumably as a result of the increase in exploratory activity after 1986.

Exploration and Development

Additions to existing reserves are linked to both the number of exploratory wells drilled and the success of this exploratory effort. Exploratory drilling is in turn influenced by oil prices, production levels relative to existing capacity and government incentives for long-term investments by oil companies. In general, the link between low oil prices, production rates lower than capacity and exploratory effort is clear. Low oil prices imply reduced absolute profits for the oil company and hence smaller sums allocated to capital investment in exploration and development. Low production rates from facilities designed to supply more provide a similar disincentive to the oil company to invest in exploration and development since the existence of large unused capacity means that there is no immediate need to add to it. In Nigeria, as in other oil-producing countries, this general relationship is complicated by the nature of government policies. For instance, if the fiscal regime is such that the tax rate responds to changes in the economic environment – i.e. compensates for adverse changes in production rates, costs, oil prices, and so on – then exploration is less likely to be influenced by these factors. Similarly, if oil company profits are guaranteed, the changes in absolute price levels become irrelevant for the company. The nature of government incentives, in such cases, assumes greater significance than either oil prices or production rates in influencing exploratory activity.

Development drilling involves either further appraisal work on existing reservoirs or the drilling of new wells to relieve pressure on old ones. More development wells than exploratory wells are drilled in any one year but development follows the same general pattern as exploratory effort. In other words, development drilling is also influenced by oil price levels, excess capacities and the nature of government incentives. Success ratios, however, are necessarily higher than in exploratory drilling because development drilling takes place within existing reservoir areas and usually adds to proven reserves.

Historical trends in exploration and development are examined below. Figure 3.1 presents the historical spot prices of Nigerian Bonny Light between 1967 and 1992 while Table 3.3 presents a time series of wells drilled in Nigeria during the period 1951–92.

In the early to mid 1960s a rapid increase in exploration and development wells occurred, largely because of the additional contribution to drilling by newcomers (Tennessee in 1962, American Overseas and Gulf in 1963, Agip and Safrap in 1964)

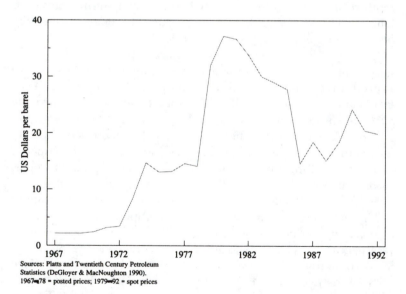

Sources: Platts and Twentieth Century Petroleum
Statistics (DeGloyer & MacNoughton 1990).
1967–78 = posted prices; 1979–92 = spot prices

Figure 3.1: Historical Spot Prices of Nigerian Bonny Light. 1967–92. US Dollars per Barrel.

Table 3.3: Historical Data on Wells Completed. 1962–92.

Year	— — — — — — — —	—	Exploration	— — — — — — —	— — — —	Development
	Total	Oil	Gas	Dry	Success Ratio(%)	Total
1962	5	2	0	3	40	31
1963	22	10	2	10	55	28
1964	37	21	4	12	68	66
1965	65	39	0	26	60	95
1966	66	24	1	41	36	149
1967	79	26	1	52	34	87
1968	38	20	0	18	53	87
1969	27	7	0	20	26	128
1970	31	11	0	20	36	137
1971	55	22	1	32	42	172
1972	61	26	0	35	43	197
1973	45	22	2	21	53	194
1974	51	18	5	28	45	198
1975	33	12	3	18	46	189
1976	21	9	3	9	57	122
1977	24	6	6	12	50	94
1978	35	21	1	13	63	69
1979	22	11	2	9	59	83
1980	31	14	5	12	61	62
1981	26	14	3	9	65	143
1982	30	15	2	13	43	114
1983	63	37	6	16	68	52
1984	42	17	4	18	50	43
1985	28	10	4	11	50	32
1986	31	18	5	8	74	30
1987	41	25	2	14	66	20
1988	46	26	5	15	67	45
1989	48	32	5	9	77	43
1990	68	42	6	18	71	56
1991	58	38	2	13	69	88
1992	53	34	6	10	75	102

Sources and Notes:

1962–1982 data from *American Association of Petroleum Geologists Bulletin*, various issues.

1980 includes 1 well of both Oil and Gas; 1981 includes 7 wells of both Oil and Gas; 1982 includes 11 wells of both Oil and Gas.

1983-1992 data from Petroconsultants, *World Petroleum Trends, 1993*.

1983 includes 4 unspecified; 1984 and 1985 include 3 unspecified each; 1989 and 1990 include 2 unspecified each; 1991 includes 5 unspecified; and 1992 includes 3 unspecified.

The success ratio in 'development drilling' averages about 85-95 per cent.

and the increased development work of Shell–BP and Mobil. The outbreak of civil war in June 1967 affected both exploratory and development efforts for two years; nevertheless, some exploratory activity took place in the offshore, where production continued throughout, and in certain areas onshore. In the years following the end of the civil war in January 1970, there was a resumption of exploratory activities in eastern Nigeria.

In the period 1970–75 when world oil prices were rising, Nigerian production levels increased with new oil companies putting their first fields on stream, and both the number of exploratory wells drilled and the success ratio of drilling going up. Crude oil reserves increased from 9.3 billion barrels in 1970 to 20.2 billion barrels in 1975. That year saw the beginning of the decline in exploratory activity in Nigeria. With the exception of a short recovery in 1978 and again in 1983–4, exploratory drilling continued to decline until 1986. Reserves decreased from 20 billion barrels in 1975 to 16.7 billion barrels in 1980. Development drilling also started to decline in 1975, and with the exception of some recovery in 1981 and 1982 (probably as a result of high oil revenues in 1980), continued to do so until at least 1987.

The first major fiscal incentives for exploration investments came in 1977 and reversed, temporarily, the decline in exploratory wells drilled. The 'Buhari Incentives' (offered during Obasanjo's military regime) were formulated to encourage exploration by a cut in the Petroleum Profit Tax from 85 per cent to 65.75 per cent until pre-production costs were amortized; both exploratory and appraisal drilling were encouraged by counting the former and the first two appraisal wells in each field as a tax deductible expense rather than capital investment. Offshore work was encouraged by lowering royalty rates and providing investment tax credits linked to water depth i.e. 5 per cent for land operations, 10 per cent for offshore fields increasing to 20 per cent for depths greater than 200 metres.[9] These incentives led to increased budgets for exploration in most companies, and certainly overall exploratory activity in 1978 was higher than year earlier levels. However, it is also claimed that the greatest amount of seismic work in this period was being contracted out by NNPC.[10]

With the exception of 1983–84, exploratory effort was relatively low in absolute terms in the early 1980s and successes did not translate into any large reserve additions. With crude oil production also plunging at the time, reserve levels in the period 1980–5 remained more or less stagnant at 16.7 billion barrels, while the R/P ratio increased. The Nigerian government attempted to reverse the flagging exploration trend, and to satisfy discontented oil companies (thereby raising crude liftings) by increasing official equity margins and production cost allowances in July 1982 and again in February 1983 (see section on the fiscal regime in Chapter 4). While production and exploration were revived to some extent, certain issues remained unresolved. The fixed production allowance did not distinguish between high-cost and low-cost concessions, onshore and offshore fields. For offshore producers whose production costs exceeded the $2.00/b cost allowance, profitability decreased by the same amount. Furthermore, the real value of official profit margins declined in line with inflation, while companies' costs increased in line with it.[11]

Exploratory drilling picked up after 1986 and success rates were also relatively higher than in earlier years. However, increasing crude oil production in this latter period and presumably the size of the discoveries meant that reserve levels remained around 16 billion barrels till 1990.

While several factors helped in the recovery of exploration and development,[12] increasingly stronger world demand and higher oil production (i.e. closer to actual capacity levels) in subsequent years were incentive enough for oil companies to increase exploration. The eventual addition to reserves, from 16 billion barrels in 1990 to 17.1 billion barrels in 1992, is thought to be the result of oil companies concentrating on previously explored areas, enhanced recovery techniques, and some new discoveries.[13] These reserve additions have been made in a period of increasing oil demand and production levels.

As a result of the increased use of the 'three dimensional seismic' instruments for successful drilling, enhanced recovery and reservoir management programmes, sizeable additions to recoverable reserves were made in 1990. In August 1990, the NNPC–Shell venture found a giant, Gbaran, in Rivers State, estimated to hold reserves of 722 mb of oil and 500 bcf of gas. In April 1990, Mobil struck oil in a new offshore tract, south east of Nigeria near Camerooni waters, in a field named Etoro-1; in

August, a discovery was made in the same tract in a field named Ekiko. These two new finds by Mobil added about 130 mb to oil reserves.[14] Again in November 1991, it was reported that Mobil's two new offshore discoveries, Yoho-1 and Omon-1, held about 450 mb of reserves. [15] By 1991, the Nigerian government was saying that all reserve estimates (17.1 billion barrels in that year), were 'underestimates'.[16] Out of an approximate 880 oil and gas fields discovered, only 180 had been developed and were producing.

An encouraging factor for future exploration and development is the revised Memorandum of Understanding signed by each producing company in 1991 for the period 1990–5.[17] This fiscal revision was basically a result of the stated goals of the government to increase productive capacity to 2.5 mb/d by 1996 and to increase recoverable reserves to 20 billion barrels by the year 2000. These government intentions essentially meant that interest would have to be reactivated in the remoter inland areas and deeper offshore. The government, therefore, had to respond to a situation where rising development costs were cutting into profit margins and where exploration in new areas was becoming more difficult and more expensive. To this end, changes were made in profit margins and production cost allowances depending on the extent of capital expenditure by the oil company on development. If total costs were kept low (below $2.50/b), then a minimum profit margin would be guaranteed at $2.30/b for equity production (after royalty and tax). If, however, average capital investment costs were equal to or exceeded $1.50/b in any one year, the notional profit margin would increase to $2.50/b and the allowance against tax for production costs would also increase to $3.50/b. The incentive for greater capital investment per barrel of production essentially meant that encouragement was being given to difficult production and exploration acreage where development is likely to be more capital intensive, and to investment in increasing the productive capacity of existing fields. Furthermore, the 1977 provisions for reduced royalty and PPT rates would also apply.[18] And finally reserve addition bonuses were also promised if additions in any year were greater than production. These bonuses took the form of 10–50 cents per barrel which could be offset against the company's PPT liability for any one year.[19]

Despite the already significant addition to reserves and as a result of the continuing official policy to work on the reserve potential of the frontier areas, open bidding rounds for onshore and offshore acreage were held in 1991, and again in 1992 for deep offshore blocks and the Chad and Benue troughs. After much delay and substantial revisions, oil companies signed production-sharing contracts in 1993 for territory originally allocated in the 1991 licensing round. These specific contracts do not benefit from provisions of the 1991 MOU, largely because the fiscal terms provided in the new PSCs were thought to be sufficient to provide an adequate return on oil company investment without the additional incentives of the MOU. The new and improved PSC terms include more flexible expenditure requirements, special royalty rates for deep water acreage and greater investment tax credits. At least six companies had signed production-sharing contracts on these terms by the summer of 1993. It should be noted, however, that these new terms are also favourable to the government for although it has access to less oil, this access is at no risk and in fact, the new tendency toward production-sharing ventures is thought to be a means of consolidating a 100 per cent ownership of reserves by the state while leaving many if not all the risks of investment in exploration and production to the contractor.

Crude Oil Production

As mentioned earlier, the first commercial oil field was discovered in January 1956 at Oloibiri. In 1958, the first year of oil exports from Nigeria, production amounted to about 5000 b/d. By 1992, average daily crude oil production was 1.85 mb/d and about 2.9 per cent of world production. In 1991, the most recent year for which detailed information is available, oil was produced from 176 fields, including forty-four offshore fields. Oil production from these latter fields represented some 30 per cent of total production.

Table 3.4 shows the historical evolution of Nigerian crude oil production. Discussed below are the most noteworthy changes to take place in the late 1960s when production took off, in 1974–5 when production declined by almost half a million barrels, and between 1979 and 1983 when production fell by almost 1 mb.

Table 3.4: Nigerian Crude Oil Production, Historical Series. 1958–92. Thousand Barrels Daily.

Year	'000 b/d	% Share of World Total	Year	'000 b/d	% Share of World Total
1958	5	0.03	1975	1,785	3.21
1959	10	0.05	1976	2,065	3.44
1960	20	0.09	1977	2,095	3.34
1961	55	0.23	1978	1,920	3.04
1962	70	0.27	1979	2,300	3.50
1963	75	0.27	1980	2,055	3.27
1964	120	0.41	1981	1,440	2.42
1965	275	0.87	1982	1,285	2.25
1966	420	1.22	1983	1,235	2.18
1967	320	0.87	1984	1,385	2.39
1968	140	0.35	1985	1,475	2.57
1969	540	1.23	1986	1,465	2.44
1970	1,085	2.25	1987	1,290	2.15
1971	1,530	3.01	1988	1,365	2.18
1972	1,815	3.39	1989	1,635	2.56
1973	2,055	3.51	1990	1,780	2.75
1974	2,260	3.86	1991	1,895	2.95
			1992	1,850	2.90

Source: *BP Statistical Review of the World Oil Industry*, various issues.

Production grew from 20,000 b/d in 1960 to 540,000 b/d in 1969. The decade saw the construction of the crude oil port and tanker terminal of Bonny in 1961 and the expansion of the pipeline system and transport; the completion of the trans-Niger pipeline in 1965 which essentially gave oil from mid-western fields access to the Bonny terminal; and the coming onstream of twelve 'giant' discoveries, including the first offshore discovery, Okan in 1964. During the Biafran war, all companies, except Gulf Oil from its offshore concern, suspended production, and output declined to 140,000 b/d in 1968. By 1969 however, production had taken off to 540,000 b/d and by 1971 had increased by about a million barrels to 1.53 mb/d.

Nigerian production in the early 1970s increased steadily to 2.26 mb/d in 1974, largely due to the government's stated aim of increasing production, continuing exploration successes, and on-going world demand for sweet Nigerian crude. Revenues in

1974 far exceeded budgetary needs and this gave rise to the realization that reserves should be conserved and production ceilings introduced on a well-by-well basis. Although ceilings were not enforced, the recognition of the limited nature of reserves eventually brought about the 1977 'Buhari incentives' for exploration. As it happened, declining world oil demand, and increasing competition from cheaper Middle Eastern crudes in 1975, caused production to drop. Production cuts were also made due to the decision of the government not to deplete reserves in such a situation. In August 1975, however, prices were cut in an attempt to make Nigerian crude more competitive. These were reversed and upward price adjustments made by October 1975.[20] In 1976 and 1977, demand for Nigerian crude and hence production stabilized somewhat. There was, however, a shift away from the European to the US market. Refinery operating costs were lower there than in Europe, and since all domestic demand was satisfied domestically, there was a greater willingness, on the part of the USA, to buy the marginal barrel of costly Nigerian crude.[21] 1978 saw production decrease further largely due to the oversupply of light, sweet crudes, and increased competition from non-OPEC supplies – primarily from the North Sea, Alaska and Mexico. Had this trend continued to the point that production was much below capacity (assuming that to be 2.3–2.4 mb/d in 1978), a large part of the capacity would have been shut in and exploration would have slowed down, despite the 1977 exploration incentives. Fortunately for Nigeria, in 1979 oil prices and world oil demand had risen in anticipation of tight crude supply as a result of the Iranian revolution and consequently, Nigerian crude output peaked at 2.3 mb/d.

Production growth in both the 1960s and 1970s had been largely due to exploration successes, the proximity of Nigerian crudes to the Atlantic Basin markets, and the high quality of Nigerian crude. Despite the two peaks in production in the seventies, the average annual growth rate of production in this period was only about 7 per cent per annum. Some analysts have attributed this relatively low growth rate to a strategy limited by the absorptive capacity and internal constraints of the Nigerian economy (Cochrane and Struthers, 1983). However, subsequent drops in output seemed to be influenced more by fluctuations in the level of world demand for Nigerian crude, than a production policy specifically responding to the limited capacity of the economy to absorb oil revenues.

Generally speaking, the declining production levels and productive capacity of the 1980s in Nigeria was due to structural changes in world oil demand and waning exploration in Nigeria itself. 1980 saw the onset of recession in the West, declining oil consumption, and the reinforcement of energy conservation and fuel-switching measures. Exacerbating this situation was the increased price competition from North Sea oil and increasingly sophisticated refining and catalytic conversion which made heavier oil more competitive with light Nigerian oil.

Between 1980 and 1983, oil production fell from 2.3 mb/d in 1979 to 1.2 mb/d in 1983. The impact on the economy was significant in that oil export revenues fell from $24.9 billion in 1980 to $9.9 billion in 1983. The decline in production was neither the result of productive capacity problems (the 1977 incentives to exploration were coming to fruition at this time and the prospect of shutting in capacity was more likely than starting production from these new developments) nor OPEC production quotas (which were implemented only after a substantial decline had already taken place); and it involved more than just a demand-led scaling back of oil operations in the country. The story of this earlier period is one of a mis-managed pricing policy in a context of declining oil demand, restrictive laws on oil company offtake, and the displacement of oil company crude production from Nigeria.

In 1980, with the price of Nigerian Bonny Light at $40.00/b, and declining world oil demand, the marketing of Nigerian oil had become increasingly difficult. Despite pressure from producing companies to lower prices, the government maintained the $40.00/b price and this consequently led to a number of large contract cancellations, plummeting government sales and reduced equity offtake. Aggravating this situation were the findings of the Irikefe committee in September 1980, set up by the Shagari government subsequent to the disappearance of substantial funds from NNPC coffers in 1979. The committee also investigated the relationship of NNPC with oil companies and found the latter guilty of 'over-lifting' between 1975 and 1978.

During these years of world oil surplus, NNPC, for lack of customers, had not always lifted its share of equity production (then at 55 per cent). Consequently oil companies, by default, had been lifting more than their 45 per cent share, since equity offtake at this time was based on allowable levels rather than actual levels. It is important to note however, that the military government, then in power, had encouraged oil companies to maintain liftings so as to uphold oil revenues. The Irikefe Committee changed the equity offtake rules, penalized the oil companies, and recommended that the future basis for the equity division of production between NNPC and the oil companies should be based on actual rather than allowable production rates. The penalty amounted to 80 mb of crude oil to be lifted over a period of time from Shell, Mobil and Gulf fields, as well as $900 million for NNPC's share of the operating costs. This meant that company offtake was limited by government sales and liftings, and specifically that in periods of world oil surplus, as in the early 1980s, Nigerian output would decline even further as NNPC clients would switch to the more competitively priced spot market, and oil companies would have to restrain liftings to comply with the actual production rate.[22]

The purpose behind this policy change was unclear. On the one hand, the government was aggravating an already bad situation of declining production by passing restrictive rules on equity offtake. On the other hand, by basing the penalty largely on barrels of crude oil, the government implicitly understood the severity of the production crisis.[23]

A comparison of the Nigerian production decline in the years 1980–83 and the production increase in the North Sea is striking. Nigerian production fell by about 830,000 b/d, while North Sea production rose by about 840,000 b/d.[24] More specifically, the Shell-led producing venture lost about 550,000 b/d of crude production between 1980 and 1983. Of this total, Shell's equity share amounted to about 220,000 b/d while its production in the North Sea rose by about 200,000. As a result of the inflexibility of the Nigerian government's pricing policy for a relatively short period in 1980 as well as its restrictive stance on equity offtake, the way was cleared for the displacement of Nigerian production by that of the North Sea. The oil companies, consequently, secured a better bargaining position *vis à vis* the government not only on price cuts but also increases in production cost allowances and profit margins.

While the price cuts of August 1981 and March 1982 made Nigerian crudes more competitive, at least with the less desirable Gulf crudes, and increased production for very short periods, the general decline in production continued till 1983. Similarly the increase in equity margins in June 1982 had little visible effect on production levels. However, with equity margins increased in January 1983, and prices cut further to $30.00/b in February, oil companies started lifting again from their Nigerian concessions. Furthermore, with effect from 1984, there was a reversion to pre-1980 rule on equity offtake according to 'allowable' production rates, and this reaffirmed the oil company's role as 'marketer' of Nigerian crude.[25] This change allowed oil companies to sustain liftings even when NNPC was unable to. In addition, the company was now allowed to offer its unsold participation crude to oil companies at equity terms (i.e. $2/b less than official prices) in return for the normal royalty, tax and government share of operating costs.[26] Lifting crude from Nigerian concessions became worthwhile again for producing oil companies and Nigerian production in 1984 and 1985 increased slightly.

At the beginning of 1985, Nigeria had abandoned the OPEC policy of defending prices in favour of a defence of market share (and in fact OPEC followed suit at the end of the year). The country's quota had reverted to 1.3 mb/d, yet Nigeria produced an average of 1.475 mb/d in 1985. While the policy in the early 1980s was to stick to its role as the marginal supplier in an oversupplied market by retaining its high pricing and targeting premium markets, by 1985 the Nigerian strategy was one of 'high volume and low prices.'[27] This attempt to recover market share led to discounting and price cuts of various crudes, different export mixes of crudes, a significant number of counter-trade deals, and discussions with equity producers to alter fiscal terms, particularly production cost allowances, so as to increase equity margins and boost company offtake.[28] Although a quota of 1.3 mb/d was reinstated by OPEC in September 1986, Nigeria produced an average 1.465 mb/d in the year. Production declined further in 1987, until the upturn in world oil demand directly influenced Nigeria. Production increased from 1988 onwards, and was very likely influenced by the revised fiscal terms of February 1987, which involved the protection of equity margins in times of falling prices (Brown, 1990, p. 320). Furthermore, a crude oil loan programme begun in April 1989 bypassed OPEC production quotas. Volumes of crude oil over and above contractual levels were loaned to US and European customers, who paid interest on the value of the barrels for 9–12 months, and then had the option of paying the principal, based on the price of the crude on the day of lifting.[29] This scheme enabled the Nigerians to acquire interest and revenues for what were essentially stocks which would otherwise be in the ground, and justify production over quota levels.

The Nigerian production quota was increased to 1.61 mb/d in January 1990, although production in the first half of the year averaged 1.8 mb/d. The extra production was supposedly for overseas storage. In reality, the loss of substantial refinery production necessitated increased exports to pay for costly product imports. 'Pressing revenue needs', therefore overshadowed 'export discipline'.[30] The commencment of the Gulf crisis in August 1990 reinforced the Nigerian comparative advantage as a source of non-Middle Eastern oil. Production quotas were abandoned for a period of time and Nigerian production averaged about 1.9 mb/d during the last few months of the year, while daily crude production averaged 1.78 mb/d in 1990. Since then, average daily production of crude oil has risen to 1.895 mb/d in 1991 and declined to 1.85 mb/d in 1992.[31]

The extent to which productive capacity has fallen or risen is unclear. It is clear, however, that capacity was at 2.4 mb/d in 1979 and had declined to 1.9 mb/d by late 1990, a fall of about half a million barrels per day. While it is true that the foreign oil company, the operator of most of the joint ventures, would have had no interest in either mismanaging or shutting in capacity, little exploration and few discoveries may have led to a gradual decay in productive capacity (the small size of Nigerian oilfields requires continuous exploration to sustain reserve and production levels.)[32] When production fell from 2.3 mb/d in 1979 to 1.3 mb/d in 1982, and the Nigerian oil industry was left with about 100 per cent over-capacity, some mis-management in the shutting in of capacity and appropriate moth-balling may have occurred. Whatever the extent of the decay in productive capacity, substantial investment and a certain amount of time (re-pressurization of shut-in wells; 3–5 year lead-time to add discoveries to capacity) would be needed in the early 1990s to re-establish adequate productive capacity.

The Gulf crisis had emphasized the need for Nigeria to increase its productive capacity as its limits were reached fairly quickly, and it was unable to benefit greatly from the crude oil price hike. In the context of OPEC, where 'influence can be measured in barrels' (Reynard, 1991, p. 181), increasing productive capacity would be necessary if Nigeria was to get higher production quotas, and an improved reserve base was crucial because of the significant role played by oil in the economy. Hence the government aims to increase both. A number of producing companies have committed investment plans for the period 1992–6 to extend productive capacity (see Chapter 4 for details). This had increased to 2.1 mb/d by 1992, and is expected to be about 2.2 mb/d at the beginning of 1993, with an increase to 2.3 mb/d in 1994 and 2.5 mb/d by 1995–6.[33]

An increase in productive capacity to 2.5 mb/d would mean that Nigeria has managed to achieve a second peak in production. While the present level of reserves is adequate to produce at 2.5 mb/d, the actual attainment of this level of capacity will depend on investment levels, the nature of the acreage, and the associated costs. If the increase is achieved by expanding existing capacity, then the second peak may not be very costly in terms of investment requirements. If, on the other hand, the peak in production is based on new discoveries from the frontier acreage, then it will be achieved at much greater expense than the one in 1979.

Types of Crude Oil

High production growth and profitability during the 1960s and 1970s were the result of two main factors: the high quality of Nigerian crudes, making them popular with Western European and North American refiners, as well as the proximity advantage that they had to these markets relative to Middle Eastern oil. The 1980s saw the emergence and growth of North Sea crudes of similar high quality, and thanks to technological advances and investments, increasingly sophisticated refining in the West. The latter made sulphur-heavy crudes more competitive than hitherto with Nigerian sweet and light crudes. The main problem facing Nigeria now is how the competitiveness and comparative advantage of its crude can be re-established.

The first discovery at Oloibiri in 1956 was that of a heavy crude with an API gravity of 23° (Schatl, 1969, p. 38). Discoveries in the following two years, however, established what would be the main characteristic of most Nigerian crudes. Afam discovered in 1956 had an API gravity of 45.6°, Ekulama, discovered in 1958, had 31.6° API gravity and Korokoro, discovered in 1959, 35.8° API gravity.[34] Presently, Nigerian crude oil, with the exception of Bonny Medium, is generally light. All commercial streams have a very low sulphur content, the highest being only a 0.2 per cent in the Forcados Blend. Furthermore, Nigerian crudes are generally classified as aromatic and distillate-rich. Due to the relatively high yield of gasoline in the straight run distillation of some of the streams, some crudes are also often classified as gasoline-rich.

Table 3.5 shows the yield structure of the main Nigerian crude streams in both straight-run distillation and catalytic cracking. Of the crudes listed above, Forcados Blend and Bonny Medium are gasoil-rich, while Bonny Light and Brass River are gasoline-rich. There is therefore a certain seasonality in the demand for Nigerian crude – with the build-up of gasoline-rich crudes for the summer and gasoil-rich oil for the winter.

The crude oil production slate is biased toward the Bonny Light type, which accounts for about 60 per cent of total production,[35] while Forcados accounts for 26 per cent, Brass River for 10 per cent and Bonny Medium for 5 per cent.[36] Table 3.6 shows the average production, domestic refinery allocation and exports of Nigerian crude oil in February 1992. Of total production, about 1.67 mb/d (or 87 per cent) is exported.

As far as the crude oil export slate is concerned, 54 per cent of total exports are of the Bonny Light type, 29 per cent are accounted for by Forcados, 11 per cent by Brass River, and 6 per cent by Bonny Medium. The share of exports by crude type follows quite closely the share in production. Allocation to domestic refineries is also completely dominated by crudes of the Bonny Light type which account for 99 per cent of the total.

Apart from crude oil, Nigeria produces some condensates. Its main project was recently completed in Oso, a field in the Bight of Biafra, 56 km. offshore from the Qua Iboe terminal. The field, which was discovered by Mobil in 1967 and remained undeveloped for many years due to high costs of production,[37]

Table 3.5: Yield Structures of Nigerian Crude. Percentage.

Crude	API Gravity/ % Sulphur	Refining	Mogas	Distillate	Fuel Oil	Sulphur Content in Fuel Oil
Bonny Light	37°/0.1%	Cracking	42.33	49.27	8.40	0.48
		Straight-Run	21.82	50.74	27.40	0.34
Bonny Medium	26°/0.1%	Cracking	29.84	51.44	18.70	0.44
		Straight-Run	n.a	n.a	n.a	n.a
Brass River	42°/0.1%	Cracking	40.76	55.58	3.66	0.33
		Straight-Run	26.25	49.32	24.38	0.20
Escravos	36°/0.1%	Cracking	39.00	52.00	9.00	0.39
		Straight-Run	n.a	n.a	n.a	n.a
Forcados	31°/0.2%	Cracking	32.59	56.05	11.36	0.52
		Straight-Run	12.10	53.54	34.33	0.35
Pennington	36°/0.1%	Cracking	26.00	71.00	3.00	0.27
		Straight-Run	n.a	n.a	n.a	n.a
Qua Iboe	37°/0.1%	Cracking	40.76	55.58	36.60	0.33
		Straight-Run	n.a	n.a	n.a	n.a
Anten	35°/n.a.					
Odudu	n.a.					

Sources: *Platt's Oil Price Handbook and Oilmanac, 1991 Prices.* See also West African Crude Oil Assays in *O&GJ Data Book*, 1991; Nigeria Supplement, *Argus*, 23/30 December, 1991 and 17 May, 1993, p. 7.

Table 3.6: Crude Oil Production, Refinery Allocation and Export by Type of Crude. February 1992. Barrels per Day.

Type of Crude Oil	Production	Allocation to Domestic Refineries	Export
Bonny Light	497,146	142,215	354,931
Bonny Medium	93,002		93,002
Brass River	186,407		186,407
Escravos	265,421	96,405	169,016
Forcados	494,131	3,325	490,806
Pennington	45,920		45,920
Qua Iboe	313,695		313,695
Anten	17,315		17,315

Source: NNPC, London.

holds reserves of about 3 trillion cubic feet (tcf) of gas and 445 mb of condensates. Once completed, it is expected to produce at least 100,000 b/d of condensates required for export, as well as 300 mcf/d of high pressure gas which will be reinjected into the reservoir to maintain pressure. In addition to the Oso field, Oredo, a field in the Bendel state being developed by NPDC, a subsidiary of NNPC, is estimated to hold, besides oil and gas, 12 mb of condensates.[38]

APPENDIX TO CHAPTER 3

Crude Oil Production, Distribution and Storage Facilities

Nigeria's crude oil pipeline system is not very large in terms of total length, but it is complex because of the small size of each link and the concentration of the system in the Niger Delta area. Total crude pipeline length, in 1990, amounted to about 2000 km.[39] Of this, the 617 km. Warri-Kaduna pipeline is the longest. Other important parts of the pipeline network include the Ramuekpe-Bonny Terminal link which is part of the Trans-Niger pipeline; the Ogoda-Brass Offshore link, and the Escravos-Warri pipeline. These links are longer and of larger diameter and therefore have greater flow capacity. Table A3.1 shows a complete picture of crude oil pipelines in Nigeria. A detailed picture of Nigeria's crude oil export infrastructure can be seen in Chapter 5. To briefly summarize here, however, Nigeria's seven crude oil export terminals include Escravos, Forcados, Pennington, Brass, Bonny, Qua Iboe and Anten. All have both onshore and offshore loading facilities, and all except Bonny onshore can handle Very Large Crude Carriers (VLCCs). Crude oil storage at the seven terminals amounts to about 29.8 mb.

In addition to crude oil storage tanks at the terminals, crude storage facilities at three of the four refineries can hold about 4 mb of crude oil. Port Harcourt I can hold up to 438,000 barrels, Port Harcourt II can hold 2,250,000 barrels of crude and Warri has storage facilities for up to 1,350,000 barrels. Information for the Kaduna refinery is not available.[40]

In 1985, NNPC had just one VLCC 'MV Oloibiri' which was used as floating storage at Pennington terminal.[41] Data from OPEC shows that since 1986, the state company owns two tankers of a combined dead weight tonnage of 406,500 dwt.[42] This is probably because the vessel Tuma was made functional again. Oloibiri, which is a 276,895 dwt vessel, was built in 1976, and has been used as a storage vessel at Pennington. Tuma, which is a 136,100 dwt vessel was built a year earlier in 1975, and is used as a storage vessel at Bonny. Tankers used for export transportation are primarily oil company owned.

Apart from these two large storage vessels owned by the NNPC,

Table A3.1: Crude Oil Pipelines in Nigeria, Current Status.

Pipeline Link	Owner or Operator	Length (Km)	Diameter (cm)
Escravos/Warri	NNPC	61	61
Warri/Kaduna	NNPC	617	41
Nkpoku/Bomu	Shell	47	61
Apara/Nkpoku	Shell	11	20
Pennington/Export Terminal	Texaco	50	18/28/76
North Apoi/Export Berth	Texaco	26	33/76
Funiwa/Export Terminal	Texaco	26	46/76
Ramuekpe/Bonny Terminal	Shell	2 x 108	71, 51/61
Alakiri/Bonny Terminal	Shell	34	61
Ramuekpe/Nkpoku	Shell	35	51
Nembe Creek/Cawthorne Channel	Shell	82	61/71
Bonny Terminal/Offshore Platform	Shell	27	122
Kwale/Ogoda	Agip/NNPC	81	25/36
Ramuekpe/Ogoda	Agip/NNPC	23	36
Ogoda/Brass Offshore Terminal	Agip/NNPC	127	61/91
Azuzama/Tebidaba	Agip/NNPC	35	30
Clough Creek/Tebidaba	Agip/NNPC	52	25
Tebidaba/Brass Manifold	Agip/NNPC	45	46
Obama/Brass Manifold	Agip/NNPC	26	46
Brass Manifold/			
Brass Offshore Terminal	Agip/NNPC	37	61/91
Izombe/Ebocha	Ashland	26	25
Akam/Anten	Ashland	23	25
Adanga	Ashland	11	28
West Isan Malu/Parabe	Gulf	14, 8	41, 30
Parabe & Meji/Valve Platform	Gulf	45, 16	20, 51
Delta South & Okan/			
Valve Platform	Gulf	3, 3	41, 41
Valve Platform/Escravos	Gulf	2 x 11	41, 66
Makarba & Abiteye/Escravos	Gulf	24, 11	41, 66
Escravos/SBM	Gulf	24	66/107
Escravos/Warri	Gulf	97	61
Etim/Odoho	Mobil	26	33/36
Utue Ekpe/Idoho	Mobil	32, 45	41, 41/51
Idoho/Qit	Mobil	21	61
Bogi/Ebughu	Ashland	2 x 3	15, 20
Mimbo/Anten Terminal	Ashland	3	15
Ukpam/Adanga	Ashland	8	15
Iyakb/Iyaka/Ekua	Mobil	14	33/46
Unamb/Ubit F	Mobil	3	33

Source: *OPEC Annual Statistical Bulletin,* 1992.

Nigeria also has two smaller (probably product) tankers owned by private tanker companies. These are the 'Ughelli Kingdom', with 2490 dwt, built in 1971, and owned by OBOLI Nigeria, Ltd. (Warri, Nigeria). The second tanker is 'Mickey', with 2515 dwt, built in 1966, and owned by the Orient Shipping Company Ltd. of Lagos.[43]

The costs of the Oso Condensate scheme will be discussed later in Chapter 4. It is perhaps important to note here the infrastructural facilities that the scheme requires and which were completed by 1993, at the time the project came onstream. At an initial production rate of 100,000 b/d, the Oso field requires a gas injection rate of 500 mcf/d, fifteen production wells and six injectors.[44] In addition, the project requires eight offshore platforms, a condensate pipeline from Oso to Qua Iboe, condensate storage tanks at the terminal, dedicated export facilities, and low pressure gas gathering facilities to connect nearby oilfields with Oso.[45]

Notes

1. Giant oilfields are those with recoverable reserves of 500 million barrels or more at time of discovery.

2. Of a total of 2,754 oil wells, 1,574 were producing and the average cumulative production per day of all these fields on 31 December, 1990 was 1,810,913 b/d (*IPE*, 1992, p. 296). Of a total of 2,335 oil wells, 2,187 were producing and the average cumulative production per day of all these fields on 31 December, 1991 was 1,891,596 b/d (Ibid., 1993, p. 313).

3. The continental shelf in this part of West Africa is very gentle, the shallow water thus facilitating initial exploration. Increasingly, however, deeper waters are being explored (Tiratsoo, 1984, p. 228).

4. Half the surface area of Nigeria is made up of igneous and metamorphic rock which potentially is not productive of oil. The other half is made up of Cretaceous-age and sedimentary rock, of which four sedimentary basins are considered to have oil potential: the Anambra basin, north of the Niger delta area; the Dahomey basin, in the Lagos area, straddling both Nigeria and Benin; the Niger Delta basin, onshore and offshore in the southern-most parts of the country; and the Chad basin, in the north-east. While initial oil and gas exploration was concentrated in the Cretaceous area north of the delta, much of the current production issues from Tertiary deltaic sands of Miocene age. The principal sources of the eastern oils, the mainly lighter, more paraffinic crudes, are the marine 'Ataka Shales', and the most productive rock for the western oils, the waxy, napthenic crudes, is known as the 'Agbada Formation'(Alazard,

1990; Barrows, *IPI Data Service, Africa* No. 31, *Petroleum Geology of the Niger Delta*, 1979, p. 32).

5.   *Shell World*, October/November 1985, p. 10.

6.   *Energy Compass*, 31 January, 1992.

7.   The R/P ratio is computed by dividing the remaining reserves at the end of any one particular year with production of that year. The ratio computed refers to the number of years the remaining reserves would last if production were to continue at the then current levels.

8.   The R/P ratio, however, increased from 22.3 years in 1980 to 31 years in 1985. This was largely because of the significant fall in Nigerian crude oil production in the early 1980s.

9.   Colonel Buhari was the Federal Commissioner for Petroleum in the Obasanjo regime. He also oversaw the merging of the Ministry of Petroleum Resources with the state oil company (NNOC). Buhari, later General Buhari, overthrew the Shagari civilian regime in 1984.

10.   *PE*, November 1978, p. 473.

11.   The oil companies, therefore, wanted some indexation of their profit margin to either inflation or oil prices (*PE*, February 1983, p. 42.)

12.   In 1988, for instance, NNPC offered a 50 per cent discount on seismic data acquired by its own crew to oil companies to encourage exploration in the Benou Trough and Anambra Basin (EIU, *Nigeria, Country Profile 1991–2*, p. 26). Perhaps more significantly, and also in 1988, the Nigerian government threatened to call in licences issued in 1968, initially forty-year licences, claiming that these had been subsequently revised to twenty years. 'This was seen as a means of pressuring the oil companies to meet their exploration commitments' (Brown, 1990, p. 320).

13.   Chevron/Gulf, for instance, in the early 1990s embarked on secondary recovery of oil by using water injection techniques. These were mainly used in Delta South and in the Meren fields. 251 mb in the former and 485 mb in the latter, of original oil in place has been removed through these processes (*PE*, Sponsored Statement, February 1993, p. 32).

14.   Barrows, *Offshore Petroleum Industry*, No. 85, 1990, p. 100.

15.   *Platts*, 8 November, 1991, p. 1.

16.   *Platts*, 25 October, 1991, p. 3.

17.   The 1991 MOU is not a new document as such in that it consolidates the 1986 MOU with amendments, sideletters, and recently agreed modifications.

18.   These, as mentioned earlier, were the incentives provided under Colonel Buhari's tenure as Federal Commissioner for Petroleum in which royalty rates of 20 per cent were reduced in swamp and offshore areas: 18.5 per cent for depths up to 100m, 16.67 per cent for greater depths; and the 85 per cent petroleum profits tax was reduced to 65.75 per cent for a maximum of five years (for new companies, covering total production) until capital expenditures were recovered.

19.   *PE*, Special Supplement, July 1992.

20.   In 1975, the consequences of over-priced Nigerian crude were exacerbated by declining demand in Europe and the USA. Overpricing was traditionally due to the proximity advantage of Nigerian crudes to western refineries.

This meant shorter haul and cheaper transportation of Nigerian crudes. In 1975, this advantage *vis à vis* Middle Eastern crudes had almost disappeared due to the slump in the international tanker market (*PE*, January 1976).

21. Ibid., February and July 1976.
22. *PE*, February 1981.
23. With a similar understanding of the difficulties in marketing crude during this period and with a view to easing some of these difficulties, in February 1981 the Nigerian government reached a settlement with BP over compensation for its nationalized assets. The compensatory sum of $135 million was to be paid in crude oil, which amounted to approximately 3.35 mb at the then current price of Bonny Light at $40.02/b.
24. *BP Statistical Review of World Energy*, various issues.
25. *PE*, November 1984.
26. Ibid., March 1985.
27. Ibid., March 1986.
28. *Argus*, 24 May, 1985.
29. The success of this loan programme was said to be waning by July, when the addition to exports through it was expected to be only 300,000 b/d (*Platts*, 15 June, p. 1; *Argus*, 7 August, 1989, p. 2).
30. *Energy Compass*, 6 April, 1990.
31. It should be noted, however, that with the commissioning of the Oso Condensate project in December 1992, and initial production of 70,000 b/d of condensate, total crude oil and condensate production had risen to 2.1 mb/d in 1993 (*Cedigaz News Report*, no. 20, 21 May 1993, p. 3).
32. Productive capacity was estimated at 1.9 mb/d in 1986, and the decay in productive capacity from 2.4 mb/d in 1979–81 to 1.9 mb/d in 1986, was forecasted to continue at a 10 per cent depreciation rate for most of the 1980s (Barrows, *IPI Data Service, Africa*, No. 47, *Nigeria*, 1986, p. 43).
33. *Energy Compass*, 29 January, 1993.
34. See Appendix 2 for detailed data on Nigerian oil fields. Information includes ownership, discovery date, production and °API gravity by individual fields (*O&GJ*, 31 December, 1991).
35. Bonny Light type crudes include Escravos, Pennington, Qua Iboe, Anten, and Bonny Light itself, and since May 1993, the new Odudu blend. Of these, Bonny Light, Escravos and Qua Iboe, alone, account for production of about 1 mb/d.
36. Generally, the Shell-led venture produces the Bonny Light, Bonny Medium and Forcados streams; the Mobil–NNPC venture produces the Qua Iboe stream; the Agip–NNPC–Phillips venture produces the Brass River stream; the Texaco–NNPC–Chevron venture produces the Pennington stream; the Ashland production-sharing venture produces the Anten stream; and the Elf venture will produce the new Odudu blend.
37. The OPEC debate on condensates (primarily a Venezuelan/Kuwaiti dispute finally resolved in 1988) was mainly concerned with agreeing on the defining characteristics of condensates which had already been designated as being outside quota restrictions. Although the Mobil–NNPC decision to develop the Oso field was taken in 1990, it had nothing to do

with the debate for it had always been clear that the field was not in fact producing what could be defined as condensates.

38. *MEES*, 32:8, 28 November, 1988 and 32:31, 8 May, 1989; *Platts*, 15 March, 1990.

39. Shell Petroleum Development is currently involved in the construction of the following pipeline links:

1. An 11 km. crude line from Belema flowstation to Nembe Creek Cawthorne Channel. Completion was expected in December 1992.
2. A 69 km. crude line from Opukushi to Forcados terminal (Trans-Ramos Pipeline). Completion expected in December 1993.
3. A 10 km. crude line from Okpokonou flowstation to Southern Forcados pipeline at Ogara Manifold. Completion expected in December 1993.
4. A 10 km. crude line from Kanbo flowstation to Trans-Ramos Pipeline at Kanbo Manifold. Completion expected in December 1993.

(*O&GJ Data Book*, 1992, p. 175). Petroleum products pipelines, storage and distribution will be considered in Chapter 5.

40. World Bank, Africa Technical Department, *Petroleum Industry Data Sheets Sub-Saharan Africa*, September 1992.
41. *OPEC Bulletin*, July/August 1985.
42. *OPEC Annual Statistical Bulletin*, 1991.
43. *Lloyd's Maritime Directory*.
44. *Platts*, 2 May, 1990.
45. Ibid., 29 June, 1990.

4 NIGERIAN CONCESSIONS AND EQUITY PRODUCERS

Oil Company Participation

As of 1 January, 1993, there were fourteen oil-producing companies in Nigeria. The Nigerian companies were NNPC, NPDC owned by NNPC, and Dubri a private sector company. The other eleven were Agip, Ashland, British Gas, Chevron, Elf, Mobil, Pan Ocean, Phillips, Shell, Sun and Texaco.[1] In 1991, exploration licences had been offered to the BP–Statoil combine; Du Pont E&P BV, an affiliate of Conoco; and to Exxon,[2] thus diversifying foreign exploration in Nigeria to an extent; and to a number of indigenous concerns, for instance Consolidated Oil. Du Pont operates under joint-venture terms with four separate indigenous Nigerian companies each of which received their acreage under concession agreements with the government. Under concessions where local companies are involved, NNPC is not present in any capacity. Consolidated Oil operates on a sole concession basis. And in 1993, the BP–Statoil combine signed a production-sharing venture with NNPC. These new E&P companies have yet to see a commercial discovery.

Currently all oil production in Nigeria has Nigerian participation, generally through the state oil company, in one case its subsidiary NPDC, and in one case through the local private company, Dubri. Oil-producing companies operate under three main types of contracts. The *joint-venture contract* is the most common and accounts for more than 90 per cent of Nigerian oil production.[3] In a joint venture the government, through NNPC or NPDC, and the producing company(ies) share the costs of investment, exploration and production, and the volume of production itself, in the proportion of their participation stakes. For the private company in a joint venture there is both entitlement to the oil and ownership of the reserves, i.e. oil in the ground.[4] The *production-sharing contract* (PSC) involves the designation of a contractor, a foreign oil company, which makes the upfront investments in exploration, development and production of an oilfield on behalf of NNPC. If commercial quantities of oil are found, the contractor pays royalty and taxes, but is entitled at some stage to recover investment costs, and then share the remaining production with the government in agreed proportions, although the precise order of this may vary. The contractor in production-sharing contracts has title to oil produced, but does not own the field's reserves. In the *risk-service contract* (RSC), the contractor funds all exploration, appraisal and development costs in a particular contract area or block. If a field is found to be commercially viable, the contractor can undertake the production operation. If the field is found not to be commercially viable within a period of five years, all contractual obligations are terminated. The contractor in the risk-service contract is similar to that in the production-sharing contract in that there is no ownership of reserves but there is entitlement to oil once it is produced, in the form of crude oil for cost remuneration, as well as a first option to purchase a fixed quantity of crude from the contract acreage at official prices. This latter 'fixed' quantity of crude oil is where the RSC differs, perhaps substantially, from the actual sharing of crude oil production in PSCs.

Joint Ventures

Joint-venture contracts arose from Nigeria taking a participation interest in the oil concessions given to foreign oil companies in the 1950s and 1960s. The entitlement to oil and ownership of reserves resulted from historical developments, and not because this feature is inherent to such contracts.

In 1992, Nigeria participated and produced from joint ventures with Shell, Agip and Elf; Chevron; Mobil; Agip and Phillips; Elf; Texaco and Chevron; Pan Ocean; and British Gas and Sun. In this year all production issued from joint ventures with the exception of the Ashland production-sharing venture and the Agip Energy service contract.[5]

Table 4.1 shows the changes in government participation in the Nigerian oil industry since the initial steps of nationalization in 1971. This process of participation or partial nationalization was a gradual one following the 1969 Petroleum Decree which gave majority ownership to the Nigerian government. However, the concession agreement with Nigerian Agip Oil Company (NAOC) in 1962, which already included an option for the

Table 4.1: Evolution of Government Participation in the Nigerian Oil Industry.

Company	Government Participation Per Cent	Date of Acquisition	Production at Date of Acquisition Barrels per Day
Elf	35.00	1 April, 1971	40,000
	55.00	1 April, 1974	85,700
	60.00	1 July, 1979	78,000
Agip/Phillips	33.33	1 April, 1971	30,000
	55.00	1 April, 1974	125,000
	60.00	1 July, 1979	230,000
Shell/BP	35.00	1 April, 1973	1,240,000
Shell	55.00	1 April, 1974	1,380,000
	60.00	1 July, 1979	1,360,000
	80.00	1 August, 1979	1,360,000
	60.00	1 June, 1989	904,900
Gulf	35.00	1 April, 1973	368,000
	55.00	1 April, 1974	390,000
	60.00	1 July, 1979	380,000
Mobil	35.00	1 April, 1973	210,000
	55.00	1 April, 1974	245,000
	60.00	1 July, 1979	270,000
Texaco	55.00	1 May, 1975	10,282
	60.00	1 July, 1979	56,000
Pan Ocean	55.00	1 January, 1978	10,000
	60.00	1 July, 1979	10,000

Sources and Notes: *Report on the Exploration and Exploitation Division*, NNPC, 1986; EIU, *Nigeria Country Profile, 1991–2*; *O&GJ*, 6 April, 1992.
Non-joint venture contracts: Ashland signed its first production-sharing agreement in 1973 and production from this concern was 30,600 b/d in 1991. The company's second production-sharing contract was signed in April 1992, which is yet to produce. Agip signed a risk service contract in September 1979. In 1991, this concern was producing 22,400 b/d.

government to participate in the equity of the company by 33.33 per cent, was exercised in 1971 when the company discovered oil in commercial quantities.[6] At the same time, the government acquired 35 per cent in Safrap (Elf). The latter was the condition under which Elf could resume production after the civil war, given the pro-Biafran stance of the French government during the crisis (Onoh, 1983, p. 22). From February 1972 onwards, no new concessions were given to oil companies, and all non-allocated and/or abandoned acreage became government property (Bach, Egg, and Philippe, 1988, p. 28).[7]

Furthermore, 'option rights for a 51 per cent interest in new concession-holders were also reserved.'[8] By April 1973, the government had acquired a 35 per cent equity stake in Shell–BP, Gulf and Mobil. A year later, the government had increased its equity stake to 55 per cent in all the above companies. Ongoing negotiations with Texaco–SoCal delayed the equity participation acquisition till 1978, which was then backdated to May 1975. In mid-1979, Marathon (Pan Ocean) interests were partially nationalized with the government taking 55 per cent. The deal was backdated to January 1978. Government participation in all producing ventures other than the production-sharing venture with Ashland and the Tenneco–Mobil–Sunray venture was increased to 60 per cent in July 1979. In August of the same year, the government nationalized all of BP's interests bringing their equity stake in the formerly Shell–BP venture to 80 per cent, with Shell participation at 20 per cent.

The nationalization of BP assets in 1979 occurred after the 'Kulu' incident when a BP-chartered tanker, with connections to South Africa, unloaded at Bonny and the company was consequently suspected of breaking the oil embargo against South Africa. 'Nigeria charged that exchanges of BP North Sea crude for Indonesian crude from Conoco resulted in some of the oil being shipped to South Africa.'[9] The nationalization came just before the Commonwealth conference in Lusaka where Britain was planning to take a softer approach to sanctions against Rhodesia. The motive behind the nationalization, therefore, might have been to influence UK policies on Rhodesia/Zimbabwe, particularly since compensation for the move would come much later. BP assets in Nigeria included pipelines, storage and export interests in eighty producing fields, 20 per cent share in the Port Harcourt refinery, a 60 per cent share in BP-Nigeria Marketing Company, and a 20 per cent share in the Shell–BP Development Company. At 1979 production levels, BP's share amounted to 276,000 b/d plus 100,000 b/d of buy-back crude from NNPC. With the company's refining commitments at 250,000 b/d, its African oil balance was seriously threatened. According to Barrows, the loss of Nigerian equity crude represented an estimated 9 per cent of the group's total crude oil supply. NNPC, on the other hand, would have very little problem in disposing of the extra oil given the political uncertainty regarding Iranian supplies, and certainly, the extra oil at the current premiums would be very profitable. Compensation for this nationalization was agreed in 1981 and was based on the written down value of the assets (in 1978 at $80 million) to be paid in crude oil. BP's 20 per cent equity in the Shell–BP–NNPC joint venture was valued at $113 million while the company's 60 per cent share in the British Petroleum Nigeria Marketing Company was assessed at $21 million. There was no 'allowance for loss of lifting rights,' a fact made clear by the total payment of $135 million which essentially implied three years production at 250,000 b/d at a price of $40.02/b.[10]

In 1989, NNPC through NPDC acquired 80 per cent interest in the Tenneco–Mobil–Sunray concern, with Mobil relinquishing its interest and Tenneco and Sun DX reducing theirs.[11] Also in 1989, NNPC reduced its 80 per cent equity interest in the Shell venture. Shell's interest increased to 30 per cent, and Agip and Elf each acquired 5 per cent. Through these changes in 1989, the government essentially reduced its equity share in production by about 18,000 b/d, and hence its share of the costs by a commensurate amount. One can say, therefore, that while the 1970s was the decade of nationalization, the 1980s saw a gradual realization that access to the marketing and investment funds of foreign oil companies would be of crucial importance to the continued growth of the Nigerian oil sector.[12] This awareness has in fact been brought home in the 1990s by NNPC's own precarious financial situation. In July 1993 plans were unveiled for the divestment of further NNPC shares, reducing its equity to 50 per cent in joint-venture operations (specifically Shell, Agip, Texaco, and Pan Ocean), in order to raise funds for other projects.

The question of why the Nigerian oil industry was not fully nationalized does arise. Up until 1974, government statements made it quite clear that the state was moving toward complete control of the oil industry, and the only possible delay in such a take-over would be a result of the lack of qualified personnel in the country. The awareness of Nigerian managerial and technical constraints in the ensuing years was probably the main determining factor of the type of participation arrangements reached in 1979.

Aggravating these problems were the fiscal constraints and production cutbacks which emerged in late 1977 and early 1978 and which made it unlikely that increases in participation would be embarked on at this stage. It is noteworthy that the increase in government equity participation to 60 per cent in July 1979 (which brought Nigeria in line with other OPEC producers who chose not to follow the 100 per cent nationalization route) and the politically motivated acquisition of BP's assets in August 1979 occurred against the backdrop of significantly improved oil export earnings in the wake of the supply crisis that occurred during the Iranian revolution.[13]

There has been little entry and exit of foreign oil companies in the Nigerian oil sector. With the significant exception of BP, which was expelled in 1979 and returned in 1992, almost all the oil companies have tended to stay on. Equity stakes in participation, however, have changed over the years. Despite these changes, the Shell consortium continues to be the most important oil-producing venture in Nigeria. In 1990, for instance, the Shell-led venture accounted for 51 per cent of total Nigerian oil production. The Chevron–NNPC venture produced 15 per cent and the Mobil–NNPC venture 13 per cent of total output. The shares of foreign oil companies in production are by definition much smaller than that of the joint venture. In 1990, these shares were as follows: Shell had access to about 15 per cent of Nigerian oil production, Chevron from its various concerns had 7 per cent, and Mobil had 6 per cent.

On top of this, the companies had access to whatever crude oil NNPC was unable to market directly by itself. Historically, the extent of NNPC's marketing role has fluctuated with evolving levels of government participation in producing ventures as well as changing legislation on the lifting of NNPC crude by other companies. In 1973, the state oil company, then NNOC, was responsible for marketing only 5 per cent of oil exported from Nigeria. By 1975, this share had increased to 40 per cent and by 1980, 61 per cent of oil exported was marketed by NNPC (Bach, Egg and Philippe, 1988, p. 33).

Government sales of crude oil, however, have not necessarily been equal to its equity share i.e. 60 per cent. Since October 1984, participation crude not sold by NNPC could be sold to producing companies on equity terms in return for which the

Table 4.2: Nigerian Crude Oil Producing Ventures as of 1992. Barrels per Day.

Producing Ventures	Production (Barrels per Day)		
	1990	*1991*	*Current Capacity (estimated)*
Joint Ventures			
Shell 30%, Agip 5%, Elf 5%, NNPC 60%	927,405	960,500	1,000,000
Chevron 40%, NNPC 60%	277,123	307,200	315,000
Mobil 40%, NNPC 60%	238,538	273,500	320,000
Agip 20%, Phillips 20%, NNPC 60%	146,324	140,500	150,000
Elf 40%, NNPC 60%	96,122	95,200	100,000
Texaco 20%, Chevron 20%, NNPC 60%	58,667	59,100	60,000
NPDC (NNPC) 80%, British Gas 15%, Sun 5%	1,816	2,800	2,000
Panocean 40%, NNPC 60%	1,157	1,200	1,200
Other Ventures			
Ashland, NNPC 100%			
Agip Energy, NNPC 100%			
Dubri 100%	908	-	1,000
TOTAL	1,812,039	1,893,100	2,015,000

Sources and Notes: *PE*, March 1992, p. 23; OPEC Library data.
Companies in bold face refer to the operator in each producing venture; the Ashland NNPC is a production-sharing concession, while the Agip Energy NNPC venture operates under a service contract.

producing company paid regular tax and royalty as well as NNPC's share of production costs.

All joint-venture companies benefit from the provisions of MOUs.[14] Both the initial 1986 MOU and the 1991 revised version have attempted to offer greater incentives for both exploration and production. These have for the most part taken the form of changes in production cost allowances and notional profit margins, although the latter had already been introduced in the period of posted prices before 1986 (see section below on the fiscal regime).

Production-Sharing Contracts

It is noteworthy that as of 1993 all new contracts signed were production-sharing contracts, and it is quite probable that this new trend may replace the almost complete reliance on joint-venture contracts. The first *production-sharing* contract was signed in 1973 with Ashland concerning two OPLs, one north-west of Owerri and the second offshore, south-east of Qua Iboe. This was amended in 1979 and again in 1986. In 1992, Ashland signed another production-sharing agreement for a further two OPLs both in the shallow offshore, south-east of the Brass River terminal. In 1993, new production-sharing terms were offered to the companies who had won exploration licences in the 1990–91 licensing round.[15] The six companies which had signed production-sharing contracts by mid-1993 were Shell, Mobil, Elf, Exxon and BP–Statoil. Table 4.3 presents a comparison of the main economic parameters in the different PSCs.

The first Ashland 1973 contract essentially gave the company 49.5 per cent of available oil production while costs were being recovered and production was under 50,000 b/d. For production above this figure the company had access to 48 per cent of available production. Once costs were recovered, however, Ashland's share was reduced to 9.5 per cent if production were under 50,000 b/d and 8 per cent if it were above this amount.[16] In 1979, the volume of cost oil as a share of total available production was increased.

The 1986 amendment of this earlier contract not only improved Ashland's royalty, PPT, investment tax credit and profit-sharing terms, it also altered the form of cost recovery.[17] Instead of allocating fixed shares of production for cost recovery (including royalty payments), payment of the PPT and then profit sharing, the 1986 amendment allowed the oil company to recover operating costs in the year of expenditure and amortize capital costs over five years, thus smoothing out the rate of cost recovery.[18]

Instead of being allocated specific shares of physical production toward the payment of taxes, the recovery of costs and the sharing of production, the amended PSC prioritized the payment of royalty and PPT, and limited the charging of capital costs in any one month to 1/60th of total recoverable costs, followed then by production sharing. The limit on the level of cost recovery in any given period was also important for the government in that it affected how quickly it could start sharing in the profits; while the prioritization of royalty and tax oil over cost recovery essentially meant that in any given period when there was not enough production for one of the three, it would be the latter that would be carried over. While the government had made a concession to oil companies regarding the rate of cost recovery, the actual order in which taxes were to be paid and costs recovered were to the government's advantage.

In 1992, Ashland signed another production contract with NNPC regarding two further OPLs in the shallow offshore. Because the location of these blocks is in water depth of between 100 and 200m, both the royalty rates and the profit-sharing terms are more advantageous to Ashland than in the previous contract. Cost recovery proceeds as under the 1986 amended PSC, i.e. after the payment of royalty and PPT and before profit sharing, and at the request of NNPC, the 1992 agreement has re-incorporated the concepts of cost oil and tax oil (by working backwards from specific revenue values, tax values, cost values, and so on, to crude oil lifting allocations or volumes associated with these specific values). The sequence in which royalty and tax payments become due before full cost recovery, even if it does not alter the total financial obligation of the company over the whole life of the project, obviously affects the investor because it shifts the financial burden to the beginning of the production life of the oilfield.[19]

In keeping with the government policy to encourage exploration in the Frontier areas, new negotiations on reducing the PPT even further and increasing investment tax credits began in 1992. New production-sharing terms were offered at the end of December and terms were finally agreed in May 1993, when oil companies started signing the much delayed exploration agreements (for territory originally allocated in the second licensing round of 1991) with the government. By June 1993, six oil companies, comprising Shell, Elf, Mobil, Exxon, BP and Statoil had signed these new contracts.[20]

A representative contract, that between NNPC and SNEPCO (Shell Nigeria Exploration and Production Company, a new subsidiary to explore in and produce from frontier areas) is presented in Table 4.3. Apart from the signature bonus, the terms of all PSCs are generally similar.[21] Royalty rates decline

Table 4.3: Comparison of Key Economic Parameters in Nigerian Production-Sharing Agreements.

Production-Sharing Contract	Royalty Rate	Petroleum Profits Tax Rate	Investment Tax Credit	Memorandum of Understanding	Profit Sharing		
					'000 bbls/day	NNPC Share	Ashland Share
NNPC—Ashland 1973 OPL 98 in <100m water OPL 118 onshore	20%	85%			0–50 > 50	65% 70%	35% 30%
NNPC—Ashland 1973 Amended in 1986	Royalty linked to water depth onshore: 20% <100m: 18.5% >100m: 16.67% so OPL 118: 20% & OPL 98: 18.5%	65.75% for first 5 years of every field, then 85%	ITC linked to water depth onshore: 5% < 100m: 10% 100-200m: 15% > 200m: 20% so OPL 118: 5% & OPL 98: 10%	Yes	0–30 30–50 50–100 > 100	55% 59% 61% 67%	45% 41% 39% 33%
NNPC—Ashland 1992 OPLs 90, 225; both in 100m–200m water depth	Per Petroleum Act: OPLs 90, 225: 16.67%	Per PPT Act: see 1973 contract	Per PPT Act: OPLs 90, 225: 15%	Yes, but not finalised	0–40 40–75 75–100 > 100	30% 40% 45% 60%	70% 60% 55% 40%

Table 4.3: Continued.

Production-Sharing Contract	Royalty Rate	Petroleum Profits Tax Rate	Investment Tax Credit	Memorandum of Understanding	Profit Sharing		
					Cumulative Mn Bbls	NNPC Share	SNEPCO Share
NNPC—SNEPCO 1993, Deep Water PSC OPLs 212, 219; both in 200-1500m water depth + 3 OPLs onshore in Benou Basin.	Royalty linked to deep water depth <200m: 16.67% 201-500m: 12% 501-800m: 8% 801-1000m: 4% > 1000m: 0%	50% flat	50%	No	0-350 351-750 751-1000 1001-1500 1501-2000	20% 35% 45% 50% 60%	80% 65% 55% 50% 40%

Sources: Barrows, *Petroleum Taxation and Legislation Report*; *O&GJ*; *PE*; *Platts*; various issues. Elf (OPLs 222, 223 in 200-1000m + 3 OPLs in the Benou Basin); Exxon (OPL 209 in >1000m water); Mobil (OPL 221 in 200-1000m); BP-Statoil (OPLs 213, 217, 218 in 200-1600m) have also signed PSCs with NNPC. Apart from signature bonus, production-sharing terms

quite rapidly from 16.67 per cent at water depth less than 200m to 0 per cent at water depth greater than 1000m; the PPT has been reduced to a flat 50 per cent for deep water blocks; the investment tax credit has been increased quite significantly from the previous 20 per cent to 50 per cent in deep water blocks; profit sharing in this acreage is based on tranches of cumulative barrels of production per contract area;[22] and finally, once royalty is paid, the company can theoretically keep all available production to recover costs before the PPT needs to be paid. In other words, in any given period if there is not enough crude oil production, it is the payment of PPT rather than cost recovery which is carried over to the next accounting period. Profit sharing can proceed once all these steps have been taken.

It has been claimed that these new contracts are more favourable to the government in that although the government has access to less oil, this access is at no risk.[23] This is true if the comparison is made with joint ventures, not with production-sharing contracts currently in place in Nigeria, in which the government has access to relatively more oil, also at no risk. While oil companies have continually claimed that the new PSC incentives are necessary for investment in exploration and production in deep water acreage, it does seem that the government has been very generous to oil companies in setting up the initial tranches of profit sharing oil.[24] For instance, an oil company that discovers only one large field of about 40,000 b/d would have access, once tax is paid and costs recovered, to 80 per cent of the field's production over a period of ten years. Given the financial straits that will continue to constrain the country in the medium term, these production-sharing terms can be seen as a signing away of Nigerian reserves and future production for a significant period. In such an eventuality, there appears to be a greater risk that Nigeria may in fact renege on the deal – for political reasons, if not economic.[25] On the other hand, one can only presume that oil companies operating under equity terms in foreign countries are in general prepared for such eventualities, and those in Nigeria must surely realize that given sufficient impetus everything is negotiable.

Risk-Service Contracts

The first three *risk-service* contracts were signed in 1979 between NNPC and Agip Energy & Natural Resources, Elf Aquitaine Nigeria Services and Nigus Petroleum.[26] The only active service contract remaining is that between Agip Energy and NNPC. Elf appears to have relinquished its acreage and Crown Central, the source for the funding of seismic work in Nigus Petroleum, left the country without any drilling. It is not clear whether Nigus continues to have exclusive rights on the acreage. The duration of the service contract was fixed at twenty years, and the time that the contractor had access to oil, after an initial exploration, development and investment recovery period of five years, amounted to fifteen years. It is felt that the structure of the risk-service contract is such that it offers incentives to exploration. Although the contractor has no title to oil, the incentives arise because, in the event of a commercial discovery, all costs are reimbursed and the contractor has assured access to crude oil supply for a long period after initial commercial production. 'The order of priority for allocation of contractual proceeds under a RSC is first to royalty; then to PPT; then to reimbursement of the contractor's costs other than production on a field-by-field basis; then for remuneration of the contractor in accordance with a formula that takes into account the market price of the crude produced and the royalty and PPT payable; and finally for reimbursement of production costs.'[27] The order in which costs are recovered are essentially similar to PSC terms.

The Fiscal Regime

The geological nature of the reservoir terrain in Nigeria and the small size of the oilfields call for a continuous programme of investment and exploration if reserve levels are to be kept high. Furthermore, the difference between onshore and offshore, accessible and frontier exploration means that varying production costs must be taken into account by the fiscal regime to ensure that profit margins remain positive in all types of ventures. In joint ventures, the production cost allowance influences the level of the company's taxable income and the extent to which its notional equity margin can be met given actual production costs on its share of production (or on that of notice oil).[28] In production-sharing ventures as well, production cost allowances and margins operate as a tax credit. Since the company's cost share of the venture, in this case, is 100 per cent and the burden of *all* initial exploration and production investment is on the contractor, the size of the tax credit affects the share of the production pie which can be taken as profit.

Although the fiscal regime has undergone several changes, it essentially consists of royalties and a tax on 'notional' profits. It involves (a) a price concept; (b) production cost allowances; and (c) tax and royalty rates. Table 4.4 shows the changing structure of the fiscal system in the 1980s.

Until 1986, the Nigerian pricing system was comprised of an artificial 'posted price' as the tax reference price and the official selling price (OSP) against which the company profit margin was assessed. The posted price, therefore, was set at a level whereby given a certain notional production cost, the company's tax paid cost guaranteed a specific notional margin against the OSP. In a period of declining OSPs, company margins were maintained and increased by successive reductions in the posted price as well as increases in the production cost allowances which reduced the company's taxable income as it did the government's tax receipts. According to *PIW*, official production cost allowances increased from \$0.35/b in 1971 to \$2.00/b in 1986. Actual production costs in 1971 were estimated to be about 0.35/b for onshore fields and about 0.55/b for offshore fields. Around 1986 estimates of production costs averaged about \$3.50/b, but were as high as \$7.00/b in some deeper offshore fields. Since actual production costs were often higher than the allowance against tax (the difference between official production cost allowances and actual production costs has increased significantly over the years), and the OSPs were often out of line with the market, the company's real margin was often lower than the government's notional guaranteed margin regardless of any adjustment made on the government tax take to ensure the latter. The extent to which notional guaranteed margins diverged from real margins remains unclear. Official profit margins increased from about \$0.40–0.50/b in the mid-1970s to \$2.00/b (\$1.00/b on notice oil) in 1990. In 1991, notional guaranteed margins were increased to \$2.30 or \$2.50/b depending on the level of capital investment.[29]

In the period leading up to 1986, therefore, when market

prices were generally dropping, the official price was higher than market prices. The 1986 MOU replaced the posted price with the netback price. Defined as 'a barrel of Nigerian crude calculated from the market prices of the refined products derived from it, less the costs of refining and freight', the netback price, adjusted every month, was more closely related to so-called 'market realisations'.[30] Where the gap between this netback and the OSP was greater than $0.60/b, the government would give the company a tax credit equivalent to 90 per cent of the loss thus guaranteeing a notional margin of $2.00/b at a netback price of $23.00/b, and of $2.70/b at a netback of $30.00. This essentially meant that for all intents and purposes, the notional margin was assessed against the netback price. The sliding equity margin provided by the January terms was very quickly made obsolete when the price fell in subsequent months. The tax reference price in February 1986 was below $20.00/b.[31] In fact, for the short period that this system was actually operating, the government was making significant losses in terms of its tax receipts since the tax reference price was being calculated the month after lifting when prices were already collapsing. This also had an impact on lifting. Changes in the 1986 MOU had made the rules for lifting government equity oil more stringent. As of 1 January, 1986, the government could theoretically call on oil companies to lift up to 100 per cent of government crude at forty-five days notice. With equity margins on notice crude at a theoretical 50 per cent of the companies' regular equity margin (ideally a $1.00/b margin on notice oil), the forced lifting of up to 900,000 b/d (the government equity share of production in this period), would have been significantly less attractive without at least a 'positive' margin protection.[32]

In 1987, in an attempt to limit the losses arising from future falls in prices, netbacks were replaced by a new tax reference price calculated on the basis of 50 per cent netback and 50 per cent spot price of BBQ (the price of a basket of three Nigerian crudes: Brass River, Bonny Light and Qua Iboe). Also at the end of the netback period in February 1987, the equity margins of producing companies were protected by a new measure. The margin was set at $2.00/b when the market price was close to the price of Bonny Light. When the market price fell below the official price, the government would adjust the 'tax and royalty

Table 4.4: Changes in the Pricing of Equity Crude Oil since 1982. Dollars per Barrel.

Tax Regime	Before 1 July, 1982	After 1 July, 1982	After February, 1983	1986 MOU	After February, 1987	1991 MOU
				Posted price replaced by realizable price:	RP now replaced by 50% netback + 50% spot BBQ	RP = 50% netback + 50% spot BBQ (divergence limited)
Posted Price	39.25	38.25	31.50 (est)	23.00		
less royalty 20 per cent	7.85	7.65	6.30	4.60		
less cost	1.10	1.60	2.00	2.00	2.00	2.50/3.50
Taxable Profit	30.30	29.00	23.20	16.40		
tax at 85 per cent	25.76	24.65	19.72	13.94	All calculations involving Royalty and PPT rates are applied as in earlier tax regimes	
royalty	7.85	7.65	6.30	4.60		
harbour dues	0.02	0.02	0.02	0.02		
Government Receipts	33.63	32.32	26.04	18.56		
plus production costs	1.10	1.60	2.00	2.00		
company tax paid cost	34.73	33.92	28.04	20.56		

Table 4.4: Continued

Tax Regime	Before 1 July, 1982	After 1 July, 1982	After February, 1983	1986 MOU	After February, 1987	1991 MOU
OSP	35.52	35.52	30.04	Netback (*)	OSP fully reinstated $2.00/b when OSP close to market price of Bonny Light; otherwise 'positive' margin	OSP $2.30/b when costs < $2.50/b; $2.50 when K costs > $1.50/b: then cost allowance increased to $3.50
Notional company profit margin	1.60	1.60	2.00	2.00		

Sources and Notes: *PIW* and Barrows, *Petroleum Taxation and Legislation Report*, various issues.
(*) In 1986, the margin was assessed essentially against the netback. If the gap between the netback and official price was greater than $0.60, the government would give a tax credit of about 90 per cent of the amount thus guaranteeing a notional margin of at least $2.00/b on a $23.00/b netback increasing to $3.00/b on a netback of $30.00/b.
In 1987, the margin was assessed against the OSP and guaranteed at $2.00/b when the market price was close to that of the official Bonny Light price. In circumstances where the market price fell below the official price, the government would adjust its tax take to guarantee a positive notional margin.
In 1991, the divergence between the spot price and the netback price in the tax reference price was limited to +/-$0.40, and profit margins and production costs were made dependent on capital investment costs per barrel. See text.

take' on company equity shares so as to keep the margin positive, while the companies would be responsible for bearing 10 per cent of the price fall.[33]

In 1987, the protected margins helped boost both equity lifting and lifting of notice oil. In the late 1980s, a period of relatively low oil prices, crude oil producers in Nigeria operated in a system which allowed for a 'protected' positive margin and which in turn counterweighed, to a large extent, any possible effect of increasing production costs on actual margins. In other words, while oil companies may not have had access to an actual margin of $2.00/b all the time, a positive margin was guaranteed.

The MOU applicable from January 1991 was not a novel document. It was the consolidation of the 1986 MOU with all its amendments, sideletters, and subsequent modifications. The incentives in this 1991 revision were essentially threefold. Firstly and perhaps most importantly, it introduced a tunnel of +/- $0.40/b on the netback element in the tax reference price, based on 50 per cent netback and 50 per cent spot BBQ prices. Although the oil companies wanted a complete abandoning of the netback element, the introduction of a floor and ceiling limited the effect of a divergence between the two sets of prices and at least during that particular time period ensured that netback prices did not pull up the tax reference price.[34] Secondly, the 1991 MOU guaranteed a minimum notional margin of $2.30/b on the company's equity ($1.15/b on NNPC equity oil/notice oil) if production costs were kept below $2.50/b. In other words if production costs were kept low, minimum margins were guaranteed, although if actual costs exceeded notional fiscal technical costs, the real margin would also decline commensurately. Finally, the revised MOU introduced the concepts of a guaranteed notional profit margin and a production cost allowance varying relative to the extent of capital investment per barrel of production. The introduction of this link has had the effect, whether intended or not unintended, of taking into account, for the first time, the varying levels of difficulty in exploration.[35] According to the MOU, where the capital investment in exploring or developing new fields is more than an average $1.50/b of oil produced in a specific year, the production cost allowance is $3.50/b and the profit margin is guaranteed at $2.50/b. In cases where exploration or development investment is less than \$1.50/b, the production cost allowance is at the lower level of \$2.50/b as is the profit margin at \$2.30/b.[36] This was essentially Aminu's attempt to achieve the government's aims of increasing both reserves and productive capacity by offering specific incentives to oil companies engaged in capital intensive work in new and/or difficult acreage.[37] One of the more important implications of this new set of incentives is that as a result of the increase in production cost allowances, there has been a further reduction of the difference between actual costs and official cost allowances. The degree of adjustment that the government had to make on its 'take' to guarantee the profit margin may have therefore also been reduced.[38]

Production Costs

Nigeria has been recognized as a high cost province since the mid-1960s. An international comparison of crude oil production costs in 1964 showed Nigerian costs to be around \$0.31/b, while those in the Persian Gulf averaged about \$0.10/b; however, production costs in Algeria (\$0.46/b), Venezuela (\$0.62/b), and the USA (\$1.56/b) were higher than in Nigeria (Schatzl, 1969, p. 31). In 1976, when profit margins for oil companies in Nigeria were reduced to about \$0.30/b (by increases in the posted and buy-back price), thus becoming closer to Middle Eastern levels, the reason for oil company discontent was obvious. Due to the shift in focus from onshore to the more difficult terrain of offshore production, investment costs per barrel were much higher in Nigeria than in the Middle East. By the mid-1980s, oil companies felt that the return on their investment and their production cost allowance were not adequate. Reservoir management techniques such as gas-reinjection were increasing the costs of production.[39] In the late 1980s and early 1990s, other enhanced recovery measures included wildcat drilling to 18,000 ft instead of 14,000 ft; 'condensate soak' schemes to reduce viscosity in heavy crude reservoirs to enable production; and pilot steam injection projects. These were all Shell initiatives. According to Shell, conventionally accessible reservoirs at 12,000 ft are becoming fewer and more complex and more sophisticated technology would be required to access these and the deep water sedimentary section of the Niger Delta.[40] The increasing need for more advanced technology in exploration and production implies that actual production costs are likely to get even higher. The current maximum production cost allowance of $3.50/b, given capital investment in developing new fields greater than $1.50/b, as prescribed in the 1991 MOU may soon be quite inadequate in oil company eyes. As it is, certain industry experts have observed that the fiscal regime brought about by the 1991 MOU may not be incentive enough for 'fresh E&P', and may only prove to be rewarding for companies which already have functioning operations in the country (Ofoh, 1992, p. 155). For the time being however, it appears that the new production-sharing ventures of 1993 will not be signing the 1991 MOU. Tax incentives in these new contracts seem to be adequate for investment in 'frontier' exploration and production and about equal to those provided in the last revision of the MOU.

Producing Companies and Investment Plans

Most producing companies in Nigeria, as mentioned above, operate on the basis of joint-venture contracts. The only exceptions are Ashland Oil which is a partner in a production-sharing scheme; Dubri, a Nigerian private company, which is the independent producer of one field (owned until 1988 by the Phillips–NNPC joint venture); and Agip Energy which operates under a service contract.

Table 4.5 presents oil production by producing venture. 'Allowable' rates of production are set by the government after negotiations with the individual producing companies. As in OPEC, these production allowables are greatly influenced by the level of production capacity (see Table 4.2 above). In March 1992, these were set at 900,000 b/d for the Shell venture; 305,000 b/d for Mobil's, 295,000 b/d for Chevron's, and 135,000 b/d for Agip's.[41] Furthermore, it was also claimed although never evidenced that in the early 1990s, the government linked production quotas to new reserves found. The aim was to find two new barrels for every barrel produced.[42] While there may not have been any such link made between production and addition to reserves, the 1991 MOU did provide incentives for further exploration and reserve additions. These stipulated that a reserve addition bonus of 10–50 cents/b could be claimed by any company where additions to oil and condensate reserves exceeded production in any one year. This bonus could then be offset against the company's PPT liability for that year.[43] It is possible, consequently, that the increasing oil company expenditure on E&P, in the early 1990s, was linked in part to these incentives.

The Shell venture is the largest and its production capacity accounts for about half the current estimated total capacity in Nigeria. The 1991–6 investment plan allocates $6.5 billion for exploration and production.[44] The annual $1.5 billion expenditure is expected to raise capacity from 1 mb/d to 1.2 mb/d by 1995, and to 1.3 mb/d by the second half of the decade. Much of the increase in capacity is expected from the Forcados fields and the joint Bonny Light and Bonny Medium fields.[45]

Mobil, in a joint venture with NNPC, produces mostly from the offshore Qua Iboe stream. The joint venture plans to invest about $850 million in this system to raise output. Projects include spending $400 million on the Edop field, primarily on a platform able to process 230,000 b/d of crude. The field currently produces about 40,000 b/d, and full capacity has been estimated at 280,000 b/d. Other expenditure plans include an outlay of $350 million on other fields in the system (Ubit, Iyak) and $100 million on expanding terminal loading and storage capacities.[46] Mobil's overall capacity plans include expansion from the 1992 capacity of 350,000 b/d to 500,000 b/d by 1995, inclusive of Oso production, and to about 700,000 b/d by the second half of the decade.[47] The Oso Condensate scheme came onstream in December 1992, with current production between 70,000 and 80,000 b/d but expected to increase to 100,000 b/d. The financial outlay in this NNPC–Mobil joint venture has been about $900 million to $1 billion with the development plan calling for the installation of twenty-one wells, eight platforms, condensate pipeline to the Qua Iboe terminal, three dedicated condensate storage tanks at the terminal, export facilities, and a low-pressure gas gathering system connecting gas-producing fields with Oso itself. NNPC and Mobil raised about 35 per cent of the cost, with the remaining sum of about $595 million arranged through the World Bank, governments, and commercial banks.[48] This was, in fact, the first upstream project in Nigeria to be sponsored by the Bank.

The Texaco–Chevron–NNPC venture produces from the

Table 4.5: Crude Oil Production in Nigeria by Producing Venture. 1966–91. Thousand Barrels per Day.

	SHELL/BP	GULF	MOBIL	AGIP/ PHILLIPS	SAFRAP	TEXACO/ CHEVRON	TOTAL
1966	366.6	51.0	-	-	-	-	417.6
1967	264.3	54.8	-	-	-	-	319.1
1968	43.0	98.3	-	-	-	-	141.3
1969	354.1	185.9	0.3	-	-	-	540.3
1970	790.3	231.8	54.2	4.4	-	2.4	1,083.1
1971	1,107.7	277.1	72.4	38.5	25.1	10.4	1,531.2

	SHELL/BP/ NNPC	GULF/ NNPC	MOBIL/ NNPC	AGIP/ PHILLIPS /NNPC	ELF/ NNPC	TEXACO/ NNPC	PAN OCEAN/ NNPC	TENNECO	PHILIPS	ASHLAND Production Sharing	TOTAL
1972	1,207.0	325.4	166.4	52.2	54.6	10.1	-			-	1,815.7
1973	1,293.8	364.8	222.5	100.5	64.4	8.3	-			-	2,054.3
1974	1,398.5	369.1	247.5	153.9	83.7	2.3	-			-	2,255.0
1975	1,118.4	227.3	196.6	156.8	73.1	7.4	-			3.6	1,783.2
1976	1,234.8	292.8	230.7	185.5	75.9	34.3	4.5			8.3	2,066.8
1977	1,211.7	291.3	223.4	214.3	74.3	53.2	9.9			7.0	2,085.1
1978	1,086.0	262.0	200.0	210.0	77.0	43.0	10.0			9.0	1,897.0
1979	1,316.0	375.0	243.0	221.0	78.0	54.0	7.0			8.0	2,302.0

Table 4.5: Continued.

	SHELL/ NNPC	GULF/ NNPC	MOBIL/ NNPC	AGIP/ PHILLIPS /NNPC	ELF/ NNPC	TEXACO/ NNPC	PAN OCEAN/ NNPC	TENNECO	PHILLIPS	ASHLAND (production sharing)	TOTAL
1980	1,167.0	341.0	214.0	183.0	86.0	43.0	8.0	5.0	2.0	9.0	2,085.0
1981	740.0	281.4	160.9	126.5	72.8	34.5	7.0	5.9	1.1	9.5	1,439.6
1982	655.0	211.0	136.0	127.0	93.0	38.0	5.0	6.0	1.0	15.0	1,287.0
1983	619.6	174.5	162.5	118.4	89.4	44.0	4.4	6.0	1.1	15.6	1,235.5
1984	698.0	186.3	178.1	126.3	97.8	65.5	5.5	4.5	1.1	24.7	1,388.0
1985	747.8	248.1	179.6	149.2	93.4	46.4	5.5	4.3	1.1	23.5	1,498.9
1986	708.4	247.1	180.4	133.7	86.1	65.3	5.5	3.3	1.0	35.8	1,466.6
1987	651.7	211.1	162.8	116.8	81.7	58.0	3.5	2.6	1.0	33.8	1,323.0
1988	700.0	220.0	170.0	100.0	90.0	65.0	9.0	5.0	1.0	40.0	1,400.0
1989	904.9	267.4	213.1	132.1	90.6	58.6	1.5	1.5		36.3	1,716.3*
1990	927.4	277.1	238.5	146.3	96.2	58.7	1.2	1.8	1.0	38.2	1,812.0*
1991	960.5	307.2	273.5	140.5	95.2	59.1	1.2	2.8		30.6	1,893.1*

Sources and Notes: *OPEC Annual Statistical Bulletin*, various issues; 1988 and 1990 figures are based on estimates from *PE*, November 1988 and October 1990. BP was nationalized in August 1979; Gulf and Chevron merged in 1984; NNPC acquired interests in Pan Ocean in 1978; Dubri acquired a Phillips field in 1988; NPDC acquired interests in Tenneco/Mobil/Sun in 1989. *1989 total production includes 10,300 b/d of 'Others'; 1990 total production includes Agip's service contract output of 25,774 b/d and 1991 total production includes 22,400 b/d from the same contract.

offshore Middletown, Funiwa and Pennington fields and has a production capacity of 60,000 b/d. Details on investment plans for the venture as a whole have not been recorded. Chevron, itself, however, plans to spend $280 million in Nigeria in 1992, increasing to $370 million in 1993.[49] It is quite probable that part of this expenditure on exploration and production may be allocated to the Texaco-led venture, in which Chevron has 20 per cent equity. The greater part of this investment, however, will be allocated to production from the Escravos stream, where capacity is expected to increase from 315,000 b/d to 400,000 b/d by 1995.[50] By 1992–93, in fact, Chevron's production was running at 340,000 b/d and production capacity was 350,000 b/d.

The Agip–NNPC–Phillips joint venture which produces from the Brass River stream expects to increase productive capacity from about 140,000–150,000 b/d to 200,000 b/d by 1994. Similarly the Elf–NNPC joint venture expects to double capacity from about 100,000 b/d by the year 2000.[51] In order to achieve this goal, Elf Nigeria has planned to spend $2 billion in the years to the end of this century to develop its offshore fields (Afia, Odudu, Ime and Edikan), where reserves total 150 mb. Afia came onstream in March 1993, producing 1,000 b/d, and has been followed by the commissioning of Odudu which came onstream in May. While the current production of the Odudu blend is only about 6,000 b/d, it is thought that 60,000 b/d will be produced from these four offshore fields by 1994, increasing to 100,000 b/d by 1998. First exports of the blend were expected in July 1993.[52]

The dominance of Shell in Nigerian production as well as in investment in future production and exploration is obvious. There have been recent attempts by the Nigerian government to encourage more diversified foreign, and increasing domestic private sector, participation in the oil industry. In the 1991 open bidding round for upstream acreage, seventeen licences were awarded to local Nigerian companies and eleven to foreign companies. The attempt to increase indigenous participation in the industry was more successful than the attempt to diversify foreign participation.[53] The only new foreign entrants in exploration were Conoco, through Du Pont; Amoco, through the farm-out with Exxon; and the alliance of BP–Statoil, which was awarded two blocks in the deep offshore and one block onshore. With Statoil the operator for all blocks, each party will own 50 per cent of each OPL. The nine other companies awarded licences were already producing in Nigeria.

In the past few years, there has been a shift of emphasis, on the part of the Nigerian government, away from joint-venture contracts to production-sharing contracts. The attraction of equity participation for oil companies is thereby retained, while the upfront costs for the government in exploration and development are considerably reduced. The need to reduce upfront expenditure in new contracts has stemmed primarily from the financial problems of the national economy since the 1980s, the extent of external indebtedness, the decline in oil revenues, and the mismanagement and mis-allocation of revenue expenditure (see Chapter 8). Since the 1980s, for instance, the government/NNPC has been involved in two large projects: the Oso Condensate project with Mobil which was estimated to cost approximately $1 billion, and the Bonny LNG project with Shell, Agip and Elf, for which costs are estimated at approximately $4.5 billion. While the first project came onstream in December 1992, the latter continues to be delayed and costs associated with it continue to rise. Apart from these two main projects, certain specific domestic factors have also exacerbated the government's fiscal problems. The reform of the federal structure from twenty-one to thirty states in 1992 necessitated an increase in federal support of 30 per cent,[54] and domestic refining problems worsened by the smuggling of petroleum products across borders has meant that more and more resources have had to be allocated to product imports. These financial difficulties have given rise to a number of possible policy changes to increase government funds. In the upstream sector, this has implications for NNPC's joint-venture participation.[55]

It is clear that while new production-sharing arrangements may ease some of NNPC's financial difficulties, the company remains heavily burdened by its financial commitment to joint ventures, which account for the greatest proportion of Nigerian production. Recent estimates show that NNPC's 60 per cent interest joint ventures cost it about $2 billion/year in development costs.[56] With bills coming in for the costly Bonny LNG project, NNPC arrears to producing companies of up to $300 million for

1992 and \$200 million for 1993 investment expenditure, and upcoming negotiations with the IMF regarding the country's \$27–30 billion external debt (at end 1993, Nigeria was about \$6 billion behind on debt-servicing payments), the ability to keep up with new exploration and development expenditure is suspect. Joint-venture companies were, therefore, asked to cut 1993 expenditure by 30 per cent, so as to reduce the state company's share of costs. This cutback has since been reduced to 10 per cent and oil companies are trying to 'hold the line at 1992 levels, if not obtain at least part of the 20 per cent or larger growth rates that they had originally hoped for'.[57] However, the same request to scale back investment expenditure (by 40 per cent of 1993 expenditure) has been made again, at the end of 1993, in relation to the oil companies' 1994 budget. Whatever the extent of the cutback, the reduction in company and NNPC outlays will have serious implications for plans and targets of productive capacity expansion to 2.5 mb/d by the year 1996 may be at risk. In July 1993, in another significant manifestation of its financial concerns, the government expressed its intention of divesting 10 per cent of its equity shares in joint ventures with Shell, Agip, Texaco and Pan Ocean. This would reduce its participation in these ventures from 60 per cent to 50 per cent. One of the actions taken already, in 1992, to ease the national oil company's financial problems (which include debts to upstream companies as well as the purchase of products during refinery shut-downs) was that the Nigerian government increased the allocation of crude oil export receipts to NNPC. Of the approximately 800,000 b/d of crude oil marketed by NNPC, the Federal government will now receive revenues worth 600,000 b/d of crude oil, while NNPC's allocation will increase by 50,000 b/d to 200,000 b/d of crude oil export revenues. At the end of 1993, there was some talk again about the necessity of increasing the allocation of oil export proceeds to NNPC.[58]

Problems of and Prospects for Government–Oil Company Relations

Although the upstream sector is less neglected than other sectors, which is a reflection of its importance, official policy is essentially short-term in outlook. It responds to market conditions generally by changing adjustment factors in the price formulae or by changing production rates for joint ventures. Incentives have been given when the market is weak and restraint shown when the market is strong. Where the market has not been followed, the strategy behind changes in policy has been unclear, and this has subsequently and inevitably misfired (see changes in rules on equity lifting in the early 1980s).

Fiscal incentives as long-term responses to the market have arisen mainly because of the need to encourage E&P. The small size of Nigeria's oilfields has meant that in order to maintain and augment proven reserves, a continuous programme of E&P is needed, increasingly in marginal frontier terrain. In recent years, the form that such incentives take has been greatly influenced by the government's financial problems. These have affected the ability of the government and NNPC to come up with their share of investment costs in joint-venture contracts, and more importantly have made it less 'affordable' for the country to grant any further concessions on beneficial joint-venture terms. This has led to changes in contractual arrangements between the government and the oil companies and in recent years has taken the form of a shift towards production-sharing agreements.

The profitability of existing JVCs is closely linked to incremental project economics. For tax purposes, these companies have been allowed to consolidate production. In a five-year development and exploration programme for instance, under the present system, the joint venture can benefit from accelerated payback and recoupment of costs through revenues from other projects. New projects for the current JVCs, therefore, are financially feasible. It appears unlikely that such favourable tax terms will be accorded to incoming JVCs at a time when NNPC and Nigeria are having such severe financial problems. Consequently, the economic disincentive of a high tax regime will just not attract further interest in JVCs in the country. The idea that on a world scale Nigeria may not be competitive for investment is reflected, perhaps, in the drastic changes made for and incentives given in deep water PSCs.[59]

If the future is to be in production-sharing for Nigeria, as seems to be the case, the terms for the contracts will have to be negotiated very carefully given the potential wealth of the Frontier acreage, the extent to which Nigeria needs these future reserves, and the significant room for policy mismanagement. In the signing of the most recent PSCs, it was evident that the state was in a much weaker bargaining position. The economic need for foreign investment in this age of capital scarcity (and many projects with investment potential) and given a country more dependent on its oil now than ever before, will need to be carefully balanced against the political viability of too advantageous exploration and production terms for non-indigenous oil companies.

It should be noted, however, that while new terms are increasingly production-sharing terms, the large proportion of Nigerian production still issues from joint-venture concerns. The future for exploration and a consistent addition to reserves therefore seems bleak. This is despite the fact that NNPC, in 1992 and again in 1993, asked joint-venture companies to scale back their forthcoming investment plans so as to reduce the government's share of the investment costs, and furthermore, in July 1993, expressed its wish to reduce its participation in certain joint-venture projects to 50 per cent. These financial difficulties, unfortunately, do not seem to be short-term ones, and more importantly may have serious implications for the government–NNPC relationship.

It seems clear that the share of oil revenues accruing to NNPC is inadequate given the company's investment commitments and responsibilities. Its debts to its joint-venture partners are already substantial. Given the dependence of the country on foreign oil companies, Nigeria will have to address this issue soon. It is likely that the structural relationship between the state and NNPC will, under these circumstances, also come under review.

Notes

1. As of 1993, Sun no longer had a Nigerian interest.
2. Amoco is also a new entrant since it farmed into Exxon's and Agip's blocks in 1993.
3. 'In Nigeria, PJVs (Petroleum Joint Ventures) are non-incorporated vehicles constituted by a Participation Agreement (addressing the issue of participation shares) and a Joint Operating Agreement (setting out the rules and procedures, rights and obligations of the two parties) between the NNPC (on behalf of the government) and a foreign producing company. Under this arrangement the NNPC purchases a participating interest – currently 60 per cent – in all the Oil Mining Leases (OMLs) held by the company; in all fixed and movable assets of the company including assets

such as its exploration, storage and transportation assets, and all associated assets such as offices, houses and welfare facilities; and also in the working capital required for operating the OMLs, including all debts due to the company . . . Each participant has the right to a certain percentage of the production of the joint venture based on its participating interest share ... A PJV may include one or more foreign participants. Typically, the foreign participant, or one of the foreign companies (if there is more than one) is designated the Operator of the joint venture. The PJVs finally executed between 1990 and 1991 (as a result of the signing of joint operating agreements) do, however, make provision for the NNPC to take over as Operator in respect of all or any part of the lease area ... Each joint venture participant contributes to the payment of all costs connected with the venture through a system of cash calls. These costs include Rent and Royalty... . Each participant is, however, responsible for paying its own Petroleum Profits Tax (PPT) and will benefit from the provisions of the Memoranda of Understanding (MOU) negotiated with each individual company.' (*PE*, Special Supplement, Energy Law, July 1992, pp. 18–19).

4.   The right of reserve ownership in joint ventures stems directly from the rights accorded to previous concession holders in Nigeria. During this latter period, such a right had widespread implications for company operations in that they could also control the rate of production. Today, one of the main advantages of equity ownership is the right to sell part or all of a particular company's equity share to other concerns. This accords the participating company greater flexibility in either raising capital and/ or simply getting out of a venture. (In PSCs, the contractor can farm out to other companies as a capital raising or risk management move, but is unable to get out of the contract with the government without making substantial losses on its initial investments.) Furthermore, the right to own 'oil in the ground' implies that should these assets be taken by the government, compensation will also account for the loss of reserves, which may not be included in the netbook value. While, this is true theoretically, compensation for 'oil in the ground' does not always occur. It is unlikely that a sovereign country will concede the principle of repaying the nationalized company for its future stream of income. For instance, while earlier increases in government participation in oil companies did include some compensation for loss of reserves, the compensation for the 1979 nationalization of BP assets (mainly 20 per cent equity interest in the Shell–BP–NNPC joint venture and 60 per cent interest in the BP marketing company) in Nigeria did not account for the loss of lifting rights. (Barrows, *Petroleum Taxation and Legislation Report*, 1981, p. 64). Finally, a factor which will have implications for the future of 'equity ownership' (albeit in its present day qualified form) is the particular aspect of the 1979 constitution which vests control and ownership of all natural resources, minerals, mineral oils, etc, in the state. (Nelson, 1982, p. 161). Bar any other legislative developments, this will ensure that once the present joint-venture contracts expire in the year 2008, future incentives of equity sharing production will not be forthcoming.

5. Ashland signed another production-sharing contract in 1992, and at least six new production-sharing contracts were signed in 1993. None of these, however, are producing at this time.
6. *OPEC Bulletin*, May 1985, p. 13.
7. Despite this, however, certain indigenous companies were granted exploration licences under concession agreements in 1991.
8. Barrows, *IPI Data Service, Africa*, No. 47, *Nigeria*, 1986, p. 22.
9. Barrows, *Petroleum Taxation and Legislation Report*, 1979, p. 63.
10. Ibid., 1981, p. 64; *PE*, September 1979 and April 1981, p. 135.
11. Tenneco has since sold its share to British Gas.
12. Changing Royalty and PPT rates are also indicative of increasing state participation in the oil industry, particularly in the 1970s. These changes in the Nigerian fiscal regime must be seen in the context of the relevant OPEC resolutions on which they are based (see Chapter 2). Based on the precedents set by the various OPEC resolutions increasing royalty and tax rates, Nigeria had, by 1975, increased its tax rate to 85 per cent and its royalty rate to 20 per cent. The next few years, however, saw a greater government awareness of the 'finite' nature of the resource and the need for increased exploration. In 1977, therefore, as part of the Buhari Incentives, the PPT was reduced to 65.75 per cent until pre-production costs were amortized (essentially the first five years for each field); royalty rates remained at 20 per cent for onshore areas but were reduced to 18.5 per cent for waters up to 100m and 16.7 per cent for waters over 100m; and investment tax credits were granted according to water depth: 5 per cent onshore; 10 per cent offshore up to 100m; 15 per cent in waters between 100–200m; and 20 per cent for waters over 200m. The most recent changes in 1993 for deep water production-sharing agreements have seen the PPT reduced to 50 per cent, royalty rates declining from 16.67 per cent at water depth greater than 200m to 0 per cent at 1000m; and investment tax credits increased to 50 per cent (see the following section). (Ofoh, 1992, p. 152; *PE*, July 1977, p. 282.).
13. *PE*, February 1974, pp. 58–9; Seymour, 1980, p. 226.
14. In fact all producing companies in Nigeria benefit from the various MOUs. The 1986 amendment to Ashland's 1973 PSC, therefore, benefited from the 1986 MOU, and the application of the 1991 MOU is currently being negotiated and finalized in regard to the 1992 Ashland PSC. The provisions of the various MOUs are essentially the same, while the form of the document is altered somewhat to take into account the PSC structure. In other words, the provisions of the MOUs are essentially a form of tax credit. The provisions reduce the extent of PPT paid on the company's share of the profit sharing oil. In an aggregate sense, the provisions of the MOU increase the size of the production pie then available for cost recovery and profit sharing.
15. Of the 136 blocks opened to exploration in October 1990, fifteen blocks are situated in the deep water extension of the Niger delta, in waters deeper than 200m. Nine of these deep water blocks were contracted out by the summer of 1993: Shell and Elf have two each, Mobil and Exxon have one each, and BP–Statoil have three deep water blocks. The

production-sharing contracts may, however, include onshore blocks as well (Barrows, *Petroleum Taxation and Legislation Report*, May/June 1993, p. 31).

16. This was based on an arrangement whereby 40 per cent of available production would be set aside for royalty payment and cost recovery; 55 per cent of the remaining oil (or 33 per cent of total available production) would be set aside for payment of the PPT; and the remaining oil, which was essentially 27 per cent of total available production was to be used for profit sharing, as shown in Table 4.3.

17. The improvements in royalty, PPT, and investment tax credit terms, however, only applied to Ashland's OPL 98. These improvements were based on the fiscal incentives of 18 May, 1977. The relevant amendments to the 1959 PPT Act and the 1969 Petroleum Regulations Decree followed soon afterwards (Barrows, *Basic Oil Laws & Concession Contracts, South and Central Africa*, Supplement 53, p. 131).

18. *PE*, Special Supplement, Energy Law, July 1992, p. 20.

19. The 1993 Deep Water PSCs have the advantage of the prioritization of cost recovery over PPT payment and it is quite probable that companies which do not benefit from this may, at some future date, attempt to renegotiate this aspect of their PSCs.

20. Frontier areas include the deep water (i.e. water deeper than 200m) and onshore blocks which are not in the Niger Delta. These latter areas include the Anambra and Chad Basins, as well as the Benue Trough. The contract area in the frontier areas varies from agreement to agreement. In the case of Exxon, the contract area is comprised of one block alone, while in the case of Shell which obtained five blocks in the licensing round, the contract area is comprised of five blocks.

21. Shell paid $30 million per deep water block, while BP–Statoil paid $42 million for their three blocks (Barrows, *Petroleum Taxation and Legislation Report*, May/June 1993, p. 32).

22. In the frontier acreage, it is expected that costs would be much higher than for Niger Delta acreage, and that the required field size for commercial development would also be much larger. In these circumstances, investors would prefer to base profit share tranches on cumulative barrels per contract area, rather than barrels per day per contract area – mainly because the former would probably ensure a larger initial profit share for a longer time (i.e. a relatively large field is likely to reach a barrels per day limit to initial profit share tranches quite soon). Similarly, for Nigeria, profit sharing based on cumulative shares of production protects the government's share of profits regardless of the stage of life of the field or rate of production. Furthermore, according to government sources, cumulative production is more measurable than specific rates of production.

23. *Platts*, 7 June, 1993, p. 4; *PE*, June 1993, p. 74. For the oil companies on the other hand, the oil industry maintains that deep water operations carry much greater risk, both geologic and technical with regard to the commerciality of the find. Furthermore, while the Nigerian government may not have as big a share in profit sharing, once production starts, they will continue to receive 50 per cent tax and royalty from the fields.

24. Another concession made to oil companies by the government in these new PSCs has been the scaling down of the initial expenditure requirements. From a demand of $176 million over ten years, the government is now demanding that companies spend $54 million over the first six years (at which point they then have a right to withdraw), and a subsequent $60 million over the following four years. A total of $114 million over ten years is now being described as *not too much to ask* by oil commentators, given the difficult acreage.

25. An interesting point to note is that in 1991, of the estimated 17.9 billion barrels of oil reserves, about 13–14 billion barrels or 70 per cent of total oil reserves were accounted for by NNPC, Shell, Elf and Agip and Chevron (*O&GJ*, 22 July, 1991, p. 24 and *PE*, Sponsored Statement, February 1993, p.32). In part, the new tendency toward production-sharing ventures is thought to be a means of consolidating a 100 per cent ownership of reserves by the state while leaving many if not all risks of investment in exploration and production to the contractor (Ofoh, 1992, p. 155). If, in fact, such a significant portion of production is signed over to the oil companies, it will matter little politically that the reserves have been consolidated under state ownership.

26. 'Elf Aquitaine signed a service contract in mid-1979 for three blocks covering 4,000 sq km off the Niger Delta . . . Agip signed a risk-bearing arrangement in exchange for 'access' to 50 per cent of any oil found on three offshore and three onshore tracts. It operates with Spain's Hispanoil in two of the offshore tracts . . . USA Independent Crown Central had a service contract on 253,594 offshore acres through Nigus Petroleum (owned by Crown Central (90 per cent), a US Independent and the local Ado Ibrahim Investments and Properties).' (Barrows, *Petroleum Taxation and Legislation Report*, 1979, p. 67).

27. *PE*, Special Supplement, July 1992, pp. 19–20.

28. The logic behind government decreed production cost allowances for the operator is that these put a cap on the effect that costs can have on the notional margin and hence limit the 'guaranteed' amount on the margin.

29. Official profit margins rose from $0.50/b to $0.80/b in 1977; to $1.60/b in 1982; to $2.00/b in 1983 and most recently the 1991 increase. Production cost allowances increased from $0.80/b to $1.10/b in 1977 (Buhari Incentives); to $1.80/b in July 1982; and to $2.00/b in February 1983. The increases in both 1982 and 1983 were possible through increases in cost allowances as well as cuts in the posted prices. (Barrows, *Petroleum Taxation and Legislation Report*, Africa, 1982 and 1983; *PE*, April 1983; February 1984). It is important to note that for some producers the actual costs of production remained higher than the 1983 allowance of $2.00/b. In 1980, for instance, when the production cost allowance was $1.10/b, Gulf, Elf and Shell production costs were lower than the allowance while Agip and Mobil costs were significantly higher (Mobil's costs were about $1.90/b). Agip produces from 'territory straddling the Niger river' and Mobil operates mostly offshore (Barrows, *Petroleum Taxation and Legislation Report*, Africa, 1982, p. 43).

30. Ibid., 1986, pp. 208–9.

31. The government take in 1986 was calculated on the basis of an adjustable tax take minus the expensing of the tax and the offsets allowed against the PPT. The 1986 agreement had also introduced the 'K' coefficient into equity pricing. This factor was the element in any new formula which provided for a specific guaranteed minimum notional margin of $2.00 by adjusting the government's tax take (i.e. royalty and tax). Cost allowances were then deducted from this to come to a specific government take allowing for a specific notional margin. The Oil Minister issued the fixed value for the 'K' factor according to the level of the netback price. However, this sliding margin arrangement did not apply to netback prices below $20.00/b.

32. *PE*, March 1987.

33. In 1987, the 'K' factor was allowed to float, adjustable relative to the level of the netback prices, allowing for a 'positive' margin.

34. This was during the earlier part of 1991, when product prices were much higher than spot crude prices and hence pulling up the tax reference price, and when the oil companies wanted to take advantage of the drop in crude oil prices following the Allied invasion of Kuwait.

35. Theoretically, where the capital costs per barrel of production are higher, it can be assumed that the exploration and production acreage is more difficult. The higher notional margin associated with such levels of capital costs indirectly gives incentives to producers for E&P in 'frontier' acreage.

36. The provisions of the 1991 MOU are essentially based on a guaranteed notional minimum margin at a realizable price (RP) of $12.50/b. The margin is 'notional' precisely because it assumes a certain cost and price. When the RP is below $12.50/b, the government applies a different schedule of notional guaranteed margins, varying according to the level of the price. When the RP is above $12.50/b, then the guaranteed notional minimum margin is as specified in the MOU: $2.30 at costs of $2.50/b or below; and $2.50/b at costs of $3.50/b or above (where capital costs are ≥ $1.50/b). In order for the company to get a higher *real* margin than the notional margin, either costs must be lower than those specified in the allowance, and/or the actual realizable price must be higher than that approximated for the tax calculations (Barrows, *Petroleum Taxation and Legislation Report*, January/February 1992, p. 33 and *Argus*, 1 July, 1991).

37. The higher notional margin and production cost allowances in the 1991 MOU have been based on the attainment of at least $1.50 of capital investment costs per barrel of production over *one year*. Also significant would be the length of time required for such capital investment to have an impact on reserve or production capacity levels. Certainly the figure of $1.50 of capital costs per barrel of production in a year would have a different economic significance if the recovery of 100 units of reserves at $150 cost took twenty years instead of ten years to recover.

38. From the oil company's perspective, in the event of low production rates, the overall profitability of Nigerian operations is lower and maintenance and capital costs take on a larger proportion of total costs. When production costs more closely reflect actual costs, even when production rates are not at capacity, the overall profitability of Nigerian operations may not in

fact be significantly reduced.

39. *PE*, July 1986.
40. *PE*, March 1992.
41. *PE*, April 1992.
42. *Statoil Magazine*, May 1992, p. 16.
43. *PE*, Special Supplement, Energy Law, July 1992.
44. *PE*, February 1991.
45. *PIW*, 19 February, 1990.
46. *Energy Compass*, 30 August, 1991.
47. *Argus*, 21 December, 1992.
48. *O&GJ*, 29 April, 1991.
49. *PE*, March 1992.
50. *Argus*, 23/30 December, 1991.
51. Ibid.
52. Ibid., 8 March, 1993, p. 7; *PIW*, 17 May, 1993, p. 11.
53. This was true in terms of number of licences awarded to indigenous companies. Of these, however, the only viable exploration and production ventures have been set up by Consolidated Oil, for which the source of foreign capital is not clear, and the Du Pont joint ventures. In 1991, Du Pont E&P B.V., a Dutch affiliate of Conoco, signed farm-in agreements with indigenous private Nigerian E&P companies for one onshore and three offshore blocks. Du Pont received 40 per cent equity in each block, while four Nigerian companies acquired 57.5 per cent in all blocks, and one company acquired 2.5 per cent in each OPL (*Platts*, 11 July, 1991). The long-term implications of growing indigenous participation are unclear at this point. Certainly if this development becomes a genuine instrument of change in the industry as a whole and in oil rent distribution issues, the government will find its historically predominant distributary role being automatically qualified. Furthermore, negotiations regarding ownership and 'rent' issues with such indigenous companies will necessarily require arguments other than those based on national sovereignty.
54. *Energy Compass*, 8 January, 1992.
55. Incentives for the downstream sector are discussed in Chapters 6 and 7.
56. *Argus*, 5 October, 1992.
57. *PIW*, 25 January, 1993, p. 1.
58. *PIW*, 5 October, 1992, p. 2; *Platts*, 29 July, 1993, pp. 1, 5.
59. It is true, however, that the new deep water terms accorded to production-sharing ventures do not include ringfencing requirements. This is compensated by the fact that the government does not have to share in the upfront investments in these ventures.

5 THE INTERNATIONAL TRADE AND PRICING OF NIGERIAN CRUDES

Introduction

The strategic nature of Nigerian crude oil arises from three main factors: its quality as a light and sweet crude, its link to other Atlantic Basin crudes through similar qualitative characteristics and the large volumes traded in the spot market. Nigerian crudes are similar in quality to North Sea varieties, their prices are related to Brent, and they compete directly with these other crudes in the Atlantic Basin market.

Nigeria's role as the interface between Gulf and Atlantic Basin crudes first arose in the early 1980s with the establishment of the North Sea market and its separate pricing system. Prior to this, Nigeria was subject to the same pricing pressures as other OPEC countries, but the development of the North Sea meant that Nigeria had to respond to new pressures. Nigeria was then affected by price under-cutting by the UK and Norway. Its situation was particularly uncomfortable in the first half of the 1980s as it belonged to one pricing system because of its location and the crude supply characteristics of the Atlantic Basin, and to another pricing system because of its membership of OPEC.

In terms of crude quality, Nigeria is in a very different situation from most Gulf producers. Furthermore, amongst OPEC crudes, Nigerian crudes are the most widely traded. While the majority of Gulf crudes have re-sale restrictions imposed on them, all Nigerian varieties are traded on the spot market (Horsnell and Mabro, 1993, p. 258). Given these large volumes of trade, especially in the Atlantic Basin, Nigerian crudes are seen as 'seasonal pointers' to refinery demand there.[1]

In this chapter we shall describe the pricing regimes under which Nigerian oil was exported, the international marketing of Nigerian crudes and the features of petroleum export and trade.

Nigerian Pricing Policies

The three main episodes in the history of Nigerian crude oil pricing are those of Official Selling Prices (OSPs), netback contracts, and spot-related crude oil pricing. The era of administered prices by the major oil companies – when the governments of producing countries or their national oil companies were compensated through taxes and royalties, calculated on the basis of posted prices set by the companies themselves, and had no say in the pricing of oil – gave way in the 1970s, to a period of direct pricing by OPEC. During this stage, export sales were mainly through long-term contracts. In periods of slack demand, OPEC held its reference price fixed and allowed demand that obtained at this price to determine supply; and in times of excess demand, OPEC could not hold the reference price fixed and the market had price explosions (e.g. in 1973 and 1979–80) (Mabro, 1986).

In the early 1980s, there was increasing pressure on OPEC's official pricing system. The world oil market changed structurally as a result of crude oil surpluses, economic recession in the industrialized West, and the growth in crude oil production outside OPEC (for example in the North Sea, the Soviet Union and in Mexico).[2] The increased production of non-OPEC oil which was being competitively priced encouraged the shift from long-term contracts between companies and OPEC producers to short-term arrangements and spot market purchases. The upstream marketing pattern was therefore diversified even further, and, in a buyers' market, with little commitment to any one supply source, prices were under much greater pressure than in similar periods of slack demand in the 1970s.[3] Increasing competition from North Sea crudes made Nigeria's position particularly vulnerable. Nigeria found itself compelled to respond unilaterally to price cuts enacted by non-OPEC producers in June 1981. Nigerian cuts in its OSP in August and again in October 1981 left OPEC with no choice but to bring the official marker price down to $34/b. In March 1982, OPEC attempted to hold its new reference price by introducing for the first time a production programme and by removing about 1 mb/d from the market. Nigerian crudes, however, remained over-valued relative to BNOC's export price of $31/b. OPEC production levels, in fact, fell below programmed levels.

Price discounting in the early 1980s (specifically in 1982 and 1983), occurred in a market environment in which the demand for OPEC exports continued to be affected by reduced consumption in OECD markets and the increase in non-OPEC crude supplies. On 18 February, 1983, BNOC which had 'recently been forced to sell North Sea oil at a loss on the spot market because of a sharp fall in producing companies' repurchases of participation crude at official prices' cut crude prices by $3.00 to $30.50/b. The Norwegians immediately followed suit, and on 20 February, Nigeria cut its crude oil price down to $30.00, thus undercutting North Sea prices. This move was then justified by the Nigerian member of the OPEC Conference on the ground that a price structure based on a $34.00 Arabian Light price had not been able to hold against the competitive onslaught of North Sea crudes, and therefore had to be abandoned. It was announced that future price cuts in the North Sea would be matched 'cent for cent' by Nigeria. The delay in an OPEC consensus on price cuts was largely due to continuing discussions on quotas and price differentials, and more importantly, the fear that BNOC would cut prices further as its customers were demanding. BNOC's conciliatory response at the end of March 1982 was to retain the reference price of $30.50 for February transactions, but to cut the price further by $0.50–0.75 per barrel in March. The price of Brent crude then fell to Nigerian levels, and the Nigerians chose not to continue the price discounting war.

In October 1984, Statoil unexpectedly decided to abandon its quarterly reference price (BNOC, two weeks earlier, had confirmed that there would be no change to its reference price) and replaced it with one month contracts at market related prices. Statoil, allegedly, did not confer with the Norwegian government on this matter and justified it by stating that the move was merely formalizing an existing situation which had been distorted by the use of 'unreal' official prices. BNOC followed suit a few days later, and a day after that, the Nigerians undercut the new British reference price by $0.65. Attempts were made by OPEC ministers to make Nigeria retract its price cuts, but to no avail. OPEC decided, therefore, to reduce production to defend their $29.00 marker crude price. Nigeria and Iraq, citing economic exigencies, refused to accept lower production quotas. OPEC eventually accepted that the higher production quotas accorded to Nigeria for August and September should be treated as permanent by the country (for at least a year), and that Nigerian prices since

March 1983 were no longer aligned to OPEC prices (Brown, 1990, pp. 615–50; Iwayemi, 1988, p. 35; Mabro, 1989, p. 46).

It was during this period when OPEC was defending official crude oil prices (1983 to 1985) that concealed discounting and counter-trade/barter deals became more prevalent amongst OPEC members. Methods of concealed price discounting to maintain volumes included offshore refining deals and counter-trade deals.

The offshore refining scheme was initiated in the mid-1970s ostensibly to correct the domestic shortage of products and was seen essentially as a temporary measure awaiting the addition of further refineries. The scheme, in fact, continued even after the commissioning of the Warri and Kaduna refineries, until at least 1989.[4] In 1985, Petrobras was refining up to 55,000 b/d of Nigerian crude oil. The crude was valued on a netback basis, light refined products returned to Nigeria.[5] In its 1986 arrangement with Total, NNPC provided about 50,000 b/d of crude in exchange for about 35,000 b/d of gasoline and kerosene (Brown, 1990, p. 321). In 1989, while 199,000 b/d of crude oil were delivered to the three domestic refineries, about 75,000 b/d was contracted out to offshore refineries.[6] The link between offshore refining and price discounting was clear, given that these schemes were initiated and continued during periods of slack demand such as in the mid-1970s and in 1985, and that netback-related pricing was used to settle accounts.

Counter-trade deals were most widely in use in the mid-1980s during which time at least five such arrangements were made. These were justified mainly as a means to overcome serious foreign exchange shortages in a period of declining oil revenues, increasing current account deficits, and an increasing debt-servicing burden. The deals were on average based on a price of $27.40 per barrel of crude exchanged. Spot prices of Bonny Light in 1984–5 ranged from $28.00 to $28.65. Since the quality of the crude exchanged is unknown, the extent of the price discount is unclear. The fact that the crude was valued on a netback basis (at least by the Brazilians), and that the agreement with France contained a provision for a 6 per cent effective oil price reduction, confirm the existence of price discounting. The main reason why these deals were suspended by the Babingida government was the common assumption that the goods being imported in exchange for the crude were being charged at inflated prices.

Further problems with these agreements related to the secrecy with which they were conducted, the lack of effective control on quality and prices, little monitoring of shipments, and bad management of escrow accounts. A first commission to investigate the agreements was set up in September 1985, chaired by Aboyade, the then chairman of Volkswagen, Nigeria. The commission recommended that although the deals were acceptable, more careful monitoring was required. The second commission set up to investigate specific deals coincidentally came to the conclusion that the deal with Brazil would be allowed to resume in July 1986.[7]

While the official justification for these deals was acknowledged as legitimate, it was also recognized that they have been used to 'disguise or falsify prices or quantities in international trade' (Obadan, 1992, p. 226). Certainly, in OPEC's eyes, counter-trade was a means to shift additional volumes of crude oil, outside of the quota restrictions, in a weak market. The risk was that these volumes would then be dumped on the spot market, depressing prices even further. While the exact amount of crude oil that the Nigerians were able to shift at discounted prices is not known, some estimates place the total value of the exchange at $1.75 billion over the two years (Iwayemi, 1988, p. 36). Estimating from Table 5.1, the total volume of crude oil exchange could not have been greater than 120,000–150,000 b/d over the two years, given that the Brazilian and Austrian deals were the only ones to survive for a relatively long period of time. The French deal ran into problems after the exchange of just one cargo, and the Italian deal was never fully implemented.[8]

Other ways by which Nigeria, as other OPEC countries, could cope with a weak market and defend market shares included the improvement of lifting terms for equity producers and the understating of the quality of the blend lifted. The former involved an increase in technical production cost allowance and equity margins for joint venture producers.[9] These were increased in July 1982 and again in February 1983, in an attempt to encourage foreign companies to increase lifting from their Nigerian concessions. Furthermore, in 1984, Nigeria improved its terms on 'buy back' crude. Equity producers were allowed to lift unsold NNPC oil at $2 per barrel below official prices. The latter method of retaining market share involved, in some cases, the reclassification of crudes, generally from Light to Medium, a 'sweetening' of the export blend to make the crude more favourable to buyers, and sometimes the offer of a competitive 'package' of crudes. Crude oil packages were offered in early 1985 in an effort by the Nigerian government to maintain its market edge. The minimum package of 20,000 b/d would be comprised of 35 per cent Forcados and 15 per cent Bonny Medium at discounted prices, and the remaining 50 per cent of either Bonny Light and Brass River at official prices or Qua Iboe, Escravos and Pennington at a premium.[10]

The period 1984–8 was essentially one of market responsive pricing, resulting in the mixed use of official prices, spot and spot-linked prices (particularly for equity producers), and netbacks. At the end of July 1985, Saudi Arabia had formally renounced its role of swing producer and was unwilling to allow the continuing steep decline in its exports. By September 1985, it was concluding netback pricing agreements to recover market share.[11] By December 1985, OPEC formally agreed that the policy of market share recovery would be given priority over that of price defence.

Nigeria formalized the use of netback pricing in its 1986 Memorandum of Understanding signed in January.[12] The concept of a 'realizable' price replaced that of the posted price on which taxes and royalties were calculated. Posted prices generally set the tax base higher than official selling rates and equity producers felt that the new concept, though not identical, would be closer to actual market realizations. The realizable price was essentially one worked out on the basis of average published product prices in the calendar month that the cargo was lifted – in effect a netback pricing formula.[13] Profit margins were also guaranteed in this 1986 agreement at a minimum of $2/b at a netback price of $23/b, increasing to $3 at a netback price of $30/b.[14] If prices were to fall significantly below $23, the Nigerian government was committed to re-negotiate its terms. In February the netback/realizable price was below $20/b and by April the average price per barrel was about $14. Pressures to stabilize and increase revenues kept oil production above the OPEC quota in Nigeria (which had been set at 1.3 mb/d in 1983) in the first half of 1986. In the summer of that year when netback values had already fallen to about $10 per barrel, the government felt unable to grant protected margins for a greater length of time. The

Table 5.1: Counter Trade Agreements Signed Between September 1984 and June 1985.

Co-Signatory in Counter Purchase Agreement (date)	Value of Agreement (Mn $)	Quantity of Nigerian Crude to be lifted	Goods Imported in Exchange for Nigerian Crude Oil	August 1985 Status of Counter-Purchase Agreements at Time of Suspension
Brazil (Sept.1984)	$500	50,000 b/d for 12 months	Volkswagen car parts; foodstuffs; industrial goods	$375 mn of eventual total $500 mn committed by Brazil
France (May 1985)	$500	50,000 b/d for 12 months	Peugeot car parts; industrial and consumer goods	$97.4 mn of eventual total $125 mn committed by France
Austria (May 1985)	$200	20,000 b/d for 12 months	Steel; agricultural & irrigation machinery; building materials; chemicals & other pharmaceuticals	$40 mn of eventual total $160 mn committed by the Austrians
Italy (June 1985)	$400	40,000 b/d	Fiat car parts; Sapien's $200 mn Escravos-Lagos gas pipeline contract	Agreement had not been implemented at time of August coup
Malaysia (June 1985)	$77	n.a.	Palm oil	

Sources: EIU, 1986, p. 47; Obadan, 1992, p. 231

terms of the 1986 Memorandum were therefore revised in 1987 to include the provision for reduced equity margins on netback prices of less than $12.50 per barrel (see Chapter 4).

Production restrictions were readopted in August 1986 as a result of the oil price collapse, and the decision to re-introduce official prices as of 1987 was taken in December 1986. The abolition of netback pricing obliged Nigeria to propose the new OPEC reference price as the official taxable price (plus or minus a differential). Although the initial proposal did not include any margin protection provisions, the revised agreement in February 1987 allowed for a protected equity margin at $2 as long as the spot market price remained close to the official price for Bonny Light. If market prices weakened further, the government would adjust its 'take' to keep the margin positive, although the companies would be obliged to bear 10 per cent of the price fall. This margin protection mechanism ensured that the lifting of notice oil remained attractive to equity producers, even in periods of market weakness.

By 1988, in an even more weakened market, however, the fact that lifting was more or less assured as a result of equity margin protection was not enough to retain the higher production levels. Nigeria's insistence on sticking to official prices for third-party buyers was no longer as feasible as before, and more flexible, market-oriented forms of pricing were considered. In 1988, product-linked pricing was re-instated. By the middle of the year, 450,000 b/d of Nigerian crude was being supplied to six overseas refineries which were processing the crude on a netback basis.[15] Besides the guaranteed downstream margins for the refiners/customers, these netback-related deals included the added incentive of a possible Nigerian acquisition of a downstream stake in their refining operations. Despite the widening spot crude and product price differentials in the summer of 1988 when product prices rose (Nigerian netback prices were $1–$2 higher than competing crudes), processing clients chose to renew their contracts with NNPC perhaps because of the lure of a downstream venture with Nigeria.[16] By November, however, some dissatisfied third-party customers had suspended lifting. Although these were resumed after Nigeria had agreed to 'sweeten' the terms, it was clear that the netbacking option had become the more costly one. In January 1989, therefore, Nigeria abandoned it in favour of pricing linked to spot crude oil. Four options were offered to customers. February and March prices could be set using either netback-style pricing based on new, standardized yields; or Brent-related pricing; or netback-style pricing with a price floor and ceiling tied to crude prices; or a 50–50 mix of the spot price of light Nigerian crudes and the netback price.[17]

Although spot crude prices rose much faster than product prices in the early part of 1989 (thus squeezing Atlantic Basin refining), about half of Nigeria's third-party clients opted for Brent-related formula pricing in February. This was mainly because Brent-related pricing was thought to be easier to hedge than netback formulae and because most buyers, in a rising market, preferred to determine crude oil acquisition terms before it was actually processed, as in netback pricing.

While Brent-related formula pricing has been the norm over the past four years, the Nigerians have periodically shifted to netback sales for their third-party clients. The option to use netback pricing was offered during the Gulf crisis when the advantage that US domestic crudes had relative to crudes priced on Brent-related terms had to be countered,[18] and more recently netbacks were re-introduced for a period of two months at the end of 1992 for Forcados and Bonny Medium. Following the collapse of gas oil prices in late November, and the increase in term prices by NNPC in December, some third-party clients refused to lift the crudes. On their insistence, and in an attempt to retain their market share for Forcados, netback pricing was introduced in December 1992 and January 1993.[19]

Price Formulae

Nigerian crude oil sales to both the United States and to Europe are linked to dated Brent prices plus or minus an adjustment factor. The point of sale is f.o.b. and the reference prices are either five- or ten-day averages of Platt's spot quotes. These can be averaged in a number of different ways relative to the date of loading: around the loading date; after the loading date; around the 5th, 10th or 14th day after loading; or after the 5th, 10th or 15th day after loading. The price timing and the market quote averages have tended to change since these reflect the degree of contango and/or backwardation in the market. In July 1990, but before the Gulf crisis for instance, Nigeria offered its term customers the option of pricing lifting around the bill of lading date. Prices based on these terms were $0.10/b higher than those based on deferred terms. This option of price triggering at the time of loading lost Nigeria potential revenue during the Gulf crisis when delivered prices (ten days after loading) were higher than those triggered at loading. Apart from this specific option offered in the summer of 1990, until June 1991, Nigerian pricing was generally of the 2–1–2 type, i.e, where the five spot quotes were averaged around the 15th day after the date of the bill of lading, two on either side. For about a year after June

---

Table 5.2: Nigerian Formula Pricing.

Bonny Light 37: Sales to the USA

Period	Market Linkage	Point of Sale	Price Timing	Market Quote Average
March'89-November'90	Dated Brent	fob	15 days a.l.	10 days
December'90-January'91	Dated Brent	fob	14 days a.l.	5 days
February'91-May'91	Dated Brent	fob	15 days a.l.	10 days
June'91-July'92	Dated Brent	fob	Loading date	5 days
August'92-Summer'93	Dated Brent	fob	5 days a.l.	5 days

Exceptions
Bonny Light 37: Sales to Rotterdam

January'90-July '90	Dated Brent	fob	15 days a.l.	10 days
August'90-October'90	Dated Brent	fob	10 days a.l.	10 days
November'90	Dated Brent	fob	15 days a.l.	10 days

Bonny Medium and Forcados: Sales to the USA

November'92-January'93	Netback Link	fob	5 days a.l.	5 days

Sources and Notes: *MEES, Petroleum Argus, PIW*, various issues.
Apart from the exceptions listed above, all Nigerian crudes to all destinations are priced according to the main Bonny Light (to the US) structure. This table shows the basic structure of the pricing formula, to which the Nigerian government either adds or subtracts an adjustment factor. These are changed on a monthly basis.

1991, when the crude market was in contango, five day spot averages were taken after the loading date.[20] Table 5.2 shows the basic structure of Nigerian formula pricing.

When formula pricing was first introduced, prices for Europe were averaged from the 11th to the 20th day after loading, while those for trans-Atlantic destinations were averaged from the 16th to the 25th day after loading.[21] In December 1990, Nigeria introduced a uniform pricing structure for its US and European clients. Cargoes from December would be priced on five consecutive quotations starting fourteen days from the bill of lading. While the price timing and the market quote average have changed since then, the changes have been applied to both US and European pricing terms – thereby leaving the basic pricing structure, at least officially, the same for both destinations.

In order to assess how the adjustment factors in the pricing formulae are set we compare the adjustment factors in the Forcados pricing formula with the Brent–Forcados spot differential (see Figure 5.1). Two observations can be made on the basis of this comparison. Firstly, there is a clear seasonality in prices. This is because the Nigerian crude is gas oil rich for which demand and prices build up at the end of the year, and generally are weaker by the spring.[22] Secondly, the adjustment factors track spot market differentials quite closely.

Ideally, however, the price differences between Forcados and

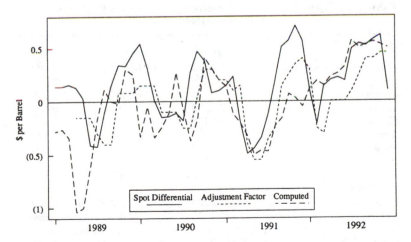

Figure 5.1: Forcardos–Brent Price Differentials

Brent depend on the following three factors: 1) the difference in the value of the crudes, i.e. differential gross product worth (GPW). This will also reflect the seasonality of the crudes; 2) the difference in freight to Rotterdam; 3) the difference in the time element in pricing. Since Brent is closer to Rotterdam than Forcados, backwardation (when current Brent prices are greater than future Brent prices) implies that the discount to Forcados is affected, and Forcados should be relatively depressed. A consideration of these three factors yields the theoretical 'computed' difference in Brent and Forcados prices (also in Figure 5.1). The relationship between the computed differential and the actual is rather weak, with the former showing a lower degree of seasonality.

The Marketing of Nigerian Crude Oil

Term Sales. Under the joint-venture participation agreements in Nigeria, the state organization NNPC has access to 60 per cent of total production, while the participating oil company(ies) have access to 40 per cent of the production. Table 5.3 shows the approximate equity entitlement of NNPC and other producing companies in Nigeria from 1989 to 1991.

Oil companies lift 40 per cent of Nigerian production. This

Table 5.3: Equity Entitlement of Nigerian Joint Venture Producers. Average Barrels per Day. 1989–91.

	1989	1990	1991
NNPC (incl. NPDC interests)	950,976	1,048,654	1,104,560
Shell	271,470	278,222	288,150
Chevron	118,680	122,582	134,700
Mobil	85,240	95,415	109,400
Elf	81,485	84,819	86,105
Agip	71,665	75,635	76,125
Phillips	26,420	29,265	28,100
Texaco	11,720	11,733	11,820
Dubri	n.a.	908	n.a.
Pan Ocean	600	463	480
British Gas	225	272	420
Sun	75	91	140

Sources: *PE*, March 1992, p. 23; *OPEC Annual Statistical Bulletin*, various issues.

has recently amounted to about 750,000 b/d. This entitlement is either run through the companies' own refinery systems or sold on the highly developed spot market in Nigerian crudes. NNPC's share of 60 per cent has recently amounted to about 1.1 mb/d. Of this total, about 300,000 b/d is allocated to domestic refineries and the remaining 800,000 b/d is allocated to term contracts. It is clear from Table 5.4 that the majority of the term contract holders are European customers.

The buyers of Nigerian crude include some equity producers, refiners and traders. Actual volumes lifted, as well as term customers themselves, tend to vary monthly largely because of the possibility of a monthly formula price change through changes in the adjustment factors. Volume changes also occur when NNPC decides to retain some of the crude itself for resale on the spot market.

Since 1988, however, the official policy line has been to sell Nigerian crude to only three groups: equity producers/joint-venture partners; local or foreign companies exploring in Nigeria; end-users willing to sell part of their refining or retail operations to NNPC. Despite this, traders were favoured in the early 1990s largely because they were willing to lift crudes out of season.[23] In 1992, the 1988 policy guidelines were reinforced and letters, threatening to cut off crude supplies, sent out to traders and or oil companies not willing to invest in Nigeria. The over-riding concern at this point was that the government wanted some serious thought put to ventures which might alleviate the chronic product shortages problem domestically. Until mid-1993 however, the 1988 sales policy that insisted that Nigerian crude oil lifters invest through joint ventures in Nigerian upstream or downstream development remained mainly tacit.[24] In October 1993, the Shonekan interim government issued new guidelines for crude oil contracts in which large oil traders were officially recognized as acceptable term buyers of Nigerian crude along with refiners, distributors, and companies investing in the country's upstream and downstream. Conditions applicable to all buyers include an annual turnover of at least $100 million, a net worth of $40 million, and a commitment to invest in the Nigerian economy – the failure to do so within six months would be penalized by the loss of the contract and the retention of a $1 million performance bond at a Nigerian bank.[25] In January 1994 under the Abacha

Table 5.4: Term Customers of NNPC Crude Oil and Destinations. Average Barrels/Day. 1991–94.

Customer	Destination	December 1991	April 1992	July 1993– June 1994
Sun	West	60,000	60,000	50,000
Elf	West	60,000	30,000	60,000
Southern Petroleum	West		40,000	30,000
Tevier (Marc Rich)	West	60,000	40,000	40,000 (30,000)*
Neste	West	60,000	40,000	30,000
Chevron (Halcon Calson)	Nigeria	50,000	50,000	50,000
Phibro	West	50,000		30,000
Attock	West	40,000	40,000	40,000
Coastal	West		30,000	20,000
Cepsa				30,000
Citizens				30,000
Dubri				30,000
Shell	West	30,000	30,000	
Texaco	West	30,000	30,000	
Wintershall	West	30,000		
Basic Resources	West/Africa	25,000	30,000	30,000
Interpetrol/Napoil	West		30,000	30,000
C.Itoh	West	30,000	30,000	
OK Petroleum	Sweden	30,000	20,000	
Ertoil	Spain	30,000	30,000	30,000
URBK	Germany	30,000		
Veba	West	30,000	30,000	30,000
Dreyfus/Duke Oil	West	30,000	30,000	30,000
Nigermed	West	30,000	30,000	30,000 (BP)
Ultramar		30,000		
Aerochem		30,000		
Ghana NPC	Ghana	25,000	30,000	30,000
Petrojam	Jamaica	15-20,000	20,000	20,000
Metalchim	Bulgaria		20,000	
Nova	Canada		20,000	
Neste/Thyssen	Germany		20,000	
Incomed				20,000
Itochu				20,000
OMV				20,000
Tosco				20,000
N.H.Rossell				20,000
Vitol/Vermont Petroleum				20,000
Consolidated Oil				15,000
ITOC/Senegal	Senegal		10,000	10,000
Total Term		**805-810,000**	**740,000**	**845,000**

Sources and Notes: *Argus*, Nigeria Supplement, 23/31 December, 1991, p. 18 and 7 June, 1993, p. 6; *PIW*, Special Supplement, Crude Oil Contracts, 27 April, 1992, p. 3, and 21 June, 1993, p. 7.
*Tevier and Marc Rich have been separated in June 1993 contracts.

regime, NNPC issued a new list of term contract holders as of March 1994. While the government insists that these newcomers comply with all the conditions stipulated in October 1993, the particular choice of companies is unclear. The new list, for instance, lacks any of NNPC's long-standing US customers and includes certain newcomers who have yet to show any evidence of spending commitments, payment of the non-refundable performance bond and the required minimum turnover.[26]

Spot Sales. According to *Petroleum Argus*, in 1991 more than 100 traded deals were reported per quarter. Information available on Nigerian spot trade shows that the primary source of liquidity in this market is in Forcados and Bonny Light. These two crudes, over the past five years, have accounted on average for 60 per cent of the reported traded Nigerian deals made.

Sellers of Nigerian crude included equity producers, the primary source of liquidity in Nigerian crude oil trade, and traders and refiners, such as Phibro which use the crude oil in their own refineries, and re-sell the rest. The pricing mechanism for this spot trade is similar to that in the North Sea. By 1991, outright

Table 5.5: Share of Total Reported Trade of Nigerian Crude by Type of Crude. 1986–91. Per Cent.

	1986	1987	1988	1989	1990	1991
Anten	1.8	2.2	1.0	1.8	3.2	1.2
BBQ	-	-	-	-	0.3	0.2
Bonny Light	21.8	17.8	21.2	21.1	20.6	18.7
Bonny Medium	20.0	23.2	9.6	13.2	10.3	11.4
Brass River	11.8	12.3	14.8	8.9	14.2	10.2
Escravos	3.6	2.2	5.8	3.2	5.8	7.0
Forcados	40.0	30.7	41.8	44.6	35.6	34.4
Pennington	-	2.2	1.9	1.8	1.2	2.4
Qua Iboe	0.9	9.3	3.8	5.4	8.7	14.4
Total Reported Traded Deals	100	269	104	280	344	501

Source: Calculated from the Petroleum Argus database by Horsnell and Mabro (1993, p. 258).
Total Traded Deals in this table include 'unknowns' and are therefore greater than those listed in Table 5.6 below.

Table 5.6: Share of Total Reported Traded Deals by Seller. 1986–91. Per Cent and Total Deals/Cargoes.

1986		1987		1988		1989		1990		1991	
Phibro	16.0	Phibro	20.6	Shell Int	25.5	Shell Int	22.1	Shell Int	18.4	Shell Int	14.0
Attock	14.0	Kaines	9.5	Addax	14.3	Elf	16.1	Agip	11.7	Phibro	7.8
Shell Int	13.0	Elf	8.0	Phibro	11.2	Phibro	10.1	Phibro	8.7	Marc Rich	7.0
Kaines	12.0	Attock	7.6	Chevron	8.2	Addax	9.0	Chevron	6.3	Elf	5.6
Marc Rich	6.0	Marc Rich	7.6	CFP	6.1	Agip	7.1	Attock	5.7	Agip	5.2
Elf	5.0	Shell Int	5.7	Elf	6.1	Vitol	5.6	Elf	5.4	Morgan Stanley	4.8
Chevron	4.0	Scan	4.2	Phillips	4.1	Texaco	4.1	Addax	5.1	Chevron	4.4
Delphi	3.0	CFP	4.2	Toro	3.1	CFP	2.6	Texaco	4.2	Addax	4.2
Enron	3.0	Delphi	3.8	Agip	2.0	Chevron	2.6	Vitol	4.2	Texaco	4.0
Ashland	2.0	J Aron		Exxon	2.0	Attock	2.2	Sun	3.3	Attock	3.2
Total Deals	**100**		**262**		**98**		**267**		**332**		**499**

Source: OIES Calculations from *Petroleum Argus* database.

deals had practically disappeared while deals priced against Brent had increased to about 81 per cent of total deals.

Trades made against the WTI price, essentially based on trade in the US Gulf Coast, accounted for about 8 per cent of total deals in 1991. Some Bonny deals are also priced against BBQ and Forcados. These trades accounted for 7.4 per cent in 1991, and since 1989 have taken some of the liquidity away from the trades priced on differentials to WTI. However since the underlying prices of these are also based on Dated Brent, traded deals against these crudes are Brent related. In 1991, therefore, Brent-related pricing of spot trade accounted for almost 88 per cent of total West African spot deals (Horsnell and Mabro, 1993, pp. 258–9, 261).

International Trade in Nigerian Crude Oil

Nigerian Crude Exports. Nigerian crude oil production, the allocation to domestic refineries, and the crude oil export slate (including that traded on the spot market) are all dominated by Shell's Forcados and Bonny. These accounted for about 50 per cent of total production in 1990. The other streams, all with average gravities of 35° or above are produced by Mobil–NNPC (Qua Iboe), Agip–NNPC–Phillips (Brass River), Texaco–NNPC–Chevron (Pennington), Chevron–NNPC (Escravos), and the Ashland production-sharing venture (Anten). The new Odudu blend, produced by Elf, and onstream since May 1993, is currently similar in quality to Bonny Light. The blend includes crude from just the Afia and Odudu fields. By 1994, when all four fields are on stream (i.e. including Ime in October 1993 and Edikan in January 1994), the crude blend is expected to be of the Bonny Medium type.[27]

Most recent data on Nigerian exports by crude stream show that about 50 per cent of total Nigerian exports are accounted for by BBQ (Bonny Light, Brass River and Qua Iboe) grades, and about 30 per cent of total exports are accounted for by Forcados, alone. See Table 5.7 for the historical evolution of Nigerian crude oil exports by type of crude.

The main export markets for Nigerian crude are the United States and Western Europe, the former accounting for 47 per cent of total exports in 1991, and the latter for 45 per cent. This

Table 5.7: Share of Total Crude Oil Exports by Stream. 1980–86, 1989.
Per Cent.

Crude Stream	1980	1981	1982	1983	1984	1985	1986	1989
Anten	n.a	n.a	n.a	n.a	n.a	n.a	1.5	1.6
Bonny Light	n.a	n.a	19.6	15.0	n.a	17.0	23.2	19.6
Brass River	n.a	n.a	13.1	12.4	n.a	11.7	10.8	9.6
Escravos	n.a	n.a	9.5	7.8	n.a	10.3	12.6	10.4
Pennington	n.a	n.a	3.2	4.1	n.a	3.4	4.9	3.8
Qua Iboe	n.a	n.a	11.8	15.5	n.a	14.1	13.7	14.0
Total 'Light' Stream	64.0	63.4	57.2	54.8	54.5	56.5	66.7	59.0
Forcados	28.9	27.5	30.1	31.0	31.2	31.4	23.7	31.6
Bonny Medium	7.1	9.0	12.6	14.2	14.3	12.1	9.6	9.3

Sources and Notes: 1980–86 data from NNPC London Library and 1989 Data
from OPEC DSD, Statistical Section, 9 December, 1992.
Total 'Light' Stream refers to Nigerian light crudes (34°-42°API) inclusive of
Bonny Light.

fairly balanced distribution of crude exports masks the quite striking
volume and compositional changes in Nigerian crude oil exports
over the past decade. Table 5.8 shows the evolution of these
exports since 1980.

The main change in export volumes occurred in the early
1980s with the onset of economic recession in the West coinciding
with the increase in North Sea production. The biggest decline
in Nigerian exports occurred over the period 1980–81 when
exports to western Europe halved (from 893,000 b/d to 493,000
b/d), those to the United States dropped by about 150,000 b/d
to approximately 400,000 b/d in 1981, and those to Latin America
(mainly Brazil and Argentina) also halved from 450,000 b/d to
250,000 b/d in 1981. While the decline in exports in general
reached its lowest point in 1983 at 935,000 b/d, exports to western
Europe bottomed out in 1982 at 482,000 b/d and exports to the
United States and Latin America bottomed out in 1984 at 173,000
b/d and 89,000 b/d, respectively. Although the decline in exports
was more significant for western Europe and Latin America
relative to the United States, the compositional change – with
one market being prioritized relative to the other – was only

Table 5.8: Nigerian Crude Oil Exports by Destination. 1980–85, 1987, 1989–92. Thousand Barrels per Day.

	1980	1981	1982	1983	1984	1985	1987	1989	1990	1991	1992
USA	553	398	357	209	154	223	530	803	786	701	701
L.America	455	253	110	96	89	215	18	25	25	40	45
W.Europe	893	493	482	608	791	832	430	567	613	730	691
of which:											
France	264	109	161	195	238	202	70	65	60	83	89
Germany	128	76	77	111	118	99	59	96	124	137	180
Italy	88	56	88	118	168	200	66	46	26	56	34
Netherlands	281	149	72	80	140	160	118	57	32	86	74
Spain	23	38	16	28	51	76	114	187	179	224	179
U.K	2	4	15	29	37	46	9	17	38	32	21
Africa	40	42	25	18	41	44	64	70	75	80	80
Far East Asia	20	26				1			1	-	10
Total	1,960	1,228	1,003	935	1,094	1,333	1,065	1,526	1,550	1,610	1,585

Sources and Notes: *OPEC Annual Statistical Bulletin*, various issues; data for Spain from IEA, *Quarterly Oil Statistics and Energy Balances*, various issues.

IEA import data is comprised of crude oil + NGLs + refinery feedstocks.

really apparent in the post-1985 period.

After 1985, crude oil exports to the United States increased until 1989, and then decreased slightly until 1992. Exports to western Europe bottomed out, for a second time in the decade, at 430,000 b/d in 1987, then increased till 1991 and declined again after that. While western Europe has managed to retain its share of Nigerian exports quite well (these stood at 691,000 b/d in 1991, only about 140,000 b/d less than the average exports in 1985), and while exports to Africa have risen by an average 30,000 b/d over the 1985–91 period, the substantive part of the increase in Nigerian exports over the past five years has been taken by the United States.

The compositional changes in Nigerian crude oil exports in the post-1985 period have favoured the United States at the expense of mainly the Netherlands, Italy and France, and Latin America. The origin of much of this structural change lies in the increased production of the North Sea crudes competing directly for Nigeria's west European market, the effects of which have only just become more visible with the ending of the recession of the early 1980s.

The overall distribution of US imports by type of Nigerian crude reflects the overall Nigerian crude export slate. Table 5.9 shows the distribution of Nigerian exports to the USA in 1990 by average API gravity. More than half of these exports are skewed toward crudes between 33° and 38° with average API gravity, and more than a quarter of the exports are skewed toward crudes with average gravities of between 28°–32° API. The first group are mainly representative of the Bonny-Light type crudes, which include Bonny Light, Anten, Qua Iboe, Pennington and Escravos; while the second group would cover the Forcados-blend.[28]

The four major US importers of Nigerian crude (BP, Shell, Sun and Chevron), accounted for about 70 per cent of US imports of Nigerian crude from 1987 to 1989, and in 1990 and 1991, about 80 per cent. Of the four companies, BP has neither equity interest in nor a significant term contract with Nigeria, and therefore the bulk of its purchases are from the spot market.[29] Sun, Shell and Chevron are importers as well as equity producers in Nigeria, and also hold third-party term contracts with NNPC. Of these, Sun purchases two-thirds and Chevron at least half of

Table 5.9: Distribution of Nigerian Crude Oil Exports to the USA in 1990 by Average API Gravity of each Crude Oil Cargo. Percentage.

Gravity Distribution	Total Exports at Specified Gravity	Share of Total Exports
27°API and Below	22.6 mb	7.8%
28°-32° API	75.3 mb	26.0%
33°-38° API	157.7 mb	54.5%
39°API and Above	33.6 mb	11.6%

Source: Calculations from *Imported Crude Oil and Petroleum Products*, American Petroleum Institute, January 1990 to December 1990.

their Nigerian crude oil off the spot market. Shell is the largest equity producer in Nigeria, and has had access to a further 30,000 b/d term contract over the past few years, and half of Shell's Nigerian production goes to its US refineries. As regards the remaining US importers of Nigerian crude oil, a comparison with a list of Nigerian term customers shows that almost none of these other refiners have any equity production in or long-term contracts with Nigeria. These imports, then, are essentially spot market purchases.

It is clear that Nigerian trade policy has changed significantly with the emergence of the North Sea market and the increased production of North Sea crudes. Prior to 1980, the quality (light characteristics) and locational (short-haul crude to Europe) advantages of Nigerian crude were being fully exploited *vis à vis* the European market. Other African producers of light crudes were shifting smaller quantities mostly to Italy. Consequently the competition was minimal. By the early 1980s, Nigerian crudes had to compete with North Sea grades, which were also light, and had the advantage of even shorter-haul. Given the economic recession in the West and the characteristics of North Sea crude (gasoline-rich), this competition was of serious concern and had implications on crude oil marketing in terms of the volume of exports and their destination.

Crude Oil Loading Terminals and Storage Facilities

An adequate export infrastructure is necessary given the large crude oil volumes exported on term contracts and traded on the

Table 5.10: Crude Oil Loading Terminals in Nigeria.

Terminal Name	Location	Max. Tanker size (1000 dwt)	Max. Draft (Metres)	Storage Capacity (1000 b)	Operating Company	Crude Type	Comments
Anten	Offshore	230	22.0	1750	Ashland/Anten	Anten Blend; Brass River	Storage & trans-shipment on tanker 'FPSO VI'
Bonny	Offshore Platform	320	22.0	n.a.	NNPC/Shell	Bonny Light & Medium	
Bonny	Onshore	100	22.0	7523	NNPC/Shell	Bonny Light & Medium	Storage on vessel 'Tuma' with 136,000 dwt
Port Harcourt	Onshore	n.a.	9.6	1058	NNPC	Bonny Light & Medium	
Forcados	Onshore & Offshore Platform	254	25.0	6000	NNPC/Agip PanOcean/ Tenneco/Shell	Forcados Blend	
Brass	Offshore SBM	300	30.0	3258	NNPC/Shell	Brass Blend	
Escravos	Offshore	350	20.0	3600	NNPC/Dubri	Escravos	
Qua Iboe	Offshore	255	22.0	3500	NNPC/Mobil	Qua Iboe	
Pennington (Oloibiri)	Offshore	250	20.0	2000	NNPC/Texaco	Pennington Light	Storage on tanker 'Oloibiri'

Sources: Guide to Port Entry, *Shipping Guides Ltd*.; OPEC Secretariat Compilation at December, 1992; *Lloyd's Maritime Directory*.

spot market. In 1991, crude oil exports averaged about 1.6 mb/d, accounting for 85 per cent of production. Nigeria has seven crude oil export terminals comprising Escravos, Forcados, Pennington, Brass, Bonny, Qua Iboe and Anten (see Table 5.10). All of these, with the exception of Bonny onshore, can handle VLCCs (tankers able to carry about 250,000–300,000 tons of crude oil). The Bonny onshore terminal, after dredging of the bar, can handle carriers of up to 90,000–100,000 dwt.[30] Each terminal has single point mooring/loading facilities about 25 km. offshore which give VLCCs easier access, and is operated and managed by producing companies on behalf of the NNPC.

Total crude storage at loading terminals is estimated at about 28.7 mb. This figure excludes certain inland storage facilities such as, amongst others, Elf's tank farm at Obagi and NNPC's own storage facilities, for instance those next to Escravos for storage of heavy oil for the Kaduna refinery (Ikeh, 1991, pp. 90–108). If the maximum crude oil storage capacity in Nigeria amounts to about 30 mb, with exports of about 1.6 mb/d, this storage capacity provides about 18–20 days export cover. While this may be adequate for operational purposes, it does not give the Nigerians any commercial flexibility (NNPC does not own any overseas storage facilities closer to export markets), nor does it give any advantage at times of crises. During the 1990 Gulf war, for instance, maximum productive capacity was attained quickly, and NNPC did not have access to any additional stocks of crude oil.

Notes

1. The widening of LLS (Light Louisiana Sweet) and WTI (West Texas Intermediate) differentials to Brent, for instance, induces US refiners to buy gasoil rich Forcados, while increased gasoline demand in the Atlantic Basin pushes them to use Nigerian BBQ grades (*Argus*, 19 August, 1991).
2. Export demand for OPEC oil fell by an estimated 12 mb/d between 1979 and 1982. 33 per cent of this decline has been attributed to the energy consumption cutbacks in the industrialized West due to both economic recession and conservation measures. 25 per cent of the decline has been attributed to the increase in non-OPEC oil supplies; 21 per cent to the increased use of alternative energy supplies; and a further 21 per cent to the shift from building stocks to drawing down stocks (Brown, 1990, p. 102).
3. The loss of British Petroleum's preferential access to a large chunk of

Iranian offtake, followed by the nationalization of its assets in Nigeria in 1979, contributed to the leadership role taken on by the company in the trend away from long-term contracts (premised on security of supply considerations) to spot market purchases (Ibid., p. 103).

4. The offshore refining scheme started in 1976, and over the first ten years contracts were signed with Shell Curacao, BP–Total consortium, Socap, Stinnes Interoil, and in 1985, Brazil's Petrobras (Eleazu, 1988, p. 210).

5. *PE*, March 1985; *PIW*, 12 August and 16 September, 1985.

6. EIU, *Nigeria*, 1991–2, p. 26.

7. EIU, Special Report No. 1072, 1986, p. 47.

8. Barrows, *IPI Data Service, Africa*, No. 50, *Nigeria*, 1987, p. 23.

9. As we have seen in Chapter 3, another means of market share protection has traditionally been managed through the improvement of tax and equity terms for equity producers, to encourage increased lifting. The Buhari incentives in 1977 were designed to fulfil this very purpose in a period of slack demand and weak prices.

10. *PE*, March, 1985, p. 81.

11. Although precise information on the extent of the discount is not known, it is known that most Saudi crude was exported to west European destinations, where the average netback value in Saudi crudes was about $2.50/b below the weighted average official rate in early October (Brown, 1990, p. 669).

12. Nigeria had been using netback related pricing since the previous year. In fact, in November 1985, a comparison of netback prices to both spot price of Bonny Light showed a price discount of about $0.91/b in its Western Europe netback price and a discount of $0.63/b in its US netback price (Ibid., p. 672).

13. Barrows, *IPI Data Service, Africa*, No. 47, *Nigeria*, 1986, p. 74.

14. In return for these new fiscal terms, the equity producers were expected to invest in exploration, production and various gas re-cycling and re-injection programmes. Furthermore, equity producers could be obliged to lift up to 100 per cent of output, i.e., their own equity volumes plus NNPC equity at 45 days notice. The equity margin for this 'notice' oil was set at $1.00/b and re-instated the attraction for oil companies to lift from Nigerian concessions (Barrows, *IPI Data Service, Africa*, No. 47, *Nigeria*, 1986, p. 74, no. 50, p. 17).

15. The overseas refineries were owned by Atlantic Richfield, Mapco, Phibro and Sun in the USA, and ERT and Petromed of Spain. These agreements were different from the Overseas Processing deals between NNPC and Petrobras, Basic Resources and Total in which light products were returned to Nigeria and yield values were used to settle the difference. (*PE*, June 1988, p. 206).

16. Meanwhile, pricing terms offered to equity producers in the Spring of 1988, were more flexible. The mechanism for pricing oil to equity producers was linked 50 per cent to the spot market value for Nigerian BBQ (i.e. Bonny Light, Brass River, Qua Iboe, adjusted for crude quality), and 50 per cent to netbacks (according to the 1986 MOU where the netback portion is based on 30 per cent special US yield structure; 45 per cent

North West Europe; and 25 per cent Mediterranean.) The spot crude component in pricing for equity producers provided a partial hedge against the growing differential between crude and product prices and was therefore a flexible means of pricing oil. In 1989, however, even when third-party customers changed to formula pricing, pricing for equity producers retained the 50 per cent netback linkage. By the summer of 1991, as a result of high product prices, the netback element in the pricing was pushing up the taxable base for equity producers. Because equity producers were dissatisfied with the netback linkage in their prices, they called for a change in the way that NNPC calculated its tax realizable price for equity exports. In the 1991 MOU, NNPC retained the netback element but introduced a $0.40/b floor/ceiling to the formula (*PIW*, Special Supplement, 29 January, 1990; *Argus*, 15 July, 1991, p. 6).

17. *PIW*, 9 January, 1989, p. 3.
18. *PIW*, 11 March, 1991, p. 5.
19. *Argus*, 14 December, 1992, p. 3; *PIW*, 14 December, 1992, pp. 1, 4.
20. Depending on the client and the degree of the contango, the Nigerian government by the summer of 1991 also offered the choice of two pricing options: five spot quotes after the loading date or five quotes after the 14th day after loading. And from the 3rd quarter of 1991, the netback option was also available to some US buyers.
21. *Argus*, 2 July, 1990.
22. In late 1991, the prospect of a warmer winter and slack demand caused oil prices to decline. Gas oil prices, built up in the late summer, collapsed in November 1992. Netbacks were therefore introduced for a short period in Forcados and Bonny Medium formula pricing to retain sales.
23. *PIW*, 7 May, 1990, p. 3.
24. BP-Statoil, for instance, won exploration rights in the 1991 licensing round. The companies were offered term contracts in 1992. Negotiations with Phibro regarding a refinery stake for NNPC broke down in 1991 and the trader/refiner's 50,000 b/d term contract was revoked at the beginning of 1992. Most press reports emphasized the political motivations underlying the various changes in policy. In the autumn of 1992, for instance, in the run-up to the elections (initially scheduled for December), it was suggested that a sales policy encouraging traders to lift out of season crudes would be counter-productive as it was associated in the public's mind with corruption (*PIW*, 7 September, 1992, p.2). By the middle of 1993, however, in keeping with the shift back to favouring refiners/traders, Phibro was reinstated as a term customer at 30,000 b/d as of July 1993.
25. *Energy Compass*, 22 October, 1993, p. 4.
26. Ibid., 11 January, 1994, pp. 1–2.
27. *Argus*, 8 March, 1993, p. 7.
28. This distribution is based on the average gravity of each crude oil cargo imported into the USA in 1990. The following lists crude oil imports in '000 barrels by individual companies. The average gravity of total imports by each company is listed in the parenthesis. Amoco 35,509 (30.05); BP 78,704 (31.95); Chevron 48,387 (35.50); Cibro 123 (36.4); Clark 1,398

(30.98); Coastal 3,192 (33.28); Crown Central 2,127 (36.59); Fina 417 (41.90); Hess 888 (29.20); Kerr-McGee 664 (36.3); Koch 319 (40.71); Lyondell 1,755 (36.03); Marathon 1,443 (34.2); Mobil 229 (33.7); Phibro 2,831 (30.85); Phillips66 9,944 (42.55); Shell 39,725 (37.09); Sun 61,501 (35.13). *Imported Crude Oil and Petroleum Products*, American Petroleum Institute, 1990 data.

29. BP's US affiliate Sohio is a large spot buyer and the largest single refiner of Nigerian crude oil.
30. Onoh, 1983, p. 44 and *OPEC Bulletin*, July/August 1985.

6 THE NIGERIAN DOWNSTREAM

Disruptions in the Nigerian downstream sector have deeper and more immediate domestic political implications for the country than those that may occur in the upstream sector. Energy supply problems have plagued the country since the 1980s. These are due to several factors: refineries are prone to breakdowns, the production slate does not always match consumption trends, and the already inadequate distribution system is also beleaguered by problems of widespread cross-border smuggling of petroleum products. Subsidies encourage both higher domestic consumption and the illegal export of products out of the country. This chapter looks at the most important domestic supply issues – domestic pricing and product smuggling. Also discussed are the perennial refinery and distribution bottle-necks, the consequent need for product exchange arrangements and the unsuccessful attempt of the Nigerian downstream to build wholly export-oriented refineries (largely because domestic supply, for obvious reasons, has always had first call on products). Finally, this chapter also considers the future for longer-term projects which the Nigerian government has embarked upon, such as petrochemicals and the acquisition of foreign downstream equity.

Domestic Product Pricing

The subsidy on gasoline and gas oil increases consumption and as a result demand is seldom met by domestic production. Significant quantities of petroleum products find their way to neighbouring countries where domestic prices are said to be at least fifteen times higher. In 1993, for instance, some oil industry sources estimated that up to 100,000 b/d of product was being smuggled overland into Benin, Cameroon, and Niger.[1]

Table 6.1 shows the results of a recent *Petroleum Argus* survey which compares domestic selling prices of petroleum products in exporting countries. The degree to which product price support constitutes a heavy burden on the economy is evident in the level of the annual subsidy (based on a three-product average).[2] In Nigeria, this is estimated to be about 17 per cent of oil export

Table 6.1: Comparative Domestic Petroleum Product Prices in Exporting Countries. 1993.

	Gasoline	Gas oil	Fuel Oil	3-Product Average	#Annual Implicit Subsidy
	(cents/USG)	*(cents/USG)*	*(US$/bbl)*	*(US$/bbl)*	*(US$mn)*
Algeria*	54	25	7.00	14.94	340
Egypt	113	34	5.81	14.04	366
Indonesia	112	67	16.13	31.25	-2,366
Iran	11	2	0.70	1.56	5,633
Kuwait	57	50	10.50	19.14	-2
Libya*	24	16	0.96	5.81	428
Nigeria*	**8**	**7**	**2.75**	**3.12**	**1,606**
Qatar	59	54	11.50	21.99	-5
S.Arabia	35	12	6.36	8.10	2,632
UAE	86	75	12.00	30.79	-336
Venezuela	24	18	6.36	7.97	1,271
USA	112	100	15.00	-	-
Bulk Spot	56	51	10.50	-	-

Source: *Argus*, 12 July, 1993, p. 4.
* At free market exchange rates; # Minus subsidy means local prices exceed bulk spot averages.

earnings. While the concession is not as high as in Iran where it represents 40 per cent of oil earnings, Nigeria's burden is aggravated by the costs of smuggling. It is important to note, however, that even the complete removal of subsidies to the level of 'bulk spot' prices, will not necessarily put an end to smuggling because taxation is high in neighbouring countries. However, pricing Nigerian products at cost will at least recover these expenditures for the state.[3] This has become increasingly significant given the constant delay in capital replacement at the refineries because of government financial constraints and the implications of the opportunity cost of such delays on the domestic supply situation.

The debate on subsidies began in 1986 and originated with negotiations between Nigeria, the World Bank and the IMF on 'structural adjustment lending and balance of payments support'.[4] Decisions taken at the time of the 1986 budget called for subsidies on petroleum products to be phased out gradually with the exception of kerosene, whose domestic use has been encouraged by the government to replace firewood and check deforestation.[5] More specifically, the new economic measures called for a reduction of 80 per cent of the price support on petrol.[6] At this time, petrol prices doubled from N0.20/litre to N0.40/litre (the price in December 1993 was N3.5/litre), while diesel prices trebled from N0.10/litre to N0.30/litre.[7] In April 1988, further cuts in product subsidies raised petrol prices by 6 per cent to N0.42/litre, diesel prices by 19 per cent to N0.35/litre, kerosene prices by 50 per cent to N0.15/litre, and engine oil prices by 62 per cent. The savings from these subsidy cuts were expected to be about $890 million, about half of the then estimated budget deficit (Brown, 1990, p. 321). The significance of these Naira denominated product price increases must not be overemphasized however, given the annual rate of depreciation of the currency. None the less, they met with strong public discontent and rioting in the same way as earlier subsidy cuts.

In 1989, NNPC in keeping with its drive toward commercialization and autonomy was allowed to fix product prices without the interference of the federal government. Product prices consequently increased by about 67 per cent after a period of three months, although subsidies were not completely removed.[8] In 1990, NNPC increased the allowable gross profit margin of oil marketing companies on products by about 30 per cent. The increase was to cover the transport allowance and the retail distributor's margin.[9] It is not clear whether this was implemented at the expense of consumer subsidies or at the expense of the NNPC budget. In early 1991, NNPC was given full permission to deregulate domestic petroleum product prices. However, the fuel riots in the summer of 1992 were more a result of price increases caused by the devaluation of the currency and coincidental gasoline shortages than deregulation on the part of NNPC.[10]

Currently, therefore, domestic price support remains high in Nigeria, and domestic product prices in Nigeria remain low, being only a fraction of world prices. In 1993, a government decision to postpone, yet again, the removal of product subsidies to after the June elections further cemented the position of politics over economics. Just before relinquishing power in August 1993, the Babingida government implemented a two-tier pricing system for gasoline which essentially increased the price of premium petrol ten-fold (to Naira 7.5/litre or $1.10/US Gallon). While the subsidy on the standard gasoline (the higher octane grade is coloured yellow to prevent illegal substitution) was maintained, the product itself was made more difficult to obtain. In September 1993, tanker drivers were refusing to load the premium fuel in protest against both the price rise and the unavailability of standard gasoline.[11] Given country-wide protests, the interim government decided not to implement this particular scheme – then in November 1993 it raised product prices approximately seven-fold (gasoline from N0.70 to N5, kerosene from N0.50 to N4.50 and diesel from N0.55 to N4.75), justifying it on the basis that it was unable to postpone reforms any further. These reforms had, of course, taken on greater urgency given the need of the interim government to secure debt relief from international creditors as well as to provide effective incentives for foreign investment in the downstream sectors.[12] While these constraints continue to exist for the new military government of General Sani Abacha, which replaced the interim government on 17 November, 1993, union strikes and public discontent have once again forced some back-tracking on the subsidy removal issue. In December, the product price increase was modified to a five-fold one, thus increasing that of gasoline from N0.70 to N3.5 instead of N5.[13]

Given the track record of public discontent and protest following the introduction of higher product prices, the new military government has a responsibility to see that it does not back down further over this move. Affected by any further delay will be one of the previous government's decisions over the summer of 1993 to allow domestic companies other than NNPC to import gasoline. This decision raised questions regarding the pricing of these imports given the disparity between local subsidized gasoline prices and the much higher international prices. It will also have implications for the government's attempt to encourage foreign participation and/or full foreign ownership of new refineries. In a market where prices are controlled, costs not recovered, full ownership is not an enticing prospect.

The Domestic Supply and Demand Imbalance in Refined Products

In 1991, 25 per cent of gasoline demand, 15 per cent of kerosene demand and 19 per cent of demand for 'other products' were satisfied by imports, while distillate and residual fuels were exported. The difference was supplied by domestic refineries and/ or product exchange arrangements.[14] Figure 6.1 provides an overview of both the supply and demand for refined products in Nigeria, and shows the years in which the three last refineries were commissioned.

From 1975 to 1989, consumption of refined products was higher than production, and their imports increased from about 21,000 b/d in 1975 to 84,000 b/d in 1981, then decreased to 34,000 b/d in 1989. Over the period 1971–91, production of refined products grew by an average 9.3 per cent per annum, while consumption grew by 10.1 per cent per annum. The average annual growth rate of product consumption was much higher in the 1970s than it was in the 1980s. This is mainly because the earlier decade was also one of rapid growth in oil revenues, but from 1982 onwards, the Nigerian economy was in a recession. Construction activity had decreased and with it road construction and the demand for asphalt. Gasoline demand had decreased, closely linked to the dwindling supply of new motor vehicles as

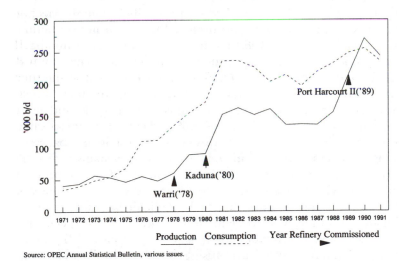

Source: OPEC Annual Statistical Bulletin, various issues.

Figure 6.1: Nigerian Production and Consumption of Refined Products. Thousand Barrels per Day. 1971–91.

well as certain stringent measures against smuggling. The latter included the closing of land borders in 1984, and a cut down in illegal bunkering by the tightening up of crude oil sales procedures. Gas oil demand was lower than in earlier years due mainly to the decrease in commercial activity, which had a severe impact on the demand for a fuel used primarily in heavy goods vehicles, ferries and construction companies. Similarly, the growth rate of heavy fuel oil consumption in the 1980s was much lower than in the 1970s, again due to the downturn in economic activity and with it the activity of the bunkering, cement and textile industries, in which fuel oil is involved. In recent years, particularly the period 1987–91, there has been an upturn in economic activity and an end to the recession of the 1980s. Consequently, the country has seen increasing demand (relative to the earlier part of the decades) for petroleum products, particularly for gasoline and gas oil.[15]

The commissioning of the Warri refinery in 1978 lessened the gap between production and consumption, but only slightly. This was because the initial gains made by the commissioning of the new refinery were quickly eroded by rising consumption after 1979. Kaduna, commissioned in 1980, made less of an impact on the gap between production and consumption. This gap started decreasing from 1981 until 1984 during which time the decline in consumption was more pronounced than that in production. It was only after the 1989 commissioning of Port Harcourt II that production of refined products actually overtook consumption levels in 1990. It is important to note, however, that at the time that Port Harcourt II came onstream, rising production was already beginning to catch up with consumption levels, and when the latter actually declined in late 1989 and early 1990, production was able to overtake it. Despite this however, sustaining a balanced supply/demand situation in refined products remains a difficult proposition. Moreover, attaining the status of a net product exporter, which Nigeria wishes to do once the export refinery at Calabar is built, also appears to be difficult (see next section). Firstly, the smuggling problem must continue to be specifically targetted and consumption growth kept under control.[16] Secondly, the structural plant problems causing shut-downs at Port Harcourt I, Warri and Kaduna will have to be reduced if production is to be near capacity. Finally, the new export refinery at Calabar will have to be built as planned and avoid having plant output diverted to satisfy domestic petroleum product requirements.

Gasoline Demand. Since 1979, gasoline has been the most important product import for the country, accounting for about 50 per cent or more of total refined product imports. While domestic demand for gasoline has always been greater than domestic production, this gap has narrowed significantly over the past five years (see Figure 6.2). Gasoline imports were highest between 1979 and 1989, with the two main increases in production occurring in 1981 and in 1990 after the commissioning of the Kaduna and Port Harcourt II refineries, respectively. Gasoline demand growth has slowed down considerably in the past decade, and since 1987 production has been growing at a much faster rate than consumption. This was due in part to improved refinery runs, increased taxes on gasoline and hence lower demand growth, as well as a clampdown on smuggling.

With the Fluid Catalytic Cracking (FCC) units at Warri and Kaduna repaired, and more recently with the old Port Harcourt

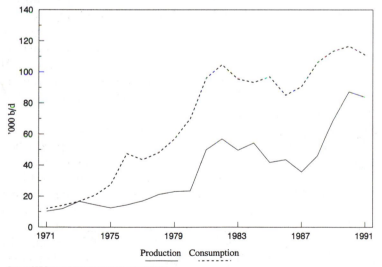

Production   Consumption

Source: OPEC Annual Statistical Bulletin, various issues.

Figure 6.2:   Nigerian Production and Consumption of Gasoline. Thousand Barrels per Day. 1971–91.

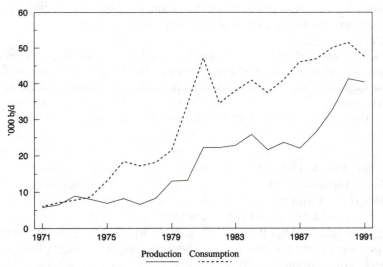

Figure 6.3: Nigerian Production and Consumption of Kerosene. Thousand
Barrels per Day. 1971–91.

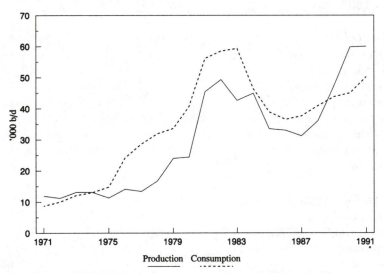

Figure 6.4: Nigerian Production and Consumption of Gas Oil. Thousand
Barrels per Day. 1971–91.

refinery coming back onstream upgraded and with greater capacity, the potential for gasoline exports is very much present. Certainly, if a new export oriented refinery is built as planned, there is a possibility for the Nigerians to increase gasoline exports, in particular to the United States. The reality of under-utilization of refinery capacity and smuggling, however, is very different. The fuel riots in early 1992 and the access to third-party processing at Port Harcourt II given in mid-1992 attest to the unfortunate fact that self-sufficiency in gasoline, let alone gasoline exports may not be achieved for some time.

In 1991, kerosene and gas oil consumption, together, accounted for roughly 39 per cent of total refined product consumption (see Figures 6.3 and 6.4).

Kerosene Demand. Kerosene production was greater than demand only in 1973. Imports peaked at about 24,000–25,000 b/d in 1981 and again in 1987. Kerosene production has grown at an annual average growth rate of 16.4 per cent over the period 1987–91. During this time, kerosene consumption grew at a rate of 0.8 per cent. Imports of kerosene stood at about 24,000 b/d in 1987 and had decreased to about 7,000 b/d in 1991.

Gas Oil Demand. The supply and demand situation for gas oil has been more balanced than for other products. Between 1974 and 1988, demand exceeded supply of distillate fuels and imports peaked at about 16,000 b/d. Since 1989, however, there has been surplus production of gas oil. The 1990 product exchange arrangements for gas oil (and fuel oil) were designed to respond to this situation. It is not clear whether the surplus gas oil, at present, continues to be either exported, or exchanged for lighter products.

Fuel Oil Demand. Figure 6.5 shows that the domestic supply of fuel oil has regularly exceeded domestic demand. In the early 1990s, the production rate has increased relative to earlier years, and consumption has been decreasing. Three possible reasons may account for this increase in the fuel oil surplus. First, the frequent breakdowns and shut-downs at the two older refineries have had an impact on the amount of fuel oil surplus used as refinery feedstock and/or actually upgraded. Secondly, the surpluses in

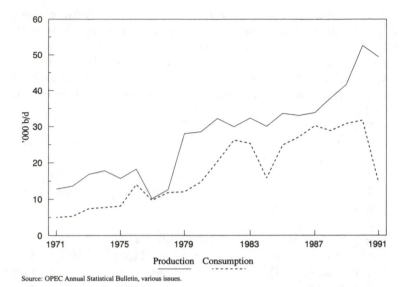

Source: OPEC Annual Statistical Bulletin, various issues.

Figure 6.5: Nigerian Production and Consumption of Residual Fuels.
Thousand Barrels per Day. 1971–91.

recent years may also indicate the end of the *ad hoc* product
exchange arrangements made in 1990 between the Nigerian
government and companies such as Addax, Chevron and Total,
where Nigerian surplus gas oil and fuel oil were exchanged for
supplies of kerosene and gasoline. Finally, the NEPA plant at
Egbin replaced its use of high pour fuel oil with gas, thus worsening
the fuel oil surplus situation.[17]

Nigerian Domestic Refineries

Table 6.2 shows the configuration of the four Nigerian refineries.
While total nameplate capacity at the four refineries amounted
to 433,250 b/d as of 1993, actual usable capacity had fallen far
below this.

This lower operating capacity severely hampered the
government's drive toward product exports, since 85 per cent of
production from the new Port Harcourt refinery, originally meant
to be dedicated to exports, has been allocated to satisfying
demand.[18] Furthermore, frequent breakdowns of FCC units in

Table 6.2: Structure and Capacity of Nigerian Refineries. As at 1 January, 1993. Barrels Per Calendar Day.

Refinery Location	Charge Capacity, b/cd						Production Capacity, b/cd		
	Crude	Vacuum Distillation	Catalytic Cracking	Catalytic Reforming	Catalytic Hydro-treating	Alkylation *Poly.	Aromatics/ Isomerization	Lubes	Asphalt
Kaduna Refinery & Petrochemical Co. (NNPC) - Kaduna[1]	104,500	36,290	[1]18,000	[2]15,300	[1]21,600 [4]15,750 [7]536		[2]291	3,878	14,850
Port Harcourt Refining Co. (NNPC)									
Alesa Eleme (old)	60,000			[6]6,000					
Rivers State (new)	150,000	54,000	[1]40,000	[6]33,000	[1]33,000	[2]7,020 [5]14,500	[4]3610 *2,274		
Warri Refinery & Petrochemical Co. (NNPC) - Warri	118,750	34,200	[1]24,700	[2]15,770	[2]15,770 [5]8,075	[2]2,850			
TOTAL	433,250	124,490	82,700	70,070	109,231	12,144	3,901	3,878	14,850

Source and Notes: Worldwide Refining, *O&GJ Databook*, 1991 edition; *World Refining Survey*, IPE, 1993.
Solvent extraction [1]9,492 b/cd. * Dimersol.
Catalytic Cracking: [1]Fluid.
Catalytic Reforming: Semiregenerative: [1]Conventional catalyst; [2]Bimetallic catalyst. Other: [6]Bimetallic catalyst.
Catalytic Hydro-treating: [1]Pre-treating cat reformer feeds. [2]Naptha desulfurizing. [4]Straight-run distillate. [5]Other distillates.
Alkylation: [2]Hydrofluoric acid.
Aromatics/Isomerisation: [2]Hydrodealkylation. [4]C_4 Feed.

Kaduna and Warri, for instance, have necessitated increasing imports of lighter products. The inefficiencies of the refining sector cause significant financial losses for the state. These include maintenance charges on the refineries themselves, the increased costs of product imports, and the loss of potential revenue from exports of premium grade crude, as these are being used domestically instead of heavy crudes.

The first refinery in Nigeria was commissioned in November 1965 and is situated at Alesa Eleme, Port Harcourt. Initial production capacity was 35,000 b/d, and was subsequently increased to 60,000 b/d in the mid-1970s. The refinery was originally a Shell–BP joint venture, but by December 1978, the government had bought all shares in the refinery.[19] With no fluid catalytic cracking facilities or vacuum distillation units, the old Port Harcourt refinery produces mostly fuel oil. The refinery has been closed due to fire damage since 1989 and after numerous delays, is finally expected to re-open in early 1994.[20]

Table 6.3 shows the refinery operations of the other three refineries in Nigeria in 1990. With one refinery completely down, and two operating much below capacity (see utilization rates), it is clear that a significant crisis situation existed in the Nigerian downstream sector in the late 1980s and early 1990s. In fact, in late 1992, refinery throughput, as a result of problems at the Alesa Eleme and Warri refineries, was restricted to 250,000–260,000 b/d.

The Warri refinery was commissioned in September 1978 with an initial crude oil capacity of 100,000 b/d. Capacity expansion to 125,000 b/d was planned for 1986 but has taken longer than expected and crude oil capacity is currently about 119,000 b/d. The Warri refinery was built to cater for some of the domestic product demand not covered by the fuel oil surpluses of the Port Harcourt refinery at Alesa Eleme. In particular, Warri was designed to increase the domestic production of motor gasoline.[21] Reforming capacity at 16,000 b/d, cracking capacity at 25,000 b/d as well as a vacuum distillation unit greatly increased the quantity and quality of motor gasoline production at the refinery at the expense of gas oil and fuel oil.

Throughput at Warri, however, has been low since 1983. This is because the 25,000 b/d FCC unit at Warri has been shut down since 1983, and came back onstream only in late 1991.[22]

Table 6.3: Refining Operations of Nigerian Refineries in 1990.

	Kaduna	*Port Harcourt II*	*Warri*
Nominal Capacity	110,000 b/d	150,000 b/d	125,000 b/d
Throughput	74,000 b/d	135,000 b/d	45,000 b/d
Utilization Rate	68%	90%	36%
Typical Crudes	Escravos,	Bonny Medium	Escravos,
	Arab.Light	and Light	Arab.Light
Typical Yields:			
LPG	0.4%	1.5%	0.6%
Gasoline	24.5%	34.5%	21.9%
Kerosene	13.8%	15.5%	16.6%
Gas oil	17.6%	24.2%	20.3%
Fuel Oil	26.4%	17.3%	29.9%
Losses/Autoconsumption	17.3%	7.0%	10.7%

Sources and Notes: World Bank, Africa Technical Department, Industry and Energy, Division Note No. 17, Summary 1990, *Petroleum Industry Data Sheets, Sub-Saharan Africa*, September, 1992.
Nominal capacity is the designed crude distillation capacity available at the refinery (for both Warri and Kaduna, these are yet to be achieved; (see Table 6.2 for actual crude capacity); the utilization rate is the nominal capacity divided by the throughput.

The alkylation unit at Ekpan which converts the effluent gases from the FCC unit into alkylate gasoline was also closed during this period. Gasoline production in Nigeria remained problematic in the 1980s despite the commissioning of the Kaduna refinery in 1980. Completed in October 1980, the Kaduna refinery had an initial capacity of about 100,000 b/d, since increased to 104,500 b/d. The refinery is yet to attain its full initial nominal capacity.[23] The 50,000 b/d Lubes Unit was installed in 1983. The three-year delay in commissioning the Lubes section of the Kaduna refinery has been attributed to the lack of port facilities to accommodate heavy imported crude oil from Venezuela. The refinery itself cost the Federal government Naira 650 million and the three-year delay has been estimated to have cost the company/government an additional Naira 540 million, a staggering sum which Nigeria could ill afford to lose.[24] Kaduna was the first refinery able to process both light and heavy crude, yielding both fuel and non-fuel products such as lubricating oils, waxes and asphalt. One of the interesting developments in the Nigerian downstream with both the Warri and Kaduna refineries coming onstream, was the renewed emphasis on using the surplus production of LPG and fuel oil as feedstock into petrochemical operations.

The configuration of the fuel section in the refinery is similar to that of the Warri refinery with a vacuum distillation unit and cracking capacity which increases the motor gasoline capacity of the refinery. Recent estimates of refinery yields show, however, that gasoline yields at Kaduna are slightly higher than at Warri. This is despite the fact that there is no alkylation unit at Kaduna which could be used to convert the FCC unit effluent gases either into gasoline feedstock or for petrochemicals.[25] It is quite probable, however, that in recent years, olefins, from these gases, have been sold to either chemical consumers or to the new Port Harcourt refinery, instead of being flared or used as a refinery fuel gas.

The Lubes Processing Unit at Kaduna, initially, used heavy/high sulphur paraffinic crude oil imported from Venezuela. The crude oil exchange arrangement between Maraven (a PDVSA subsidiary) and NNPC began on 1 December, 1982 and ended on 30 June, 1988. Initially 25,000 b/d of Forcados was exchanged for Venezuelan Lagomar crude oil (for the Kaduna refinery) at Curaçao. Nigeria paid freight to and from Curaçao as well as storage there. This was presumably due to the quality differential between the two crudes. The maximum amount of crude exchanged was 30,000 b/d. In 1988, of the 3.4 mt of crude oil processed at Kaduna, Lagomar accounted for 1.1 mt, or about 32 per cent. The official reason given for the end of the exchange arrangement in 1988 was that the Kaduna refinery had been upgraded. Unofficially, the agreement lapsed because of the problems that NNPC faced in disposing of the asphalt produced from the Lubes Unit with Lagomar.[26] Presumably, the market prices for asphalt at this time did not justify the costs of the exchange arrangement. In 1988, with the end of this arrangement with Venezuela, Saudi Arabian Light was used as a substitute (of which 35,000 b/d were supplied by the trader Attock).[27] Recently, Chevron Nigeria has found substantial quantities of heavy crude oil in the Ewan field in the Niger Delta area. Tests have suggested that the reservoirs could produce about 40,000 b/d. Further tests are still needed, however, to fully ascertain the potential of this find to substitute imports of heavy crude oil.[28]

The Kaduna refinery has not had the sort of problems plaguing the Port Harcourt and Warri refineries. However, there have been frequent 'maintenance' shut-downs, some problems with the FCC unit, and a fire in 1992–3 which damaged part of the refinery. Operating at a 68 per cent utilization rate in 1990, the Kaduna refinery is more efficient than Warri, but only slightly higher than the average operating rate of sub-Saharan Africa, considered by the World Bank to be uncompetitively low at 63 per cent.[29] The discrepancy between refinery output and local market requirements, however, continues to exist. The increased production of fuel 'white' products in 1981, with Kaduna coming onstream, was unable to match significant increases in consumption. And this was to be the case until 1989.

The second refinery at Port Harcourt came onstream in March of that year with an initial crude oil capacity of 150,000 b/d and at a cost of about $800 million.[30] It is apparent that this refinery is significantly more upgraded and more efficient than the other Nigerian refineries. In addition to significantly higher cracking, reforming and vacuum distillation capacity, Port Harcourt II also has greater capacity in its alkylation unit and in 1990 was operating at a utilization rate of 90 per cent. One of the advantages of such an upgraded refinery was that it would be able to process the residuum from its own cracking unit as well as any excess from Port Harcourt I, thus reducing 'the amount of low-value petroleum fractions' produced by the existing, older refinery.[31]

Port Harcourt II was initially envisaged as one dedicated to satisfying domestic demand. However, with higher domestic taxes on gasoline thought to be cutting domestic demand for gasoline, the focus shifted to a refinery dedicated to exports. Expected yields of greater than 40 per cent USA quality unleaded regular gasoline would enable exports of gasoline and LSFO to the USA and high pour gas oil to West Africa, the Caribbean and South America.[32] The refinery was designed to produce 64,000 b/d of gasoline, 43,000 b/d of fuel oil, 17,000 b/d of diesel and 123,000 tonnes/year of LPG.[33] At the time of its commissioning in 1989, with Port Harcourt I damaged by fire, the FCC unit at Warri down since 1983 and Kaduna closed temporarily for maintenance, the crisis situation necessitated that production from Port Harcourt II be reallocated to domestic use.[34] Despite this, 50,000 b/d of crude was set aside to be processed at Port Harcourt II for export through the refinery's joint venture marketing and technical service arrangement with Chevron (the joint venture is known as Calson).

In 1990, with a view to resolving some of the problems of product shortages, the Nigerian government made *ad hoc* product exchange arrangements with Addax, Chevron and Total. These arrangements allowed for Nigerian surplus fuel oil and gas oil to be exchanged for the supply of kerosene and gasoline. In October 1993, the Shonekan interim government, in an attempt to reduce the corruption and costs involved in the import of petroleum products, issued an international tender for a contract to supply refined products and purchase Nigerian fuel oil. Thirty companies have registered to either supply the products or to purchase fuel oil. Of these, Mobil and Total are trying to displace Marc Rich, the largest supplier of Nigerian product imports. Mobil has offered to assist Port Harcourt refinery in its technical and maintenance audit, presumably as part of an attempt to strengthen its case *vis à vis* the contract tendered for product imports.[35]

The product supply/demand imbalance has become more acute in recent years. As mentioned earlier, 1992 was one of the worst years for the country's four refineries. Early in the year, Nigeria was producing only 107,000 b/d of product and during this period, NNPC was paying almost $16 million/day for fuel imports.[36] The drastically deteriorated situation in the production and distribution of products culminated in the fuel riots of May 1992. Two reasons for the protests were continuing gasoline and heating oil shortages as well as price rises.[37] In June 1992, the government gave access to third-party processing at Port Harcourt II in order to increase the domestic availability of light petroleum products. One-third of the refinery's 150,000 b/d capacity was set aside for companies refining foreign crude at a fee of $2.00/b and supplying products locally.[38] This scheme had the advantage of increasing the supply of requisite products domestically without increasing the runs of what are essentially premium export crudes, which are collectively known as BBQ.[39] Cracking and reforming capacity at Port Harcourt II ensured that poorer quality, heavier Nigerian crude could be processed instead.

In addition to the product exchange arrangement of the early 1990s and the more recent third-party processing scheme, renewed emphasis has been placed on plans to build a new export-oriented refinery at Calabar.[40] These plans were initially unveiled in September 1991. The refinery is expected to run about 100,000 b/d of crude oil. Developing Asian and African countries are thought to represent 'ready' markets for Nigerian product exports. Preliminary estimates place the costs of construction at about $1–1.2 billion, and there has been some discussion of private sector participation – a first for the otherwise wholly-owned Nigerian refinery sector.[41] In order to encourage foreign investment, the government plans to create an export processing zone in the Calabar region, with tax advantages. Some sources mention a probable return of 18.6 per cent on a $1–1.2 billion project if the refinery is located in a free-trade area. Furthermore, the payback period on such an investment would be reduced from 8.5 to 6.5 years.[42] Possible partners include a consortium of Lonrho–Chevron–Bechtel and/or Elf. Distribution and access problems have already been foreseen for the planned refinery, and more importantly, it is quite likely that if domestic supply problems persist, output from this refinery too can be diverted to the domestic market.

The Distribution and Storage of Petroleum Products

The Nigerian product distribution network includes about 2,500 km. of product pipelines, twenty-one storage depots, and capacity of about 1,422,000 cm (or about 8,950,000 barrels) of product storage. Additionally, the products jetty at Lagos is capable of receiving a products vessel with a maximum capacity of 30,000 mt and at Warri, the maximum allowable capacity in a products vessel is 5,000 mt. Port Harcourt II has a bigger allowance and can accommodate the following: two vessels of 25,000 mt and two vessels of 5,000 mt for clean fuels; and one 50,000 mt vessel for dirty fuels.[43]

Table 6.4 shows the current pipeline network for petroleum products. A further 500 km. expansion is planned to enable the distribution of products from Port Harcourt II to all parts of the country and to specifically deal with product shortages in the Lagos region. The planned system is known as System 2F.[44]

NNPC does not sell refined products directly to final consumers. The corporation through its subsidiary Pipelines and Products Marketing Co. Ltd. (PPMC) sells to marketing companies from

Table 6.4: Product Pipelines in Nigeria. Year end – 1992.

	Owner/Operator	Length (km)	Diameter (cm)
System 2A			
Warri/Benin/Ore/Mosimi	NNPC	314	40/35/30
System 2B			
Atlas Cove/Mosimi	NNPC	64	40
Mosimi/Lagos	NNPC	3x40	30/25, 20/25, 15/20
Mosimi/Ikeja	NNPC	43	20
Mosimi/Ibadan	NNPC	69	30
Ibadan/Ilorin	NNPC	151	15
System 2D			
Kaduna/Kanol/Gusau	NNPC	359	25/15
Kaduna/Jos/			
Gombe-Maiduguri	NNPC	1056	25/30/15
System 2E			
Port Harcourt/Enugu/			
Makurdi	NNPC	335	30/15

Source and Notes: *OPEC Annual Statistical Bulletin*, 1992.
System 2B handles refined products from local and overseas refineries.
System 2C, not mentioned above, runs from Warri to Kaduna, and carries both
Escravos and imported crude oil. (Ikeh, 1991, p. 35)

its network of seventeen depots and three major pipelines, and
the companies in turn sell to final consumers through their own
network of filling stations. Three hundred and fifty independent
distributors account for 25 per cent of domestic sales while the
eight major marketing companies account for 75 per cent of
domestic sales (see Table 6.5).

Although operational problems at the refineries are partly
responsible for fuel shortages, product distribution and storage
problems as well as domestic subsidies and product smuggling lie
at the heart of an inefficient downstream and growing public
discontent. To give a few examples, the Warri refinery, apart
from being plagued by breakdowns in its FCC unit, also has to
contend with restricted and delayed product evacuation. This is
mainly because the port cannot handle tankers above 5,000 dwt.
Port Harcourt I, when operating, has pipeline links to the docks,
but its inland distribution is severely restricted by the standard of
roads in the surrounding area. Kaduna refinery has been, to a
large extent in the past, left as the singular supplier and distributor

Table 6.5: Share of Domestic Sales. By Company.

Independents	25%
Major Companies	75%
of which:	
Total Nigeria	17%
National Oil & Marketing Company	14%
Mobil Oil Nigeria	10%
Texaco Nigeria	9%
African Petroleum	9%
Agip (Nigeria)	7%
Unipetrol Nigeria	6%
Elf Nigeria	4%

Source: World Bank, Africa Technical Department, Industry and Energy, Division Note No. 17, Summary 1990, *Petroleum Industry Data Sheets, Sub-Saharan Africa*, September, 1992.

of products in the north. With inadequate depot and storage facilities, it has been unable to meet demand requirements. Port Harcourt II although initially envisaged as an export refinery does not have the infrastructural support of a good export terminal. Efforts are currently underway to construct an efficient ocean terminal at Bonny. Since its commissioning, however, the refinery's production has been allocated to satisfying domestic demand. Because it was not constructed for this purpose, the refinery lacks the infrastructure to deliver products internally. With no link to the other refineries there is a tendency for the artificial accumulation of products. The planned export refinery at Calabar has already raised concern on the issue of product evacuation. This, it is thought, may be difficult because of the shallow nature of the Cross river estuary, and the numerous oil installations in the area.[45] If the distribution and product distribution problems of the Port Harcourt II refinery are not to be duplicated, the government will have to ensure that not only are the necessary export facilities constructed but also the necessary infrastructure for inland distribution – should the need to reallocate production domestically ever arise. Hence, the major challenges for the Nigerian downstream industry include both an increase in the operating capacity of the different refineries, greater efforts to reduce the breakdowns of various units, and radical improvements in the internal distribution network of petroleum products, the export facilities for products as well as in domestic pricing schemes.

An attempt has been made by the state to address some of these problems in recent years. The most concrete investment plans concern the expansion of the pipeline network to link the four refineries. Initial plans for this new pipeline grid were made in 1990, and the expected investment cost of linking the two Port Harcourt refineries with Warri and Kaduna was estimated at $150 million.[46] The first phase will link Port Harcourt with Warri, and Enugu with Auchi/Benin in the north. The second phase will link the Warri refinery with Kaduna.[47] Pipeline contracts of about $500 million were awarded in late 1991 for the third phase of network expansion, and these included in some cases, the construction of storage depots as well.[48] Work is expected to be completed in 1993, with a total capital outlay of approximately $750 million. Additionally, the Calabar jetty project is to be completed (abandoned since 1986), and the $30 million products depot, constructed in 1979 but lying idle since then, is to be made functional again.[49] Investment plans for a new refinery, dedicated to exports, at Calabar presumably had a bearing on this decision.

Apart from pipeline expansion to link the four refineries, there have also been efforts recently to plan pipeline links between the heavy crude oil fields and the refineries. This has become necessary in order to increase crude runs for domestic needs. If Nigerian light crude is to continue to get the premiums it does as export crudes, the domestic refineries will need to replace light crude runs with Bonny Medium and Forcados. Currently, the pipeline links to Port Harcourt II encourage the use of Bonny Light. New pipelines will have to be laid to take full advantage of the country's premium export grades.

Due to the inadequate product pipeline network, internal product distribution has been frequently carried out with tanker fleets. These are easily diverted to Cameroon, and the much higher product prices in this neighbouring country offer enough financial incentive to do so.[50] With the expansion of the pipeline system and an increase in product storage and distribution depots, particularly in the north, it is expected that the fuel shortages in the country caused by insufficient storage facilities and smuggling, will be significantly reduced.

The Nigerian Petrochemicals Industry

In the early 1980s, the petrochemical industry was conceived of as one of the core economic projects that would both diversify foreign exchange earnings and reduce import expenditure in an economic environment of decreasing oil export earnings and increasing external debt. Due to the capital intensity of petrochemical projects, the government chose to 'embark on a phased implementation' of the petrochemical programme.[51]

Phase I of the programme, initially costed at $500 million, was finally commissioned in 1988 after a delay of three years. The petrochemical plants of Phase I are located at Ekpan (near Warri) and Kaduna and use FCC decant oil, benzene, ethylene, kerosene, and refinery off gas/LPG as feedstock. Production capacity at these plants is as follows: 30,000 mt/year of linear alkyl benzene (LAB), 18,000 mt/year of carbon black, 15,000 mt/year of benzene, and 35,000 mt/year of polypropylene.[52] In more familiar terms, the end-use applications of these products include detergents, lubricants, insecticides, woven sacks, bottle crates, tyres and tubes and so on. Two main shortcomings have been discussed in relation to this first phase of the programme. Firstly, the production capacity of polypropylene and LAB falls significantly short of domestic demand, and in this sense there is less foreign exchange saved and/or earned through import substitution and/or export to west African markets than initially envisaged. Also, it is unclear whether the downstream conversion industry of petrochemical products is developed and large enough to actually deliver the end-products, mentioned above, to the domestic market and/or as exports to neighbouring countries. Secondly, since the plant operations of Phase I are based on refinery feedstock, capacity production of the relevant products is closely linked to the functioning of the Warri and Kaduna refineries, and particularly of the FCC units. For instance in 1991, when the FCC unit at Warri came back onstream after major rehabilitation work, it was also expected that the polypropylene unit at the refinery, commissioned only recently in 1988 and run on solvent from the FCC unit would also be fully operational by the end of the year.[53]

Phase II of the petrochemical programme is sited near Port Harcourt, Rivers State and known as the Eleme Petrochemical Complex. The complex was initially expected to produce primary petrochemicals, plastics, fibres and agrochemicals, and seen as a way to absorb associated gas surplus and reduce $650 million/year worth of chemical imports.[54] However, these initial plans have been significantly modified by the World Bank, in keeping with Nigerian domestic demand and financial capacity.[55] Phase II plant operations are based on feedstock extracted from Natural Gas Liquids from nearby gas fields and from the new Port Harcourt refinery. At the end of 1990, feedstock agreements were signed with Agip and Phillips with the NGL sourced from Obrikom, about 70 km. away from Eleme.[56] Export agreements for the finished products were also signed at this time with Du Pont (Canada) for polyethylene and Technimont for polypropylene. Completion of Phase II is expected in 1993, and capital costs for the project have been estimated at $1.2 billion, significantly less than the $1.5–2 billion estimated for the initially envisaged larger scale venture.[57]

Phase III of the petrochemical programme which remains very much on the drawing board is expected to involve the production of advanced aromatic intermediates such as benzene, tuolene, phenol, polystyrene, and so on. Possible end-use applications include the satisfaction of specific domestic demand in the building, automotive, agricultural, textiles, packaging, and electrical industries. This aromatic-producing complex will be based on feedstock from refineries and the petrochemical plants of Phases I and II.[58] It is important to note that at this stage, there is no certainty that Phase III will in fact be executed. Nigeria, as other exporters, officially announces a long list of planned projects which may never be implemented if foreign investment partners find more lucrative projects elsewhere.

The delay in the start-up of the petrochemicals programme in Nigeria has been held partly responsible for the continuing poor linkage between the petroleum industry and the Nigerian economy. The petrochemical industry, in this argument, is seen as the catalyst, the link between an economy based primarily on its oil and gas industry and an economy diversifying into small-scale manufacturing. The multiplier effect of petrochemicals on the Nigerian economy would manifest itself through the growth of satellite industries (insecticides, paints, polish, packaging, carpets, textiles and footwear), foreign exchange savings through import substitution of both petrochemicals and end-products, and the diversification of oil and gas revenues through the value added to these resources.[59] The benefits of the petrochemical programme to the Nigerian economy will only really emerge towards the end of this decade. It is noteworthy, however, that there has been some recognition of the important role that petrochemicals can play in the development of the economy in that in April 1993, the government approved certain incentives aimed at attracting investment in the sector.[60] These include the possibility of full foreign and/or private equity participation; five-year tax holiday; guaranteed export earnings and the permission to hold escrow accounts in the country of the investor's choice; competitively priced feedstock and capital allowances; unrestricted allowances for the import of intermediate feedstock; and preferential consideration for crude oil lifting contracts for investors in 'priority areas'. It is yet to be seen whether the possibility of full private and/or foreign ownership of new projects will remove the high risks associated with downstream investments in which NNPC was the majority shareholder.

Outlook for the Nigerian Downstream Sector

The main problem with the Nigerian oil industry has been the lack of an efficient framework and efficient implementation of a plan to diversify revenues away from crude oil exports. The downstream sector is a case in point: a value-added programme through domestic refining operations was embarked upon in the Third Development Plan 1975–80; almost twenty years later, exports of refined products have yet to be realized. Leaving aside what now seems to be quite an idealistic aim, domestic refining in Nigeria is plagued with far more immediate problems. These have arisen as a result of a number of factors. For some refineries, the problems are structural, and the delays in turn-around maintenance just worsen the domestic supply situation. Also aggravating structural problems is the severe lack of capital replacement. Combined with what are essentially institution-breaking subsidies, there is the strong possibility of a complete breakdown of the system. And finally, there is the problem, common to the entire oil industry, of inadequate and ineffective executive supervision.

One of the main problems targeted in the shake-up of the

NNPC by the interim government in September 1993 was that of domestic petroleum product distribution. In an attempt to generate public support and show political accountability at the highest levels of the organization, the government dissolved the boards of NNPC and four of its subsidiaries. The members of the boards were held responsible for the widespread product smuggling and shortages within the country.[61] Greater transparency in government and/or NNPC expenditure may in fact be the only change needed to make the removal of subsidies economically palatable and acceptable to the Nigerian people.

While the petrochemicals programme has been a relatively more successful attempt to diversify revenues within the oil industry, NNPC has also made numerous unsuccessful efforts to acquire equity assets in downstream overseas ventures.[62] These were seen essentially as 'crude oil for equity' swap sort of arrangements. NNPC participation in foreign refineries would not only increase foreign revenue, it would also ensure confirmed long-term crude oil contracts. While the attempts to secure downstream equity stakes abroad have failed, product marketing arrangements with overseas refineries have met with some success. These are based on the supply of crude oil from NNPC in exchange for the use of the product-marketing outlets of the refinery. Arrangements currently operating include those with Nigermed and ERTOIL, and the marketing venture with Argentina's Interpetrol, known as Napoil.[63]

After the failure to acquire refinery assets abroad, there was a renewed emphasis on the *domestic* expansion of the downstream sector. It is more likely, in fact, that the change in perspective stemmed from the urgent need for domestic investment in both the upstream and the downstream sectors. This renewed emphasis can in part be seen in NNPC's changing relationship with its crude contract holders – whether third party or term. In 1992, under Okongwu as Oil Minister, term contracts were retained and renewed for those willing to invest in the downstream (and/or upstream).[64] In other words, crude oil sales to end-users were being encouraged, while sales to re-sellers (for instance traders) were being discouraged. The only term or third-party contracts not to be cancelled were those where NNPC has either processing agreements or marketing agreements – for instance Petromed, ERTOIL, and Interpetrol – or where the partner, for instance

US Sun, bought significant amounts of Nigerian crude on the spot market to refine itself.[65] As of October 1993, the Shonekan interim government issued a new set of guidelines for crude contract holders. Large oil traders were recognized officially as acceptable term buyers of Nigerian crude oil for the first time, and while investment in the Nigerian upstream and downstream remained as conditions, those linking crude term contracts in exchange for foreign downstream refinery or retail outlets for NNPC were dropped.[66]

The main problems in the Nigerian downstream have been touched upon above. These include rampant refinery breakdowns, domestic subsidies, internal distribution problems and smuggling of up to 100,000 b/d, and most importantly the state's own investment constraints. Possible savings in the Nigerian downstream sector have been estimated by the World Bank to be greatest in refining.[67] Poor maintenance and the under-utilization of capacity are the biggest problems in Nigerian refineries. Some potential savings can also be made in inland distribution. The inefficiencies in this sector are largely due to the greater use of road transport instead of railways and inadequate storage depots. If Nigeria is to become a net-product exporter in the coming century, substantial investments in the sector, and a concerted effort to reduce the losses from inefficiencies in refining and distribution will be required. It is timely, therefore, that the government has offered the incentive of full private ownership of *new* refineries (an offer largely geared toward current equity producers), and that it has asked a few foreign firms for technical and maintenance audits of its refineries.[68] What is discouraging is that although these audits were carried out in 1990, their recommendations were never implemented.

Notes

1. However, the World Bank and the Energy Sector Management Assistance Programme (ESMAP) have estimated that about 20–25,000 b/d of product is smuggled. In 1992 at a time when both Port Harcourt I and Warri were down, this amounted to 10 per cent of operating capacity. It is important to note though, that the Bank has indicated that it is more than likely that this was in fact an underestimate given the new forms of smuggling, such as to offshore tankers (ESMAP, 1993, p. 36). It has been stated that in 1992, Cameroon closed down its main refinery because domestic demand was being satisfied by smuggled Nigerian product (*Argus*,

15 June, 1992, p. 3). Furthermore, the extent of the problem is made particularly evident whenever the Nigerian government decides to clampdown on smuggling. Recently, Chad appealed to Nigeria for emergency oil aid during a period of time when the Nigerians had banned official exports of product and tightened border controls. Chad gets 90 per cent of its oil from Nigeria, of which 80 per cent arrives through unofficial channels (*Platts*, 13 May, 1993, p. 6).

2. It has been estimated that the annual product subsidy in Nigeria is about $1.9 billion. This is based on a five-product average which includes gasoline, gas oil, fuel oil, kerosene and LPG (ESMAP, 1993, p. xix). It should be noted that the extraordinary difference between domestic product prices and bulk spot prices may be due in part to exchange rate devaluations, particularly in 1992 and 1993.

3. ESMAP and the World Bank have estimated that on the basis of 1992 domestic product prices, Nigeria would have to increase gasoline prices by 411 per cent, gas oil prices by 502 per cent, fuel oil prices by 287 per cent and kerosene prices by 534 per cent in order to recover costs. In order to attain world parity prices, on the other hand, gasoline prices would have to be increased by 584 per cent, gas oil prices by 711 per cent, fuel oil prices by 373 per cent and kerosene prices by 744 per cent (ESMAP, 1993, pp. 37, 40).

4. Barrows, *IPI Data Service, Africa*, No. 47, *Nigeria*, 1986, p. 53.

5. *PE*, December 1987. In fact, the large reduction in petroleum product subsidies in the 1986 budget was possible because Babingida had in 1985 postponed negotiations with the IMF on a $2.5 billion loan. There had been strong popular resistance to accepting the conditions of the IMF loan, and once talks with the Fund had been abandoned, Babingida's popularity increased to the point that the reductions of subsidies met with very little protest (EIU, *West Africa: Economic Structure and Analysis*, November 1990, p.139).

6. *Statoil Magazine*, May 1992.

7. Barrows, *IPI Data Service, Africa*, No. 47, 1986, p. 54.

8. *OPEC Bulletin*, 1990, p. 10.

9. *Platts*, 23 May, 1990.

10. The 43 per cent devaluation of the Naira in March 1992 was prompted by IMF demands that gasoline subsidies be phased out, and the withholding of EC and IMF grants (*Argus*, 15 June, 1992, p. 3).

11. *PE*, September 1993, p. 42.

12. *FT*, 9 November, 1993, p. 6.

13. *PE*, December 1993, p. 38.

14. See Appendix 3 for production, consumption, and average annual growth rate statistics of refined products in Nigeria, 1971–91. It is important to note here that import figures are in fact net estimates. Even when production of a specific product is less than consumption and there are necessarily net imports, there may still be some exports, e.g. in the case of gasoline.

15. As Appendix 3 shows, domestic demand for all refined products, except kerosene, decreased in 1984 (See also Barrows, *IPI Data Service, Africa*, No.

47, *Nigeria* pp. 45–46, 51).

16. It is interesting to note that a substantial portion of the increase in product consumption since 1986, particularly in gasoline and diesel, has been attributed by the World Bank and ESMAP to increased levels of smuggling (ESMAP, 1993, pp. 21–2).

17. Ibid., p. 21.

18. *Energy Compass*, 6 April, 1990.

19. *OPEC Bulletin*, July–August 1985, p. 30.

20. Initial costs to rehabilitate the gutted refinery and to expand capacity to 120,000 b/d has been estimated at $25 million. At the time of its re-opening, capacity at the old Port Harcourt refinery will be 75,000 b/d and the unit will also have been upgraded to yield high octane gasoline. It is unclear whether the latter will be exported or domestically consumed. In September 1993, the government decided *not* to implement the two-tiered pricing system and phase in high octane grade gasoline at close to international market prices. In December 1993, however, product prices were raised at least five-fold. It remains to be seen whether this increase will enable the government to introduce the high octane, more expensive gasoline (*Argus*, 8 November, 1993, p. 7; *PE*, December 1993, p. 38).

21. *O&GJ*, 17 June, 1985, p. 112.

22. *Platts*, 31 December, 1991.

23. According to some sources an initial crude oil capacity of 100,000 b/d at Kaduna was increased to 110,000 b/d in December 1986. During this period, Warri's capacity of 100,000 b/d was being expanded to 125,000 b/d. Currently, however, crude capacity at Warri and Kaduna is 118,750 b/d and 104,500 b/d, respectively. It is clear, therefore, that the former nominal capacities have not been reached (Ikeh, 1991; Ola, 1987).

24. Another reason put forward for the delay in the start-up of the Lubes section is that the demand for asphalt, a by-product of the Lubes section, was in decline during this period. This was thought to be because with decreasing crude oil sales and revenues, economic activity in the road construction sector in particular, was also in decline. The very high asphalt stock level was partly responsible for the delay in the start-up of the Lubes section of Kaduna. Kaduna, at this time was using only 43 per cent of installed capacity and the implications for the rapidly increasing domestic demand for lubricants was significant (Abba, 1985; *O&GJ*, 17 June, 1985, p. 117).

25. *O&GJ*, 17 June, 1985, p. 112.

26. *Platts*, 21 July, 1989; PDVSA.

27. *Argus*, 5 February, 1990.

28. *OPEC Bulletin*, February 1993.

29. World Bank, Africa Technical Department, Industry and Energy Division Note no. 17, Summary 1990, *Petroleum Industry Data Sheets, Sub-Saharan Africa*, September, 1992, p. 5.

30. EIU, Country Profile, *Nigeria, 1991–2*, p. 26.

31. *O&GJ*, 17 June, 1985, p. 117.

32. *PIW*, 20 March, 1989.

33. EIU, 1989, p. 57.

34. In 1989, Kaduna, Warri and Port Harcourt took delivery of an average 199,000 b/d of crude oil. Given that Port Harcourt alone was functioning more or less at capacity during this period, deliveries to the refinery probably accounted for 70 per cent of the total. About 75,000 b/d of crude oil was allocated to offshore refineries in 1989 (EIU, Country Profile, *Nigeria, 1991–2*, p. 26).

35. *Energy Compass*, 6 April, 1990; *PIW*, 25 October, 1993, p. 2.

36. *O&GJ*, 27 April, 1992.

37. Maintenance at Port Harcourt II has consistently been delayed to compensate for the breakdowns in the other two refineries. When the former was finally shut down in May 1992, Warri broke down at the same time, resulting in a severe product supply crisis (ESMAP, July 1993, p. 23).

38. *PE*, June 1992.

39. Bonny Light, Brass River and Qua Iboe are collectively known as BBQ. These crudes are not blended. BBQ grades face very strong demand in the summer, the peak gasoline season. Third-party processing in the summer would allow the country to take advantage of BBQ premiums in the market.

40. In one of the earlier attempts to address the growing domestic demand for petroleum products, NNPC was involved in an offshore refining scheme, where Nigerian crude has been processed in foreign refineries, and light products returned to Nigeria (See Chapter 4). This scheme, initiated in the mid-1970s, has lasted at least ten years up till 1985. Acute products supply/demand imbalances are not a new phenomenon in Nigeria. In 1975, the OPUTA Judicial Commission of Inquiry was set up to investigate the sporadic shortages of petroleum products. The supply crisis in the mid-1970s had occurred due to the rapid increase in economic activity in the post civil war period, the consequent increase in product demand, and the increasing inability of Port Harcourt I (given its crude capacity of 60,000 b/d), to satisfy domestic demand. By 1978, in fact, Port Harcourt's refining capacity and production satisfied only 49 per cent of domestic demand. It was in this context that the offshore refining scheme was initiated and plans were made for the construction of the Warri and Kaduna refineries (Ola, 1987, p. 6).

41. *PE*, June 1992.

42. *OPEC Bulletin*, April 1992, p. 49.

43. World Bank, Africa Technical Department, Industry and Energy, Division Note No. 17, Summary 1990, *Petroleum Industry Data Sheets, Sub-Saharan Africa*, September, 1992.

44. Ikeh, 1991, p. 35. The following product pipelines under construction may not belong to the planned system 2F but are important additions to the current pipeline network. NNPC is currently completing two 55 km., 16 inch product pipelines – one for mogas/gas oil and one for fuel oil – from the proposed Bonny crude oil terminal to the Port Harcourt refinery. Completion is expected in June 1993 (*O&GJ Databook*, 1992 edition, p. 175).

45. *PE*, March 1992.

46. *Energy Compass*, 6 April, 1990.
47. *Platts*, 5 April, 1990.
48. Technit of Argentina is to construct a 685 km. (20 cm diameter) pipeline from Enugu through Makurdi to Yola. This will cover the eastern flank of the country. France's Spie Capag is to construct a 486 km. (30 cm diameter) pipeline from Port Harcourt through Aba and Enugu in the east, cutting across the Niger river to Benin City, north of Warri. This contract also includes the construction of product storage tanks at Aba and Benin City with a total capacity of 128,000 mt. The third contract awarded to a British-Lebanese company involves a 400 km. (30 cm diameter) pipeline from Auchi east of Benin City, north east through Suleja, and across the Benue river to Kaduna. The contract also involves a 265 km. (20 cm diameter) pipeline link between Jos and Gombe, repair work on the Niger river crossings and a 105,000 mt storage tank at Sulega (*Platts*, 5 November, 1991; 21 January, 1992).
49. *Platts*, 5 April, 1990.
50. In 1984, during the crackdown on smuggling, specific companies were licensed to 'bunker shipping under strict conditions' in order to prevent the illegal export of petroleum products. These companies included African Petroleum, Unipetrol, National Oil and Chemical Marketing, Texaco and Total (*PE*, July, August 1984). This restriction did have some impact in that domestic demand estimates were significantly reduced, as was the amount of crude refined overseas for domestic use.
51. Nzelo, 1987, p. 32.
52. *O&GJ Databook*, 1992 edition, p. 40.
53. *Platts*, 31 December, 1991.
54. *O&GJ*, 2 July, 1984.
55. The production capacity of the main plants under construction now are 270,000 mt/year of ethylene and 260,000 mt/year of low and high density polyethylene; 82,000 mt/year of propylene and 80,000 mt/year of polypropylene; and 20,000 mt/year of butadiene (EIU, 1989, p. 63.)
56. *O&GJ*, 3 December, 1990.
57. *O&GJ Databook*, 1992 edition, p. 166.
58. *OPEC Bulletin*, July/August 1985, p. 35; Nzelo, 1987, p. 33.
59. EIU, 1989, p. 63; Nzelo, 1987, p. 34.
60. These downstream incentives also apply to gas development. See Chapter 7 and Barrows, *Petroleum Taxation and Legislation Report*, May/June 1993, pp. 34–5.
61. The dissolution of the boards was initially justified mainly on the basis of the acute problems of internal product distribution. Also important, however, was the interim government's claim that it was targeting the 'endemic corruption' in the industry. To this end, certain crude oil term contracts were suspended, and a thorough audit was ordered into NNPC books and accounts organization (*Argus*, 20 September, 1993, p. 6 and *OPECNA News Service*, 16 September, 1993).
62. The following is a list of NNPC's forays into the downstream sector abroad:
    1. In 1989, a letter of intent was signed between Farmland Industries

Inc., Kansas City, Mo. and NNPC regarding the latter's attempted acquisition of a 49 per cent interest in the 60,723 b/d refinery at Coffeyville, Kansas in exchange for the supply of 60,000 b/d of crude oil. The joint-venture terms were to last twenty years (*O&GJ*, 9 October, 1989). This arrangement has yet to be finalized.

2. NNPC negotiations with Elf, stalled since 1988, were re-opened in mid-1990. These concern the acquisition of a 30 per cent stake in the Elf Refining and Distribution system outside Africa (*Platts*, 31 July, 1990). As in the above case, these negotiations have not progressed much further.

3. In 1989, NNPC began negotiations with a Polish refinery in Gdansk regarding participation rights in exchange for the supply of 3 mt/year of crude oil (*Platts*, 23 August, 1989). These talks have since fallen through.

4. Also in 1989, NNPC claimed to have signed a letter of intent with Petromed regarding a stake in the Spanish refinery. This was later clarified as 'Nigermed', a joint venture arrangement involving a crude processing/product marketing deal (*Platts*, 23 March, 1990). Similarly, the 1990 negotiations to acquire a 25 per cent stake in Spain's ERTOIL in exchange for crude supply were not successful, and the relationship of NNPC and ERTOIL remained a 'crude processing and marketing' one (*PE*, April 1990).

5. In 1990, negotiations for a downstream stake in the Irish National Petroleum Corporation failed as did the 1991 negotiations for a 47 per cent equity stake in Windhoek, the Namibian refinery (*Platts*, 23 March, 1990 and 11 September, 1991). The long ongoing talks with Phibro US for a 20 per cent stake in their downstream operations also ended by February 1992 (*Platts*, 17 January, 1992).

63 *PIW*, 7 September, 1992.

64 In 1991, under Aminu as Oil Minister, traders were appreciated as Nigerian crude oil lifters due to their willingness to take certain crudes out of season.

65 *PIW*, 7 September, 1992.

66 *Argus*, 25 October, 1993, p. 6.

67 Potential savings in the downstream sector are defined as the difference between the actual cost of supplying petroleum products to consumers (either through imports or by refining crude) and a benchmark cost corresponding to the procurement of these products from world markets under competitive conditions; and are subdivided into three categories: procurement, refining and distribution (World Bank, Africa Technical Department, Industry and Energy, Division Note No. 14, 1992, pp. 3–5).

68 Elf is to look at Kaduna, Mobil at Port Harcourt and Neste at Warri (*PIW*, 9 August, 1993).

7 THE NIGERIAN NATURAL GAS INDUSTRY

Introduction

The importance of the gas sector in the Nigerian economy arises mainly from the size of the country's reserves. There are two interesting issues: one relates to the infrastructural and pricing problems that constrain the development of the much needed domestic gas market, and the second to investments for an LNG export chain.[1] At current rates of gross production, Nigeria's gas reserves will last 104 years but at current rates of marketed production (plus reinjection), Nigerian gas reserves will last over 400 years. The extent to which Nigerian gas is flared is spectacular: in 1992, the equivalent of about 400,000 b/d of oil was flared daily. The two possible alternatives to flaring are the development of a domestic gas market and exports. As we shall see, both options have their own specific problems. While gas exports, primarily through the LNG scheme have the advantage of generating foreign exchange revenues, they are unlikely, by themselves, to resolve the gas flaring problem. The bulk of associated gas production which is now flared can only be absorbed by large-scale domestic demand, given of course, that the higher costs of processing associated gas are somehow compensated.

Natural Gas Reserves, Exploration and Production

With natural gas reserves currently estimated at between 3–3.4 trillion cubic metres (tcm), Nigeria ranks eighth in the world and fifth within OPEC. The country, and more specifically the Delta area, is frequently referred to as a natural gas province with some oil in it. West of the Niger river, reserves are estimated at over 1 tcm, and east of the river, at more than 1.6 tcm.[2] Approximately half of these reserves are thought to be in the form of associated gas. The reserves/production ratio has increased from seventy years in 1971 to 104 years in 1992, largely because of the very slow rate of production increases relative to that of reserve additions. Reserves, therefore, are ample, and may undoubtedly under-estimate the gas wealth of the country given that the volumes found were yielded by oil exploration. Nigeria has yet to explore for gas as such.[3]

Table 7.1 shows the historical evolution of natural gas reserves in Nigeria. The average per annum rate of increase in proven reserves in the 1971–92 period was 6.5 per cent, with a higher rate in the 1980s compared to the 1970s (9.4 per cent and 2.5 per cent respectively). In the 1980s gas started being perceived as an important national resource, and consequently greater attention was paid to the delimitation of fields and definition of reserves. The pace of increase in gas reserves of the 1980s has been maintained in the early 1990s and this has of course coincided with a high rate of crude oil discoveries.[4] New government incentives to exploration, and larger oil company expenditure commitments to oil exploration (if these are not drastically scaled back given the financial problems of NNPC in the early 1990s and its inability to come up with its share of investments) are likely to yield significant additions to gas reserves.

The majority of natural gas accumulations have been discovered in the Niger Delta area. Most onshore gas discoveries are in the Mobil (in the far eastern region around Eket), the Shell (Port Harcourt and the Ughelli region), and the Agip ventures (north of the Obiafu-Obrikom region around the banks of the Niger river). Most offshore gas discoveries, both the predominantly gas and the oil and gas, are in the Texaco–Chevron–NNPC venture in the west, and in the Shell venture in the east. Table 7.2 lists the main gas, and oil and gas, fields in the country.

Table 7.1: Historical Natural Gas Reserves. Billion Cubic Metres. 1971–92.

Year	Reserves	Year	Reserves
1971	909.1	1982	1385.0
1972	909.1	1983	1345.0
1973	909.1	1984	1330.0
1974	1022.7	1985	1340.0
1975	1006.8	1986	2400.0
1976	1000.0	1987	2407.0
1977	1217.8	1988	2476.0
1978	1189.5	1989	2832.0
1979	1172.5	1990	2840.0
1980	1161.1	1991	3400.0
1981	1147.0	1992	3400.0

Sources: *OPEC Annual Statistical Bulletin*, various issues; 1992 data from *BP Review of World Gas*, August 1993.

Table 7.2: Main Gas Fields in Nigeria.

	Gas Fields	*Oil & Gas Fields*
Onshore	Nsukwa, Ameshi, Matsogo, Aboh, Okopolo, Ukpichi, Kumbowei, Uzi, Aba-Town, Koroana, Manuso, Ika, Ebeziba, Tema, Akata, Teeba, Soku, Bomu, Oshi, Ubeta, Ibewa, Obagi, Idu	Ubetai, Ndelle, Egbomie, Buguma, Ebubu, Eket, Alakiri
Offshore	Agge, Akarino, Forupa, Ala, Ato, Ka	Bilabri, Pennington, Apoi

Sources: *OPEC Annual Statistical Bulletin*, 1992, see map; *O&GJ*, 14 December, 1987, p. 28.

Natural gas production began in 1958 with the start of crude oil production from Oloibiri and Afam and increased from 45 million cubic metres (mcm) in 1958 to 481 mcm in 1962 (Schatzl, 1969, p. 223). Gas production was used commercially for the first time in 1963, when 5 per cent of gross production was marketed. By 1992, production had increased to 32.7 bcm/year, of which 15 per cent was marketed. The greatest increases in the gross production of natural gas, as those in crude oil, occurred in the 1970s. Since 1988, we seem to be in another period of gas production growth, largely due to increasing exploration expenditure and crude oil discoveries by oil companies (see Table 7.3).

Gas Flaring

In 1963, when gas was first used commercially, 95 per cent of gross production was flared. By the early 1970s, flared gas accounted for 99 per cent of total production. By 1992, marketed gas accounted for 4.9 bcm/year, and combined with gas re-injected into fields to maintain pressure, total utilized gas accounted for about 24 per cent of gross production.[5] 76 per cent of total production, however, was still being flared. This is currently the highest flaring rate in OPEC.

Most of the gas flared in Nigeria is associated gas (see Figure 7.1). This waste is due in part to an inadequate infrastructural

Table 7.3: Production and Utilization of Natural Gas in Nigeria. Million Cubic Metres per Year. 1963–92, Selected Years.

Year	Gross	Marketed	Flared (per cent of Gross)	Re-Injected
1963	619	29	590 (95)	
1969	4,126	64	4,102 (99)	
1970	8,093	111	7,982 (99)	
1973	20,561	303	20,258 (99)	
1974	26,623	404	26,219 (98)	
1975	18,955	402	18,553 (98)	
1979	30,049	1,378	28,671 (95)	
1980	24,552	1,070	23,482 (96)	
1981	16,572	2,155	14,346 (87)	71
1985	17,500	3,100	13,000 (74)	1,400
1986	18,739	3,299	13,917 (74)	1,523
1987	17,169	3,493	12,257 (71)	1,419
1988	20,250	3,770	14,740 (73)	1,740
1989	25,129	4,322	18,784 (75)	1,980
1990	28,430	4,010	22,410 (79)	2,010
1991	31,460	4,400	24,660 (78)	2,400
1992	32,700	4,900	24,900 (76)	2,900

Sources: *OPEC Annual Statistical Bulletin*, various issues; 1963 data from Schatzl, 1969, pp. 137, 223.

support system, an inadequate number of feasible gas utilization schemes, and most importantly to the high costs of the extraction, processing and separating of associated gas production. The costs involved in associated gas use have been estimated to be ten times higher than those for the non-associated variety. The latter is cheaper to use because the capital costs involved include drilling and treatment without any extra outlay on compression and/or re-pressurization for transport. Furthermore, these costs are spread over a larger reserve base compared to those in associated gas production.[6]

The government had come to realize the enormity of the waste by the early 1970s. In 1979, anti-flaring legislation appeared for the first time with the promulgation of the Associated Gas Reinjection Decree No. 99. This required oil companies to check gas flaring by developing ways of utilizing the associated gas production from their fields. It was also stated that if gas flaring continued after January 1984, without the specific permission of

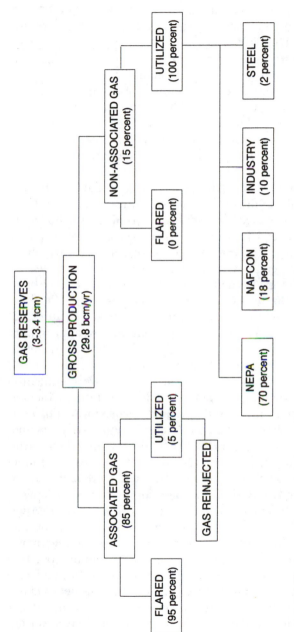

Sources and Notes:
Flared and Utilized shares of total gas production based on 1989 estimates in ESMAP, 1993, p. 45. Shares of non-associated gas production utilized in the power, fertilizer and industrial sectors based on estimates made for the late 1980s in *World Gas Intelligence*, February 1990, p.5.
NEPA: Nigerian Electric Power Authority; NAFCON: National Fertilizer Corporation of Nigeria

Figure 7.1: Associated and Non-Associated Gas Production and Utilization in Nigeria

the Petroleum Ministry, the oil companies would be fined $0.13 per cm of gas flared. This was later reduced to $0.026 per cm. In many ways, the 1979 legislation was the least appropriate way of checking increasing levels of gas flaring since it penalized oil company actions without offering alternatives.

By 1984, the government had realized the problems in enforcing such legislation, and in December 1984, amendments were made to Decree 99 of 1979. The implementation of the original gas reinjection decree was postponed to 1 January, 1985 and exemptions were made for certain fields in the paying of flaring fines.[7] As a result of these exemptions for instance, only twenty-nine of the eighty-four Shell fields, eighteen of the twenty-two Agip fields, five of the fifteen Mobil fields, two of the nine Gulf fields, two of the five Texaco fields, and two of the six Elf fields would be fined. If after 1 January, 1985, the oil companies initiated projects to reduce flaring, then according to the 1984 modifications, the penalties would be lifted.

These modifications in the mid-1980s were deemed necessary because both the Bonny LNG and the Escravos–Lagos Pipeline (ELP) projects seemed to be running into trouble at this time and risked being delayed.[8] Without any viable gas utilization proposals of its own, the government could not credibly enforce stringent anti-flaring legislation. Exemptions were made for eighty-six of the 155 active fields in Nigeria at that time and were evidently generous. The remaining sixty-nine fields were responsible for about 62 per cent of the flared gas, and according to the new legislation, 40 per cent of the gas flared was essentially beyond the government's control.[9] Furthermore, the fine of 2 Kobo/cm was fairly insignificant. In 1986, the Nigerian government made only $2.21 million from gas flaring fines (Ikeh, 1991, p. 42). A 1985 statement by Gulf Oil of Nigeria is an interesting reflection of how significant the amendments were to oil company operations. Gulf Oil stated that while gas flaring would cost the company about $1 million in fines, the capital costs of switching from water injection to gas reinjection techniques would cost the company an 'unacceptable' $56 million (Brown, 1990, p. 323). Any project requiring the re-pressurization and pipelining of associated gas would have cost even more. The economics, therefore, for gas utilization, were just not acceptable to most oil companies.

There was some evidence in early 1992 that the Nigerian government was attempting a new approach to the problem of gas flaring, essentially one that was pro-gas utilization rather than anti-gas flaring. Reports at that time claimed that the package of incentives contained therein had been approved by Babingida. Whether these incentives have been formally ratified is, however, not clear. In keeping with the fact that much of the flared gas is in fact associated, these incentives were mainly directed toward associated gas production. The main idea behind the new approach is to reduce the flaring fines, and announce a package of fiscal incentives to encourage commercial use of natural gas. From a level of $0.026/cm in 1984, the flaring fine has been reduced to $0.0011/cm. Some of the more important aspects of the incentive package include firstly, the provision that 85 per cent of capital invested in the development of associated gas can be offset against income. This has been increased from the previous 40 per cent offset. Secondly, the separation costs of oil and gas can be included in development costs, and transport costs of delivering associated gas to utilization points will be considered as capital investment for oil development. Finally, revenues from sales of gas or products derived from gas will be taxed at 40 per cent.[10] This is the first time that incentives have been included in the context of anti-flaring legislation, and if these rules are actually implemented, they may be relatively more successful than previous legislation.

Much more recently in April 1993, the government issued a formal decree outlining incentives for the downstream sector, specifically for the development of the petrochemicals programme and of natural gas. The incentives relevant to the latter included an amendment to the Associated Gas Reinjection Act of 1979 to the effect that all gas not utilized by the operator must be made available to the government free of charge at the operator's fence for delivery on agreed terms to third-party investors.[11] All other things being equal, this decree essentially means that the Nigerian government continues to feel that the gas infrastructure is not adequate to stringently enforce gas flaring legislation and fines.

An important aspect of the Nigerian gas flaring problem which has not been mentioned earlier concerns its implications for global warming. It has been estimated, for instance, that in 1989 the flaring of approximately 17–18 bcm of associated gas resulted in the release of 30 million tons of CO_2. The marginal damage caused by these carbon emissions has been estimated by one source at \$7.5/ton. However, the replacement of the cheaper non-associated gas by associated gas, which would otherwise be flared, has been estimated to cost \$15/ton.[12] The Nigerian government will find that its minimal cost strategy involves continued flaring, which in itself is a better option environmentally, than releasing the gas in its raw form. While this issue has not attracted or benefited from any great degree of attention until now, it is bound to gain in significance once environmentalist lobbies in oil companies themselves become more vocal.

The case for gas flaring in Nigeria, therefore, is a strong one, despite conventional wisdom against the waste of a natural resource and its implications on global warming issues. Given a situation where non-associated gas reserves are as ample as associated gas reserves and where any expansion in domestic demand can be satisfied by the former, the cost discrepancy between using the two varieties of gas is the main determining factor to the greater use of the former.

Domestic Gas Use and Supply Systems

The four main options for gas utilization in Nigeria have been electricity utilization, industrial use, petrochemicals and LNG exports. The latter two options have acquired significant and realizable status only since 1985. For the first twenty-five years of independence, the main consumers of natural gas in the country were the electric power plant sector and the industrial sector. In the 1960s, Nigerian natural gas was mainly marketed to the Electricity Corporation of Nigeria (ECN), and the Eastern Nigeria Development Corporation (ENDC), the industrial end-users. In the early 1960s, ECN took delivery of 91 per cent of total marketed production for its various power stations. By the late 1960s, ECN was using 69 per cent of total marketed gas production while ENDC had expanded its industrial consumer network and was utilizing 31 per cent of total marketed gas production (Schatzl, 1969, p. 139).

By the mid 1980s, the electricity sector in the form of the Nigerian Electric Power Authority (NEPA) had reasserted its place as the main gas consumer in Nigeria and accounted for 95 per cent of total marketed gas. The refinery at Alesa Eleme accounted for 2.3 per cent as did industrial usage at Aba and Ughelli. By the late 1980s and early 1990s, gas consumption had increased to about 4 bcm/year. Of this total amount of marketed gas, NEPA's share was about 70 per cent, the National Fertilizer Corporation of Nigeria (NAFCON) used approximately 18 per cent, the industrial complex at Aba accounted for 10 per cent, and the Delta Steel company at Aladja accounted for 2 per cent.[13]

The greatest increase in marketed production occurred after 1979, in the 1980s.[14] This increase in gas utilization was largely a result of the completion of various gas supply systems and the commissioning of different gas utilization projects by either NNPC or the individual oil companies operating in Nigeria. These included gas processing plants, gas recycling plants, gas re-injection plants as well as new gas-fired power stations, steel complexes, other industrial complexes, new refineries using NGLs as feedstock, and so on.

Tables 7.4 and 7.5 show the existing and future gas delivery systems in the country. Total flow capacity from all existing pipeline systems amounts to about 50 mcm/day (18 bcm/year). Judging from total marketed production in recent years, it is clear that the systems do not function at capacity, and there is significant room for growth in the demand for gas from the industrial and the power sectors. This also confirms that at least in the south of the country, primarily in the delta region, the lack of viable gas projects rather than the lack of pipelines is the main reason behind a low gas utilization rate.

The commissioning of the Escravos–Lagos pipeline in 1988 more than doubled existing flow capacity by adding 31 mcm/day (11 bcm/year), and boosted gas utilization quite significantly. The ELP project involves the gathering of both associated and non-associated gas from the Escravos area. The importance of this line also lies in the fact that the commissioning of the basic line in 1988 has ensured that smaller links can now be built integrating the gas facilities both north and west of the Niger river.[15]

In fact, as Table 7.5 shows, the majority of proposed gas supply projects consist of smaller pipeline links to the ELP line. In terms of flow capacity, these linkages will account for 81 per

Table 7.4: Current Gas Supply Systems.

Pipeline System	Operator	Gas Consumers	Length (km)	Diameter (cm)	Flow Capacity (mcm/day)
Eriemu-Aladja	NGC	Delta Steel, Aladja	33	40	1.8
Oben-Sapele	NGC	NEPA, Sapele	35	45	n.a
Oben-Ajaokuta	NGC	Ajaokuta Steel	195	60	5.6
Sapele-Ajaokuta	NGC	NEPA, Sapele	43	40	5.6
Obigbo North-Afam	NGC	NEPA, Afam	18	40	2.5
Bomu-Afam	Shell	NEPA, Afam	2 x 10	20, 25	n.a
Imo River-Aba	Shell	Various Industries in Aba(*)	27	30	0.9
Alakiri-Onne	NGC	NAFCON, Onne	14	35	2.5
Escravos-Lagos (ELP)	NGC	NEPA-Egbin, NEPA-IV Ughelli, Warri Refinery	341	90	30.8

Sources and Notes: Ikeh, 1991, p. 48; *OPEC Annual Statistical Bulletin*, 1991, pp. 114–15.
NEPA: National Electric Power Authority; NGC: National Gas Corporation; NAFCON: National Fertilizer Company of Nigeria; * Various industries in Aba include International Glass Industries, Aba Textile Mills, Nigerian Breweries, International Equitable, etc.

cent of the total projected 20 mcm/day. In terms of pipeline length, however, the proposed linkage to Abuja and Kaduna in the north of about 420 km., constitutes 85 per cent of the total pipeline length of the proposed projects. At present, there is a complete lack of pipeline infrastructure in the north of the country, despite the potential industrial usage in Abuja, in Kaduna, and near the northern border.[16] The main constraint to the development of this inland market is financial. The pipeline link alone was estimated at $500 million in 1990. Besides this, the development of the residential grid would require further assistance. In total the planned expansion of flow capacity by about 20 mcm/day, and the proposed increase in the supply of gas for power generation, the steel industry, the fertilizer plant, industries around Lagos, and industrial usage in the North will increase total marketed gas by about 14 bcm.[17] Unless the higher cost of processing associated gas is somehow compensated for, it is unlikely that it will supply any significant proportion of this

Table 7.5: Proposed Gas Supply Systems.

Pipeline System	Gas Consumers	Length (km)	Flow Capacity (mcm/day)
ELP-Ughelli	NEPA Delta IV: fuel for gas turbines	1	5.60
Ajaokuta-Abuja-Kaduna	NEPA Industrial Consumers: fuel	420	5.60
Oben-Ajaokuta (modification)	Ajaokuta Steel: fuel for power plant	2	2.90
ELP-Aladja System	Delta steel: fuel for power plant	14	2.80
Eriemu-Agbara-Otor	Super bru: fuel for boilers	2	0.04
Okpella Spur	Okpella cement: fuel for kilns	27	0.17
ELP-Shagamu	Shagamu Cement: fuel for kilns	11	0.73
ELP-Iwopin	Iwopin Paper Mills: fuel for boilers	30	0.42
ELP-Eyean	Coca-Cola, Benin: fuel for boilers	3	0.08
Warri Refinery and Warri Housing Estate	Warri Refinery/ NNPC Housing Estate: fuel for processing and cooking	2	0.70
ELP-Lagos Industries	Lagos Industries: fuel	40	1.18

Source: Ikeh, 1991, p. 48.

projected demand and the impact on the level of gas flaring in the country will thus be minimal.

New Projects

The gas supply system extensions and the subsequent gas supply to specific projects, as mentioned in the preceding section, constitute one aspect of the Nigerian government's renewed attempt to develop the gas industry more fully as a means of export revenue diversification. The other part of this two-sided approach involves the continuation and completion of longer-term, larger-scale projects, such as the LNG scheme, the ELP Gas Gathering and Processing project, and various other projects associated with the petrochemicals industry.

Apart from the LNG scheme, which will be considered in further detail in the following section, there are other proposed gas projects which will increase marketed production of gas and which in some cases may even increase the utilization of associated gas. A recent idea concerns the pipelining of unused associated gas from Nigerian fields to neighbouring countries. The advantages of such a project are thought to be two-fold. Firstly, flaring would be reduced considerably; and secondly, exporting the gas may encourage the government to deregulate domestic prices. The World Bank (in the financing of the $260 million project), US Chevron and RD Shell are all interested in participating in this project.[18] Its main disadvantage concerns the security costs of pipelining gas to neighbouring countries. In comparison, exporting LNG appears to be the safer option.

The other new development concerns the Chevron/Gulf proposed project to reduce the flaring of associated gas by establishing a gas processing and distribution system at Escravos. Estimated expenditure for the two phases will be about $1 billion phased over eight years. The gathering system, which may be tied into the Escravos–Lagos Pipeline system, will bring together about 4.8 mcm/day (1.8 bcm/year) of associated gas from fields around Escravos. The processing plant is expected to extract propane, butane and other NGLs from the gas for export and supply the remaining gas domestically. Domestic supplies are estimated at 4.2 mcm/day and Chevron is expected to recoup its initial costs by exporting the LPG. The project was given a boost in June 1993, when Chevron announced that it had secured funding for its part (40 per cent) of the project. NNPC is expected to approach the World Bank to fund about 60–70 per cent of its share (60 per cent) of the project.[19] The initial gathering and processing stage is expected to be completed in 1996, with the entire project fully operational by the year 2003.[20]

Nigeria's first major gas processing plant is already under construction by the Agip–Phillips–NNPC venture at Obiafu and Obrikom in Rivers state. Completion of the project is expected in 1993 at a cost of $300 million. The plant is expected to produce about 25,800 b/d of NGLs from the associated gas being re-injected into the Obiafu and Obrikom oilfields.[21] Recovery volumes of ethane, methane and butane are expected to be significant and the NGLs will be used as feedstock in the Eleme petrochemical outfit.[22] Phase II of the Eleme Petrochemicals programme, therefore, is another indirect potential consumer of Nigerian natural gas. The plant is expected to produce primary petrochemicals, plastics, fibres, and agrochemicals using NGLs from nearby gas fields, particularly Obrikom as well as feedstock from the Port Harcourt refinery.

The Oso condensate scheme, operated by Mobil, was commissioned in December 1992. The project uses 14 mcm/day of associated gas from Oso and nearby Mobil fields to maintain pressure in Oso.[23] Another project to increase gas utilization in the country was the MTBE plant 'jointly conceived by NNPC and a consortium of foreign firms' in 1990.[24] The project entailing the production of NGLs and methanol/MTBEs was stalled for two years due to the lack of a guaranteed source for the butane feedstock required. With the commissioning of the Oso Condensate project and access to its large gas-gathering capacities as well as the expected completion of the Agip gas plant in Obiafu and Obrikom, there is the increased likelihood that the quantities of butane required may now be available. The possibility of future projects in middle-distillates and methanol production can now be investigated.

LNG Projects: Past and Present

The LNG scheme has been considered a possible way of diversifying Nigeria's energy base and commercializing its gas resources for almost three decades now. The first LNG project collapsed in 1981 after five years of negotiations, and the second is in 1994 in its eleventh year of planning. Commissioning of the project is expected in 1999, at the earliest. For the cynics, of course, the present status of the project is more or less similar to that of the original scheme before it collapsed. At that time, sales contracts had been finalized, complete financing had yet to be arranged, and there was some tension between the technical leader of the project and the confirmation of certain contracts.[25] An optimistic view, however, contends that the Nigerian context in 1993–4 is significantly different from that of 1981. First, the infrastructural network supporting the project is far more advanced. This network includes the gas gathering supply systems, the gas processing plants, and the LNG vessels which were acquired for the project in 1989. Secondly, the government is far more aware today that the economy needs to diversify its energy base, increase foreign exchange earnings and reduce the stranglehold of the external debt. The realization, therefore, that the country must take advantage of a natural resource whose reserves are estimated to outlast significantly those of oil, is far more acute in the early 1990s than it was in 1981. Allowing for the requisite Nigerian delays, therefore, it is likely that the LNG scheme, in some form or the other, will come onstream within the next decade.

The Phillips Bonny LNG Project. The first LNG project was introduced initially in Nigeria's Fourth Development Plan 1975–80, and started taking shape in early 1976 when the government approved plans for the construction of a gas liquefaction plant at Bonny with a total capacity of 8 bcm/year. The agreement signed later that year by Shell–BP set up the 'Bonny LNG' company which would manage the project. The state took a 60 per cent interest in the project, with Shell and BP dividing the remainder equally. Costs were estimated at $3.2 billion, which included plant construction as well as transportation and infrastructural plans. During this period, feasibility studies were being carried out by Agip–Phillips–Elf for the construction of another liquefaction plant sited at Peterside, near Bonny.[26] By 1978, the two projects had been merged.

The modified project entailed the construction of a very large liquefaction plant with total capacity of 16 bcm/year, a very large infrastructural network capable of supplying what was essentially 80 per cent of gross production in 1988, and the necessary shipping facilities (fourteen to sixteen LNG carriers). The state took a 60 per cent interest, Shell and BP took 10 per cent each, Phillips (the technical leader) and Agip took 7.5 per cent each, and Elf took 5 per cent interest in the new venture.[27] During 1979, certain operational issues were sorted out with participants in the venture agreeing to explore and produce gas individually, sell at the well head to a transmission company (probably wholly government financed but with a possible 10 per cent share offered to international pipeline companies), which would then sell the gas to the Bonny LNG company for processing and marketing (with a 50 per cent government share). Total estimated investment costs for the project had risen by now to over $10 billion,[28] with the government's share of these costs substantial. Furthermore, deliveries from the six-train plant were to begin by 1984–5. By 1980, sales contracts for at least half the projected LNG output, or 8 bcm/year, had been finalized with

European companies, while sales contracts for the remaining production, in the form of draft sales agreements with four American companies, awaited confirmation from the US government.

In January 1981, the Fifth National Development Plan 1981–5 was unveiled, showing that the government had not come up with the requisite financial commitment to the project. In fact, the $561 million allocated to the project for initial construction purposes was to be used only at the end of the plan period in 1984–5.[29] The completion of the project had essentially been deferred to the end of the decade. This financial set-back to the project was followed by government dissatisfaction and review of pricing and shipping arrangements.[30] By October 1981, after the development plan was formally finalized, Phillips had relinquished technical leadership of the project. Despite attempted negotiations on the part of the three remaining members to rescue the project, the consortium finally broke in early 1982.

The Current Bonny LNG Project. Negotiations immediately started between the government and independent consultants in a concerted effort to re-start the LNG project, with the main change from the earlier scheme being the scale of the project. In late 1983, Shell was designated the project leader and by the end of 1985, 'Nigeria LNG' was formed as a project company to launch Nigerian LNG. The agreement formalized the shares of the various partners: NNPC at 60 per cent, Shell Gas Nigeria at 20 per cent, and Nigerian Agip and Elf Nigeria at 10 per cent each. The new scheme was to be sited at Bonny, and would supply 3.6 mt of LNG to customers each year. Costs were estimated at $4 billion for the 13.7 mcm/day (5 bcm/year) project. The agreement emphasized that the project could only be taken further when the various partners were fully satisfied as regards its feasibility and viability. A 'go no-go' decision was expected by early 1987.[31] This essentially meant that the following two years would be spent setting up the appropriate sales contracts and the financing arrangements.

At the end of 1987, the project's cost had been reduced to $2 billion. This was mainly achieved as a result of decisions to use non-associated gas supplied by the joint venture partners themselves, to buy second-hand LNG tankers, and to take advantage of the keen competition between plant designers and contractors. First deliveries of LNG to customers were expected in 1995, with maximum capacity of 6 bcm/year being reached by 1997. The fields selected to provide the gas included Oshi and Idu (Agip), Ubeta, Obagwi, Ibewa (Elf), and Soku and Bomu (Shell). Initial discussions with potential customers and financial institutions had already occurred, and finalization of this aspect of the negotiations was expected from mid-1988 onwards.[32] In October 1988, NNPC set up the Nigerian LNG Project Co., (NLNG) a subsidiary company which formalized the company's brief to oversee gas transmission, liquefaction and shipping in a corporate structure.[33]

Considerable progress was made on the project in 1989. In May, sales contracts were agreed to in principle. These accounted for 5.5 bcm/year of the proposed LNG output. Although by 1991 the German customers as well as Columbia Gas of the USA had dropped out, the 1989 contracts had narrowed potential customers to the four who would eventually sign contracts for the gas. These included Gaz de France, Enel of Italy, Enagas of Spain, and Distrigas of the USA.

In September 1989, in an attempt to keep the momentum of the project going, the oil ministry implemented a package of fiscal incentives and guarantees for the partners in the LNG scheme. The government offered a 5–10 year tax holiday tied to LNG sales prices. In terms of foreign exchange restrictions, the joint operating company would be allowed to base its accounts on the US Dollar rather than the Nigerian Naira. Offshore bank accounts could also be established to facilitate a more efficient clearing of outstanding debts, and the NLNG would operate as an autonomous entity.[34]

By the end of 1989, Shell Gas Nigeria BV, acting on behalf of the LNG company exercised its purchase options on two carriers, and Enellengee, a subsidiary of the LNG project company acquired two tankers. These were refurbished as LNG Finima and LNG Bonny and were chartered to Malaysia LNG and Pertamina LNG, initially for four years. Presumably the contracts will now have to be renegotiated until the project is commissioned. The loan to purchase and refurbish the carriers was made by a consortium of banks, including Citibank, Crédit Lyonnais, and the Hong Kong Shanghai Banking Corporation. Enellengee was to use the remainder of the loan to purchase two more vessels.[35] By 1990, the gas supply for the liquefaction plant at Finima had been arranged.[36] A total 20 mcm/day would be required to supply the two-train plant. Although seven fields had initially been earmarked for the supply, in late 1991 it was decided, after a re-estimation of Soku's reserves, that the Shell field would be able to supply the four contracts signed and the remaining fields' production would be kept in reserve in case of project expansion.

By late 1991, four LNG carriers had already been acquired by the venture. The chartering of the first two was seen to have two advantages. Firstly it served to recoup some of the cost of buying the vessels, and secondly it meant saving, for the time being, on storage space.[37] The other two carriers were to be chartered to Algeria for the Algerian LNG–Cove Point haul. It is unclear whether this has actually occurred.[38]

Also by the end of 1991, sales contracts had been agreed to with four buyers taking the plant's entire output for a period of 22.5 years. Table 7.6 lists the customers, with whom memoranda of understanding had been signed. Actual contracts were signed only in mid-1992.

Pricing was also arranged by mid 1992 with these customers. The Nigerians took a sector-by-sector approach alongside negotiated 'escalation clauses' to suit the individual customer. Enel, which will use the gas for electricity generation, agreed to a base price of $3.02 per mBtu (cif), and escalation linked to oil products, clean coal, electricity and Italian inflation rates. Enagas and Gaz de France base prices, on the other hand, were set at about $2.32 per mBtu (cif) and would escalate in line with heating oil and two grades of residual fuel oil prices.[39] USA Distrigas

Table 7.6: LNG Sales Contracts.

Gas Utility	Volume (bcm/year)
Gaz de France	0.5
Enel (Italy)	3.5
Enagas (Spain)	1.0
Distrigas (USA)	0.7
Total	5.7

Source: *FT International Gas Report*, 19 September, 1991, p. 8.

would buy Nigerian LNG on a netback basis, 'reflecting the depressed US gas market'.[40] LNG would, in this case, be sold at an actual sales price, or at a reference price based on competing oil products, whichever was higher.

At these contractual sales prices, the commercial basis of the LNG venture is not very clear. The base prices at which contracts were agreed are too low for the government to expect a commercial return of about 15 per cent on the investment. While the government itself may in fact accept a low, utility return of about 4–5 per cent, it is unlikely that the other more commercial partners in the LNG project, in particular the oil companies, would be happy with this. The degree to which these pricing terms have influenced the various delays in the project would be interesting to assess, even though the terms had been accepted in principle. It is quite likely, however, that by the time the project's other problems are resolved, its contract structure will also have changed. Certainly, the Italian prices will have to be renegotiated, if only because of the political upheaval in the country.

As far as financing is concerned, this had become a fairly serious matter with estimated costs for the project at the higher level of $4.5–$5.0 billion. With shareholders' equity covering 40 per cent of the costs or $1.8 billion, the 60 per cent covered by borrowing amounted to $2.7 billion. This has not been an easy sum to find from the international financial community, particularly since the prospective lenders did not initially have a large equity in the project. NNPC's share is also significant at $1.1–$1.2 billion.[41] Financing arrangements had still not been finalized at the end of 1992. Although the six-month delay, caused by the missed deadline for construction bids on 22 December, 1992, may have given the government extra time to come up with its share, it has also risked alienating the little interest that has been raised so far. The Import-Export Bank seems to be reconsidering its $300 million to the project, 'citing Nigerian political instability' and uncertainty over project accounting to date.[42] Certainly the delay in the project shows every likelihood of causing an increase in its costs. If or when this happens, it will constitute another set of pressures on the price terms of the sales contracts already signed, especially given that the contracts have yet to be made 'unconditionally binding' both from the buyer's and the seller's perspective. Recent indications from the operator of the LNG venture, Shell, have pointed to the likelihood that contracts, for whatever reason, will have to be re-bid in 1994.[43]

The main obstacle, however, when the NLNG board was dismissed in 1992 was the little progress made in finalizing the selection of both a construction team, and even the process to be used.[44] Initial agreement was made between the NLNG board with the French engineering company, Technip, to develop the technical specifications and liquefaction process (known as Tealarc) at the LNG plant. However no contracts were actually signed. In October 1992, the government replaced its representatives on the NLNG board claiming its preference for the rival consortium led by the US company, Bechtel, in its bid for the $2 billion plus contract. 'Overriding interests of state' were cited.[45]

The December 1992 deadline for choosing the technical contractor for the project was initially delayed for six months, and was extended till December 1993, largely because both contractors have been asked to submit revised bids to allow for a change in the liquefaction technology, and this revision requires a significant amount of re-working and re-negotiation. Whatever the reasons cited for or against specific construction companies and specific technologies (and a number of accusations and counter-accusations have already been exchanged between the government and the NLNG board), the problem lies not in the disputes themselves but in the delay to the entire project and the consequent re-questioning of all contracts already signed. NNPC, in late 1992, was now saying that the contract prices may in fact be unjustifiably low. Whether these were mere delaying tactics, as in 1981, or real issues of contention is not yet clear. Pricing issues will also be brought to a head with the recent declaration by Shell that LNG output at the plant may be greater than 5.7 bcm and that all present customers are willing to negotiate an increase in their contractual supplies.[46] What is clear is that the new military government of General Abacha, which took power in November 1993, will have the enormous responsibility of sifting through issues of US versus European engineering rivalries, European versus US/Japanese lobbying power and most importantly project financing, if the NLNG project is not to lose its momentum completely.

It is also quite evident that these delays are straining NNPC's credibility in its support for the LNG project. As we have seen, the project is at risk financially. In May 1993, the government decided that coming up with its share of the funding – about $1–1.2 billion – was impossible. NNPC therefore decided to sell off part of its stake to reduce its share of the almost $5 billion project. The new ownership structure is said to look as follows: NNPC 49 per cent; Shell 24 per cent; Elf 15 per cent and Agip 10 per cent. The remaining 2 per cent equity share is being offered to the International Financial Corporation in the World Bank as a 'balancing stake'. Such a move is bound to prove popular both with the participating oil companies and with the Bank for the following reasons: (a) with the oil companies because a lesser NNPC stake and therefore influence in the project may ensure against sudden decisions and changes in plans due to the 'overriding interests of the state'; (b) with the World Bank, because it serves to reassure a potential creditor by allowing it a stake in the project. Financial credibility on the part of shareholders has been enhanced by the setting up of an escrow account in which the NNPC initial share will be $500 million.[47] In addition to ceding majority holding in the project itself, the government, in 1993, also decided to reduce its equity stake in upstream joint ventures to raise financing for the LNG scheme. The level of funds to be raised and the actual logistics of this proposed divestment are unconfirmed as yet.[48]

While it is likely that the Nigerian LNG project will get off the ground, there are several problems associated with further delays. Firstly, the present gas customers must constantly adapt to the delays in the project. For instance, Bechtel had also been working on an LNG terminal in Montalto di Castro in Italy, where it was intended to land some Nigerian supplies. Work here has since stopped as a result of a government order that the entire project be environmentally reviewed.[49] Secondly, if delays persist beyond the year 2000, the potentially strong competition (especially from Algeria and Qatar) will make it increasingly difficult for Nigeria to establish a secure niche for itself as an LNG supplier.

Issues and Future Prospects in Natural Gas Utilization

The credibility of the government's policy on increasing the utilization of the country's gas reserves is invariably questioned as a result of the much delayed LNG scheme, mainly because of the scale and public exposure of this project. It is worth noting, however, that the successful implementation of the government's gas policy and the development of an efficient gas market has been mainly constrained by inadequate investment in gas projects and infrastructure as well as ineffective pricing policies and incentives. The credibility of the government's policy on gas use, therefore, depends more on whether these issues are addressed.

LNG exports are one important solution to the currently low utilization of gas in the country. The project's gas use, however, is only about 7 bcm/year and moreover entails the utilization of non-associated gas. While this scheme remains significant for export revenue purposes, and while it would increase marketed production to 11 bcm/year, it does not address the issue of gas flaring. In such a context, other projects may be more significant.

The proposed extension of existing supply systems in itself can increase gas use significantly. If pipelining to the North is included, gas utilization in industries and power generation in Abuja and Kaduna would increase the present level of marketed gas at least three-fold. This increase would arise largely from the expansion in power generation, for which there is enormous potential in the country. Presently, the country has one of the lowest per capita electricity consumption levels amongst developing countries.[50] In this context, the domestic market holds the greatest potential for expansion in the utilization of gas.

Another important option that can be developed further is that of LPGs, especially for exports. The development of a LPG market within the country is constrained by the high cost of accessories and equipment such as storage tanks, gas cylinders, the adaptation of cookers and so on. The potential for LPG exports, on the other hand, appears to be greater. The Chevron operated gas gathering project at Escravos has recently raised part of its financing requirements; and the completion of the gas processing plant at Obiafu–Obrikom is imminent. The latter is expected to provide feedstock (ethane and methane) for the Eleme plant, but the recovery of butane, potentially exportable, is also expected to be significant. On a related note, gas based petrochemical production will not only replace the current imports of these products, but can also be considered as possible sources of export revenue in the future.

Whatever the potential in the domestic market, the effective utilization of the country's gas reserves is only possible if the issue of domestic product pricing is addressed, in terms of both the substitutes for gas and gas itself. At present, for instance, the heavy subsidies on petrol and heating oil make it unlikely that consumers will shift to gas. Furthermore, if the level of flaring is to be reduced and greater use made of associated gas, then the pricing of gas itself will have to take into account the higher production costs associated with the latter. A further complication exists in the form of the power industry and the implications of its pricing on gas pricing. Besides reflecting costs, gas pricing in Nigeria must also reflect what NEPA (now known as Nigerian Electric Power, PLC), the biggest gas consumer, can pay, given its electricity tariffs. The government has understood the importance of pricing reflecting the costs of projects if gas industry development is to be seriously pursued, and has raised gas prices. Since June 1989, there has been a new uniform price at which power stations and industry must buy gas: this is $0.75 per mBtu at official rates or $0.45 per mBtu at parallel market rates.[51] This is significantly higher than the old price of $0.10-$0.15 per mBtu. Whether this increase is adequate to cover production costs (i.e. the commercial rates payed by NGC to producers) or to encourage the use of the costlier associated gas is not clear.

Inefficiencies in the sector arise mainly from the pricing structure but also from the way the system operates. The main producers of gas are the oil companies through joint ventures. NNPC is involved primarily in the distribution and sales of gas through NGC, which buys gas from the producers at a commercial rate and sells to the consumers at the new uniform rate. This chain invariably causes delays (even if payments are being made in full) and sometimes these may take the form of erratic NGC payments to producers. In these circumstances, oil companies feel that in supplying gas they get a negative return on their investments.[52] In general, however, the delays in payment are ultimately at the expense of NNPC's budget.[53] A reflection of the inefficiencies in the sector is that NAFCON continued to pay the old price of $0.10-$0.15 per mBtu instead of the new rate for at least 6 months after it was implemented. This was apparently an oversight and not transitional relief.

Notes

1. By infrastructural, we refer to both pipeline and transportation inadequacy, particularly in the north of the country, as well as the paucity of viable gas projects.
2. *Energy Economist*, September 1991, p. 12.
3. The Gbaran structure was discovered in 1967 by Shell. The field, thought to be a gas field, remained undeveloped till 1990. In May 1990, Gbaran-4 was drilled uncovering about 700 mb of crude oil reserves and 14 bcm of gas at the site. The field will now be developed. In the earlier years of oil exploration in Nigeria, the abandonment of large gas accumulations in the search for oil was a frequent occurrence.
4. In 1990, Shell made three other delta discoveries (besides the giant Gbaran) while Mobil, Gulf and Elf also made significant crude oil discoveries, presumably with some associated gas. Most reserve increases, however, are generally a result of the redefinition of reserves and/or fields.
5. Of total marketed production of natural gas in 1992, 35 per cent issued from offshore fields (*BP Review of World Gas*, August 1993).
6. ESMAP, 1993, p. 45.
7. According to the 1984 Gas-Flaring Penalties Legislation, exemptions cover the following fields:
   (1) Where 75 per cent of the produced gas is 'effectively utilized'.
   (2) Those operated as a result of a specific directive from the Nigerian government.
   (3) Where the gas contains 15 per cent of 'impurities' that could render the gas unsuitable for industrial purposes.
   (4) Where the volume of gas produced is small as related to the distance to the site where the gas could be utilized.
   (5) Where the gas reinjection is not feasible and where an ongoing gas utilization programme is temporarily disrupted (Barrows, *Petroleum Taxation and Legislation*, 1984, p. 72).
8. The Bonny LNG scheme at this time was still planning to use associated gas production and the ELP scheme was to provide the much needed pipeline linkages and transportation for both associated and non-associated gas fields.
9. Barrows, *Petroleum Taxation and Legislation*, 1985, p. 58.
10. *OPEC Bulletin*, May 1992.
11. The more significant of these downstream incentives include the opening of the gas industry to a 100 per cent private and/or foreign ownership; competitive pricing of primary feedstock; guaranteed export earnings; unrestricted import allowances for intermediate goods; and preferential consideration for crude oil lifting contracts for investors embarking on projects in priority areas (see Barrows, *Petroleum Taxation and Legislation Report*, May/June 1993, pp. 34–5).
12. ESMAP, 1993, p. 46.
13. *World Gas Intelligence*, February 1990, p. 5.
14. The following outlines the main reasons behind some of the increases in marketed production of gas and/or reductions in gas-flaring in the 1980s:

The increase in marketed production between 1982 and 1983 was largely because of the commissioning of the Aladja and Ajaokuta steel complexes and their complementary gas supply systems. In 1985, two main factors may have contributed to the reduction in flaring and increase in marketed production. Firstly, the Obigbo-Afam gas supply system was commissioned in 1984, resulting in a significant increase in marketed production to industries in and around Afam. Secondly, there was a big increase in natural gas re-injection in 1985. This was due to the commissioning of the $80 million Obiafu-Obrikom Gas Recycling Plant in March 1985 built by the NNPC–NAOC venture which allowed for the reinjection of some 8 mcm/day (or 3 bcm/year) of previously flared gas (*FT International Gas Report*, 28 June 1991, p. 8). The increase in 1988 was mainly due to the commissioning of the fertilizer plant at Onne, supplied by a Shell-built gas plant at Alakiri, which increased gas utilization by about 2 mcm/day. The increase in 1989 can be mainly attributed to the commissioning of the Escravos–Lagos Pipeline in October 1988 as well as the 1989 start-up of the $56 million Utorogu gas gathering and processing plant in Bendel state. The gas plant, built by a Shell/NNPC venture to supply the ELP pipeline, has a production capacity of about 7.6 mcm/day or 2.8 bcm/year (Barrows, *IPI Data Service, Africa*, 1986, No. 47, *Nigeria*, p. 55; Ikeh, 1991, p. 43). This significantly raised gas utilization by power plants in the Lagos/Egbin and Ughelli areas.

15. The $600 million Escravos–Lagos Pipeline Project was finally commissioned in October 1988. It was initially conceived of as another one of Shagari's show-piece projects. Bids for the pipeline contracts in the associated gas project were accepted at the end of 1983. Commissioning was, at that time, planned for the end of 1985. As it happened, the Nigerian government, by the mid-1980s was largely caught up with negotiations with the IMF regarding its massive foreign debt, an important legacy of the civilian regime of Shagari. Financing and construction of the project were finally facilitated by the government's 'quiet agreement' to the economic reforms demanded by the Fund, and the finalization of the IMF loan by 1987 (*PE*, March 1987, p. 90; November 1988, p. 366).

16. Developing residential gas use along the border is recommended as one of the ways to cut wood-burning and check deforestation in and desertification of the area. It is evident from statistics on Nigerian fuelwood use, that the partial replacement of this fuel with natural gas would significantly increase gas utilization in the country. In the mid 1980s, of total domestic fuel use in urban areas, fuelwood use accounted for 44 per cent, kerosene accounted for 52 per cent and LPG for 4 per cent. In rural areas, wood accounts for 80 per cent of domestic fuel use, kerosene for 18 per cent, and LPG for 2 per cent. Even if the share of wood in domestic fuel use has decreased over the past seven years, the potential for fuel switching remains enormous (*World Gas Intelligence*, February 1990, p. 5; Ikeh, 1991, p. 44).

17. Projected Gas Requirement: Aladja Steel Plant 0.7 bcm/year; Ajaokuta 2 bcm/year; NEPA Lagos and industrial usage 6.5 bcm/year; NEPA Afam IV Extension 1.4 bcm/year; NEPA Sapele Phase II 1.5 bcm/year;

Abuja Federal Capital Territory 1 bcm/year; Fertilizer Plant at Onne
0.6 bcm/year; and Warri Refinery 0.3 bcm/year (Ikeh, 1991; p. 43).
18. *World Gas Intelligence,* June 1993, p. 19.
19. *Platt's,* 22 June 1993, p. 6.
20. *World Gas Intelligence,* May 1990, p. 3; *FT International Gas Report,* 25 May,
    1990, p. 16; *PE,* Chevron Sponsored Statement, February 1993, p. 34.
21. While gas reinjection techniques to maintain pressure may be substitutable
    for water injection techniques, the extent to which using the former can
    reduce flaring may not be significant. Nigerian oilfields, by and large, do
    not require such re-pressurization.
22. *IPE,* 1992, p. 140.
23. *IPE,* 1991.
24. *OPEC Bulletin,* February 1993, p. 19.
25. In 1981, these tensions concerned sales or customer contracts; in 1992,
    these concerned the actual contractors of the project or construction
    contracts.
26. *PE,* November 1976, p. 439.
27. Ibid., January 1978, p. 27; March 1978, p. 107.
28. *World Gas Report,* 10 March, 1980, p. 4.
29. *PE,* February 1981, p. 51.
30. The Algerians were unhappy with Nigerian contract prices to their
    European customers: $4.50–$5.00 per Million British Thermal Units (mBtu)
    c.i.f. Europe as opposed to the Algerian demanded price of $6.10 per
    mBtu and above for f.o.b. cargoes. These contract prices, negotiated by
    the partners in the LNG project, may not have met with the approval of
    the government, since they were too low and did not reflect either the
    costs of the project or the level of the crude oil price. As regards the US
    customers, the Nigerians appeared to be insisting on a $5.50 per mBtu
    c.i.f. price; the Americans were unhappy about this given that accepting
    these prices would openly signal other gas exporters to the USA, such as
    Canada and Mexico, to increase their prices (*World Gas Report,* 26 May,
    1980; 1 September, 1980, pp. 1, 12). It is quite likely that the government
    was not, in fact, really unhappy about prices, and was now just thinking
    of a project on a much smaller scale.
31. Barrows, *IPI Data Service, Africa,* No. 47, *Nigeria,* 1986, p. 80; Barrows,
    Petroleum Taxation and Legislation Report, Africa, 1985, p. 53.
32. *World Gas Report,* 4 December, 1987, p. 6–7.
33. Barrows, *Petroleum Taxation and Legislation Report,* Africa, 1988, p. 167.
34. Ibid., 1989, p. 179.
35. *O&GJ,* 29 January, 1990, p. 38.
36. Shell/NNPC's Soku field would supply 11.2 mcm/day; Elf/NNPC's Ubeta,
    Ibewa, and Obagi fields would supply 4.9 mcm/day; and Agip/Phillips/
    NNPC's Idu and Oshi fields would supply 4.9 mcm/day as well (*World
    Gas Intelligence,* February 1990, p. 6).
37. *Energy Economist,* September 1991, p. 13.
38. *FT International Gas Report,* 22 March, 1991, p. 17.
39. Pricing terms for Spain and France are more favourable than for Italy for
    two main reasons. Firstly, Nigerian LNG supplies would have to contend

with greater competition from North African suppliers in the former two countries. Secondly, Italy has been known to pay inflated prices for its gas contracts with Algeria. Presumably kick-backs have a significant role in the setting of these prices. Certainly, the present charges of corruption facing the old Italian management of national utilities attests to this.

40. *Energy Compass*, 24 December 1992, p. 3; *PE/GWI*, Special Report, March 1992, p. 7.
41. NNPC's equity contribution to the LNG project has apparently been going into a special escrow account since 1984. With proceeds from 20,000 b/d of crude oil sales, NNPC's equity contribution can theoretically be fully met from this special account (*Energy Economist*, September 1991, p. 13).
42. Ibid., January 1993, p. 12.
43. *FT*, 14 December, 1993, p. 4.
44. *Energy Compass*, 5 March, 1993, p. 3.
45. Ibid., 24 December, 1992, p. 3. The NLNG board is comprised of six Nigerian members, two members from Shell, and one member each from Agip/Phillips and Elf. The Bechtel consortium includes the US Bechtel, the Japanese Chiyoda (the Kaduna refinery contractors), the German Thyssen and the French company Spies Batignolles. The Technip consortium includes the French company Technip, the US company M.W. Kellog, Japan Gasoline Corporation and the Italian Snamprogetti.
46. *FT International Gas Report*, 7 January 1994, p. 242/2–3.
47. This amount has apparently come from the sale of 5 per cent of its stake to Elf. NNPC is also reported as setting aside 20,000 b/d from crude sales worth about $10 million/month, to finance its share. The sale of a further 6 per cent of its equity to the World Bank and to Shell have still to be finalized (*World Gas Intelligence*, July 1993, p. 1; August 1993, p. 3; *FT International Gas Report*, 7 January 1994, p.242–3).
48. There are some unconfirmed reports, for instance, that besides the 5 per cent stake buyout by Elf in the Shell–NNPC venture which essentially reduces NNPC's stake to 55 per cent and increases Elf's to 10 per cent, a further 4 per cent of NNPC's stake is also up for offer. The latter may either be taken up by Shell itself, increasing its stake to 34 per cent, or sold to another company altogether, such as Mobil (*PIW*, 9 August, 1993, p. 3).
49. *World Gas Intelligence*, June 1993, p. 3.
50. *UN Energy Statistics Yearbook*, 1991.
51. *World Gas Intelligence*, February 1990, p. 5.
52. However with clauses in their joint-venture contracts to the effect that NNPC will be allowed to take over the gas reserves if operators fail to develop them, oil companies will continue to supply gas.
53. In 1992, for instance, NEP's debt to NNPC amounted to $40 million. It cannot be over-emphasized, however, that these payment delays and/or problems of non-payments occur in a vicious circle. It has been reported, for instance, that in 1993 the Delta Steel Company had amassed debts to government agencies, NEP and NGC of over $18 million. (*OPEC Bulletin*, November/December 1993, pp. 43–4).

8 OIL AND THE ECONOMY

Introduction

The story of the impact of oil revenues on the Nigerian economy begins with the oil boom period of the 1970s when 'Dutch Disease' symptoms set in to establish an economy that was unable to accommodate the OPEC production cuts and the reverse price shock of 1986. It is a story of increasing dependency on oil revenues, tremendous expansion of the public sector, increases in public expenditure, higher indebtedness, and a collapsing non-oil economy.

The Nigerian economy has become increasingly dependent on oil revenues over the past decade. During the 1986–92 period oil export revenues increased at an average 13 per cent per annum, while GDP, measured in current US Dollars, decreased by an average 7 per cent per annum. This slow but obvious recovery in oil export revenues alongside the continuing decline of the non-oil economy implies higher dependency. By the early 1990s, petroleum production accounted for over 90 per cent of foreign exchange receipts (oil exports accounted for 97 per cent of total export receipts), 70 per cent of budgetary revenues, and 25 per cent of GDP. More importantly however, the rising oil revenues and declining GDP of the late 1980s suggest that the impact of the oil boom in the earlier decade was so detrimental to non-oil economic activities, that even increasing oil revenues after the low of 1986 were not sufficient to initiate or sustain a GDP recovery.

Some structural aspects of the economy reveal the failure of Nigerian oil revenues to provide the impetus for growth in other sectors, and describe the basis for what has been an essentially uneasy marriage between energy and economic growth in the country. Per capita income has declined from about $1000 (in current dollars) in 1980 to about $240 in 1991. The evolution in the structure of production shows that the share of agriculture in GDP has declined to 37 per cent in 1991 from 41 per cent in 1986, despite the introduction of the structural adjustment

183

programme which emphasized the need to re-establish agriculture as a growth sector. The share of industry (manufacturing plus mining), however, increased from 29 per cent in 1986 to 38 per cent in 1991, but more importantly, there has been almost no change in the share of manufacturing (around 7–8 per cent) over the past ten years. Oil revenues, it is clear, have not succeeded in strengthening either the agricultural or the manufacturing base of the economy. Furthermore, the oil boom years, and massive government expenditure on what was primarily infrastructure and other non-tradables, did not prepare the economy for the oil production cutbacks of the early 1980s and the oil price shock of 1986. The external debt has consequently increased from a manageable $9 billion in 1980 to about $30 billion in 1992. The servicing of this debt is, as the economy as a whole, highly dependent on oil revenues.

Table 8.1: Oil Export Revenues and as Share of Total Export Receipts. Various Years 1970–92. Million Dollars and Per Cent.

	Oil Export Revenues (Million $)	Oil Revenues as Share of Total Export Receipts Per Cent
1970	724	58.01
1973	3,054	84.67
1974	9,006	92.87
1975	7,761	93.18
1979	15,702	93.44
1980	24,933	96.14
1985	12,564	95.80
1986	5,667	94.21
1987	7,011	92.92
1988	6,286	91.14
1989	7,469	94.90
1990	13,180	97.01
1991	11,781	96.14
1992	11,642	97.94

Sources and Notes: IMF, *International Financial Statistics*, Various Yearbooks. 1992 figures are Naira based and converted at 1992 period average exchange rates.

Oil Revenues and Government Expenditure

Table 8.1 shows the growth in oil export revenues over the past two decades and its high share of total export revenues. Oil price increases in 1973–4 and again in 1979–80 as well as the expansion in crude oil production during this period induced boom years in the Nigerian economy. Revenues increased by 200 per cent in 1974 and by 60 per cent in 1980. This surge in oil export revenues has been linked to the complete loss of economic and financial control of the Nigerian economy and the beginning of 'financial indiscipline and corruption in the public economy' (Forrest, 1993, p. 55). As a result of greater state ownership of the oil and higher royalties and taxes, the increased oil revenues meant an explosion in government expenditure and public consumption.[1] Before government expenditure allocation is assessed, however, it is important to see how the price increases and production expansions of the 1970s affected the income of the economy as a whole. To this end, we estimate windfall export income, windfall income (GDP) and the approximate allocation of this to consumption and investment.[2]

Although the boom years actually lasted from 1973 to 1981, the various estimates on windfall gains cover the period 1973–83. The present value of the stream of windfall exports (i.e. oil revenues) during this period is estimated at around Naira 6.4 billion which was equivalent to about 13 per cent of total actual exports. During the same period, the present value of windfall GDP was estimated at Naira 36.2 billion, which amounted to approximately 16 per cent of total actual Nigerian GDP over the period 1973–83. Of this windfall income, 54 per cent was allocated to consumption and 46 per cent to savings – and of the latter, domestic investment accounted for about 50 per cent, 4 per cent of which was financed by foreign debt.

According to Oyejide, these estimates show that contrary to the declared objectives of the government, income allocation during the years 1973–83 did not prioritize investments, but was biased toward consumption (Oyejide, forthcoming, p. 20). It is also noteworthy that the income windfall was mainly domestically consumed, with no investment of revenues abroad. Large oil revenues accrued directly to the federal government, thus increasing expenditure for which in turn there were strong claimants. The massive increase in government expenditure was essentially a way for the government to acquire legitimacy in the eyes of the public. This was true of the military governments in the mid to late 1970s as well as Shagari's civilian government. The expansion of the public sector generally took the form of wage increases for the employees, the creation of more jobs in the public sector, and the increased provision of urban services. These were thought to be the easiest and most obvious ways of spending the oil wealth on the nation, as well as convenient means of repaying political debts which were largely urban-based. However, the most negative consequence of this surge in oil revenues was the neglect of non-oil tax revenues (of which some were abolished) and of accounting procedures, which opened the way for fiscal indiscipline and corruption (Forrest, 1993, pp. 134–5).

Government capital expenditure in the 1970s was heavily biased towards economic services. Of these services, significant expenditure increases occurred in the power, mining and manufacturing, and transportation & communications sectors. In 1973–4, expenditure in these sectors accounted for 31 per cent of total capital expenditures. By 1979–80, this share had increased to 53 per cent.[3] The share of expenditure in agriculture, however, decreased from 5 per cent in 1973–4 to 3 per cent in 1979–80. Other important increases in expenditure occurred in the water and education services. Olayiwola confirms this service-based expenditure pattern in his tabulation of average annual growth rates in the various sectors over the period 1970–81. Growth in the agricultural sector averaged only -0.4 per cent over this period, while the utilities sector (electricity, gas, water) grew at 16.3 per cent, construction at 13.1 per cent, manufacturing at 12.4 per cent, and transport and communications at 8.3 per cent. Most importantly, imports grew at an annual average rate of 15.9 per cent (Olayiwola, 1987, p. 137).

The Agriculture Sector

That classical Dutch Disease symptoms had set in during the so-called boom years was made evident by the pattern of government capital expenditure, the growth of the non-tradable sectors, and the decline of the only other main tradable sector besides oil, agriculture.[4]

In a forthcoming paper Oyejide has compared the projected and actual sectoral allocation of capital expenditure by the government during the Third Development Plan period 1975–80 and has found that in the proposed plan, there is a strong bias toward capital expenditure in the non-tradable sector. Furthermore, actual capital allocation in the same period has shown this bias to be even stronger, with expenditure in the non-tradable sector accounting for almost 80 per cent of total public capital expenditure. Nigeria did not balance its capital expenditures between infrastructure, industry and agriculture, and capital expenditure in the agricultural sector itself accounted for only 7 per cent of the total during the years 1975–80.

It has been estimated that between 1970–82, yearly production of the main Nigerian cash crops, cocoa, rubber, cotton and groundnuts, fell by 43, 29, 65, and 64 per cent respectively (Gregoire, 1988, p. 84). Addressing the same issue, Forrest disputes the claim that the switch in consumption in favour of wheat and rice exports was due to a production crisis. In his view, the decline in agricultural output for export had started before the surge in revenues and was exacerbated by the latter as well as by the drought of 1973–4. The oil boom increased the relative prices of mainly 'labour-intensive export crops of the southern states'

Table 8.2: Projected and Actual Sectoral Allocation of Capital Expenditure 1975–80. Per Cent

	Third Development Plan 1975-80	*Actual Expenditure 1975-80*
Tradables	**31.0**	**20.8**
Agriculture	6.6	7.1
Mining & Quarrying	8.2	5.0
Manufacturing	16.2	8.7
Non-Tradables	**69.0**	**79.2**
Public Utilities	31.3	36.9
Education	7.5	10.2
Health	2.3	2.0
Other (including Defence)	27.9	30.1
Total	**100.0**	**100.0**

Source: Oyejide, forthcoming, p. 30.

due to increased demand, thereby causing a consumption switch to cheaper imports (Forrest, 1993, pp. 184–6). Whatever the timing and influence of the oil boom on the agricultural sector, it is clear that the loss of agricultural productivity, particularly after the boom, was severe.

In addition to the inadequate capital expenditure in the agricultural sector, the Nigerian government did little to reverse the effects of an appreciating currency on a declining sector even on the micro-economic level. Arresting this decline may have been possible through measures such as price support, market protection, and perhaps even linking foreign investments in the oil industry to either specific or general agriculture projects. It has been pointed out that even within the sector, there were three main problems in Nigerian agricultural policy which could have been addressed more effectively. First, there was little encouragement to establish private price setting and marketing channels and mechanisms; secondly, there was an inadequate credit system financing farming and ancillary services; and finally, there was inadequate infrastructural support for machinery maintenance, repair and training. Furthermore, the continuing system of government-installed commodity/marketing boards ensured that exports were both taxed heavily, and significant amounts of producer export earnings were retained, ostensibly for development purposes. This system discriminated against the agricultural sector in general and small-holder production in particular (Pinto, 1987, p. 432; Bienen, 1988, pp. 231, 247). Adding to the existing problems in the sector was the fact that even the proposed allocations to agriculture were only seldom fully disbursed. There are records of instances where at the state level funds directed toward agriculture have been diverted away. And other factors reinforcing the neglect of the agricultural sector were the movement of labour away from the sector to construction and other urban services, and the spread of primary education which served to reduce the use of child labour on farms (Bienen, 1988, p. 253). Employment incentives, for instance, in the rural areas may also have slowed the decline in the agricultural sector.

The legacy of the oil boom years, therefore, can be described from several different perspectives. Nigeria, in 1980, was to a large extent and primarily a nation of consumers. The productive element in the economy had been over-shadowed by the massive increase in imported goods, both capital and consumer, the availability of cheap energy, and the tremendous increase in public services, in particular education and public utilities. The fast growing population, particularly urban, had acquired a taste for a high quality of life, and social well-being was emphasized at the expense of developing linkages between the oil sector and the rest of the economy.[5] Industrial development was dependent on imports and therefore on the continued strength in the oil market. While lip service continued to be paid to the importance of agriculture, the country could no longer feed itself and was dependent on food imports. Capital investments were largely geared toward largely show-piece construction projects such as the new federal capital at Abuja, or complex, capital-intensive projects such as those pertaining to the steel industry or to educational projects.[6] Other than the investment in the steel industry, there was little effort made to establish a solid development base, and no investment project had the potential to replace oil earnings should this need arise in the future.

The Introduction of the Structural Adjustment Programme (SAP)

The structural problems of the economy were masked by a decade of high oil revenues, high GNP per capita, substantial foreign exchange reserves and a national economy spending rapidly what it thought could be borrowed against future oil revenues. By 1980, therefore, the year that oil export revenues peaked at $24.9 billion, external indebtedness had increased to $9 billion, oil exports accounted for 27 per cent of GDP, about 80 per cent of government revenues and expenditures, and 96 per cent of total export receipts. The Nigerian economy with practically no diversification in its productive base and high dependency on oil revenues entered the decade of the 1980s ill-equipped to handle production and oil price shocks.

From a peak production rate of 2.3 mb/d in 1979, Nigerian crude oil production decreased to 1.24 mb/d in 1983 as a result of a combination of factors including the slump in world oil demand, the scaling back of oil company operations in the country. Crude oil export revenues fell from a peak of $24.9 billion in 1980 to $9.9 billion in 1983. These had recovered to about

$12.5 billion by 1985. However, the price shock of 1986 more than halved oil prices in the first quarter of the year and consequently oil revenues fell to their lowest point at $5.7 billion in 1986. Oil exports in 1986 were less than half the value of these in 1985, and about one-fifth the level of oil export receipts in 1980.

The decline in the Nigerian economy is perhaps most spectacularly apparent in the collapse of the country's GDP and GNP per capita (in current dollars), and in the significant devaluation of its currency (see Table 8.3). The price shock of 1986 and its immediate aftermath constituted the lowest point for the economy in the 1980s. By 1987, GDP (in current dollars) was less than one-third that in 1980 and GNP per capita was less than one-quarter the level in 1980.[7] By 1986, the respective shares of exports, imports and gross capital formation all halved relative to 1980 levels. And from a position of parity in the Naira/US$ exchange rate up to 1985, the currency had devalued to about N9.9 per US$ in 1991, N17.3 per US$ in 1992, and finally fixed at N22.0 per US$ at the end of 1993 by the new military government of General Abacha.

The severity of the economic crisis in the mid-1980s and the urgent need for change led to the introduction of the Structural Adjustment Programme (SAP) by the government. The austerity programme aimed to move towards a liberalized and market-determined exchange rate and thus devalue the national currency; remove domestic fuel subsidies; liberalize trade by terminating import licensing, disbanding commodity boards and removing price controls; prioritize investments in the agriculture sector so as to increase production of food, raw materials and exportable cash crops; reform public enterprises by privatizing and commercializing inefficient public sector enterprises; regulate fiscal policy so as to keep federal budget deficits to below 4 per cent of GDP by, for instance, restraining government budgetary allocations and reduce the size of the large public sector; and liberalize rules governing foreign participation and private investments in Nigerian industrial and manufacturing activity.

How favourable the impact of the SAP has been on the economy has remained unclear in the years since its introduction in 1986. In 1992, GDP in current dollar terms was not significantly different from its 1987 level, in fact slightly lower.[8] GNP per

Table 8.3: Historical Data on National Accounts. 1980, 1985–92. Current Billion Naira and/or Dollars and Per Cent.

	1980	1985	1986	1987	1988	1989	1990	1991	1992
Exports of Goods & Services									
In Naira	14.3	12.0	9.4	30.0	32.0	95.0	129.9	181.0	238.3
In Dollars	26.0	13.4	5.4	7.5	7.0	12.9	16.2	18.3	13.8
Share of GDP	28.8%	18.3%	12.9%	27.6%	22.0%	42.2%	49.8%	62.7%	52.3%
Government Consumption									
In Naira	5.1	5.7	7.5	7.4	9.3	10.1	11.5	12.7	20.1
In Dollars	9.2	6.3	4.3	1.8	2.0	1.4	1.4	1.3	1.2
Share of GDP	10.1%	8.6%	10.3%	6.8%	6.4%	4.5%	4.4%	4.4%	4.4%
Gross Capital Formation									
In Naira	10.8	6.3	7.7	9.6	9.4	18.4	31.1	36.6	66.7
In Dollars	19.7	7.0	4.4	2.4	2.1	2.5	3.9	3.7	3.9
Share of GDP	21.8%	9.6%	10.6%	8.8%	6.5%	8.2%	11.9%	12.7%	14.6%
Private consumption									
In Naira	31.7	49.7	56.2	78.3	113.1	138.8	146.4	128.2	294.5
In Dollars	57.6	55.6	32.0	19.5	24.9	18.9	18.2	12.9	17.0
Share of GDP	63.7%	75.9%	76.9%	71.9%	78.0%	61.8%	56.2%	44.4%	64.7%
Imports of Goods & Services									
In Naira	-11.6	-7.0	-7.8	-16.5	-18.4	-37.5	-58.3	-70.0	-164.2
In Dollars	-21.2	-7.9	-4.4	-4.1	-4.1	-5.1	-7.3	-7.1	-9.5
Share of GDP	-23.4%	-10.7%	-10.7%	-15.1%	-12.7%	-16.7%	-22.4%	-24.2%	-36.0%
GDP									
In Naira	49.8	65.5	73.1	108.9	145.2	224.8	260.6	288.6	455.5
In Dollars	91.1	73.4	41.6	27.1	32.0	30.5	32.4	29.1	26.3
GNP per Capita									
In Naira	618	685	700	959	1,262	1,973	2,198	2,359	n.a
In Dollars	1,131	767	399	239	278	268	273	238	n.a

Sources: IMF, *International Financial Statistics Yearbook*, 1992 and *International Financial Statistics*, July 1993 (See Period Averages of Official Exchange Rates in National Accounts).

Table 8.4: Nigerian Federal Budget. 1985–89. Per Cent.

	Share of GDP (per cent)				
	1985	*1986*	*1987*	*1988*	*1989*
Total Revenue	11.2	14.7	17.5	14.6	16.9
Total Expenditure	13.6	17.4	27.4	26.0	24.1
Overall Balance (Commitments)	-2.5	-2.7	-10.0	-11.4	-7.1
Adjustments		-0.4	0.7	3.7	0.6
External Borrowing (net)	-0.5	-0.4	5.5	0.9	3.6
Domestic Financing (net)	2.2	3.4	3.8	6.9	2.3

Source: IMF staff estimates from World Bank, *Trends in Developing Economies*, 1990, p. 403.

capita has also remained around $240. While investment as a share of GDP has increased over the years, the real increase seems to have occurred as a result of greater oil revenues during the 1990 Gulf crisis.

The extent to which public finance was tightened and regulated can be seen in Table 8.4 which presents a breakdown of the Nigerian federal budget over the period 1985–9. It is apparent that the gap between government revenues and expenditures grew even larger after 1986, and the federal budget deficits were not reduced to the 4 per cent of GDP level aimed for in the SAP.[9] The deficits were financed both by external borrowing and by adding to the domestic debt of the government.

The latter also involves the debts of the state government and parastatals and includes large arrears to contractors, suppliers and banks. About 15 per cent of the total external debt in the early 1980s was a result of state and local governments' borrowing abroad and domestically.

In fact, by 1982 when the external debt began to acquire 'crisis' proportions, state deficits were controlled by means of federal ceilings on the extent of foreign borrowing allowed to the states. As a result of these borrowing constraints, however, federal loans to the states increased. Since the federal government has no control over state expenditure, these loans were not used to rescue ongoing development projects but to maintain previous levels of current expenditure. In other words, the particular nature of the federal government and state relationship, in which the states enjoyed political autonomy from the federal government

yet relied on federal funding, had led to increasing fiscal irresponsibility as regards public expenditure at the state level (Forrest, 1993, p. 51; 1988, p. 108). No authority, therefore, existed to regulate either domestic indebtedness or Federal foreign borrowing. Both, in fact, continued to increase significantly even after the introduction of the SAP.

Any complete evaluation of the extent of success of the SAP must take into account the growth of the non-oil economy, since in the final analysis, this is what the programme had attempted to promote. As mentioned at the beginning of this chapter, the share of agriculture in GDP has actually declined since the SAP was implemented in 1986.[10] The share of services also declined, and while the share of industry increased, the share of manufacturing in GDP stayed at more or less the same level. Furthermore, non-oil exports remained insignificant as contributors of foreign exchange earnings. The increase in exports of goods and services in the past five years can be mainly attributed to the strengthening of world demand for oil, the 1990 Gulf crisis, and consequently increased oil exports. In fact the period during which the SAP has been implemented has seen an increase in the dependency of the economy on oil revenues both in terms of its share of GDP and as a source of foreign exchange and government revenues. Oil revenues and the developments in the oil market, which are largely outside the control of the Nigerian government, remain the main determinants of the country's external financial status, i.e. its balance of payments and its external debt status.

Nigerian External Accounts

Table 8.5 points to two important facts regarding Nigeria's external accounts. Firstly, the current account balance has closely followed the trade balance and therefore oil price and production developments over the years. Secondly, the capital account continues to be heavily burdened by the economy's debt servicing commitments and relative to the latter, foreign direct investment flows can only have a minimal impact on the capital account. As Table 8.6 shows, the debt burden had become unsupportable in 1986 when oil prices and revenues collapsed, and debt rescheduling and new capital inflows had to be re-negotiated to avoid Nigeria

Table 8.5: Historical Balance of Payments Data. Million Dollars. 1980,
1985–91.

	1980	1985	1986	1987	1988	1989	1990	1991
Current Account	4,269	2,566	366	-69	-194	1,090	4,988	1,203
Trade Balance	11,180	5,616	2,313	3,448	2,626	4,178	8,653	4,441
(% Share of GDP)	(12.3)	(7.7)	(5.6)	(12.7)	(8.2)	(13.7)	(26.7)	(15.1)
Capital Account	-4,429	-2,432	-205	375	409	-981	-5,224	-1,110
Direct Investment in Nigeria	-739	478	167	603	377	1,882	588	712
Repayments on Other Loans Received	-385	-2,642	-1,770	-3,759	-3,798	-3,439	-2,240	-3,331

Source: IMF, *Balance of Payments Statistics Yearbook*, 1992 and previous issues.

Table 8.6: Historical Series of External Debt Statistics. 1980, 1985–91.
Billion Dollars and Per Cent.

	1980	1985	1986	1987	1988	1989	1990	1991
Debt Stock (US $ Bn)	8.9	19.6	23.6	30.9	31.5	32.8	36.1	34.5
Debt/GNP Ratio (%)	9.0	22.2	51.7	133.9	113.2	119.1	117.9	108.8
Debt/Export Ratio (%)	32.2	144.6	373.2	395.2	431.8	381.7	242.7	257.1
Debt-Service/ Export Ratio (%)	4.2	33.3	32.7	13.4	29.4	23.2	20.3	25.2

Sources: World Bank, *World Debt Tables and World Development Report*, various issues;
EIU, Country Profile, *Nigeria, 1991–2*.

unilaterally defaulting.[11] By the early 1990s, largely as a result of
the increased oil revenues in 1990, the debt service/export ratio
had decreased from 33 per cent in 1986 to 25 per cent in 1991.
In late 1993, however, after the military takeover by General
Abacha and the announcement of a 'regressive' 1994 budget
which would fix the exchange rate and restrict the repatriation
of export proceeds, debt relief negotiations with the IMF appear
to be threatened. The current debt status of the country leaves it
with a $30 billion debt and arrears of up to $6 billion for debt re-
servicing commitments to the Paris Club of creditors.[12]

Over-spending, high levels of public consumption and the
willingness of the international financial community to lend to
'oil-exporters' in earlier years were the main determinants of the

increased indebtedness of the country in the early 1980s. However, even in these years production constraints and falling oil revenues were not offset by a commensurate drop in expenditure, and government borrowing, domestic and external, necessarily increased. The external debt more than doubled during the years 1980–85. It was clear therefore, that even after the introduction of the SAP in 1986, the debt stock would increase for lack of savings and continued borrowing. This increased by over 50 per cent to $35 billion in 1991.

External debt indicators provide one of the main vulnerability indicators for an economy. In recent years with the increase in exports, both debt/export and debt-service/export ratios have also improved – although they do not disguise the extent to which Nigeria's indebtedness constitutes a drag on the economy. Investment and capital inflows must increase significantly if there is to be any compensation for an annual debt-servicing outflow of about $3 billion. These capital inflows, in turn, depend on the continued buoyancy of the oil market, since much of the investment is made in the oil industry, the main productive sector of the economy. With the strength of the oil market determining the extent of investments and the national oil sector the obvious recipients of this investment, it is unlikely that the neglect and/or decline of the non-oil sector can be easily arrested or reversed.

Therefore, the reform programme launched in 1986 had left the economy, in 1993, with a $30 billion external debt, increasingly sceptical creditors, budget deficits in 1991 and 1992 at over 12.5 per cent of GDP, domestic inflation at 60 per cent, foreign exchange reserves at $1 billion, barely six weeks import cover, and an exchange rate collapsed to about Naira 18 per US dollar.

Policy Failure and the Lack of Public Accountability

While the size of the external debt has drained the economy of significant resources needed for the SAP, there are also institutional and political failures to blame for the present state of the economy. Institutional failures include the lack of accountability in public finance and therefore the lack of real control over government spending. Uneconomic military and industrial projects remain a possibility as long as there is no independent, unofficial regulator. In early 1993, there was some tension between the Nigerian transitional council government and the IMF and World Bank over the failure of the Nigerian government to remove the domestic subsidy on petroleum products and float the national currency. This affected Nigeria's chances of securing debt relief through the Enhanced Structural Adjustment Facility loan. Furthermore, there was little evidence that investment in and expenditure on unproductive investments was being controlled by the transitional council government, in place since January 1993. Oil revenues in the first quarter of 1993 were budgeted at Naira 45 billion. Revenues reported to the Fund and to the Bank totalled Naira 39 billion. The discrepancy is thought to be due to payment into 'dedication accounts' which finance large infrastructure projects and Nigeria's military involvement in Liberia. The Shonekan interim government, installed in August 1993, promised government accountability and an end to corruption. While there was some managerial reshuffling, ostensibly to remove corrupt officials, the lack of financial disclosure and transparency of government finances continued.[13]

The future does not look bright. According to the World Bank, without further rescheduling, the debt burden is likely to become unsustainable. Interest payments of $5 billion per annum in the period 1993–6 will be financed by 36 per cent of export revenues. The average debt-service/export ratio for all developing countries in 1992 was 19 per cent, and for severely indebted countries, this ratio was 30 per cent (Balls, 1993).

This debt burden in the context of little or no economic reform within the country had put at risk the attempted transition to democracy. A worsening economic situation for the population was certain to cause regional and religious tensions to come to the surface. Riots have, in the past few years, been the most frequent form of protest against fuel shortages, price increases, and so on. These forms of protest if they acquire regional, ethnic and/or religious overtones will not encourage any form of transition to a non-military government. Besides the internal Nigerian implications, of course, the international implications are also severe. The West's fears for political stability given the growing fundamentalism in North Africa can only be magnified, if Nigeria appears to follow the same route. And certainly, Nigeria's creditors will have much to lose if the government follows the path of economic populism. Babingida's statement that 'it is a rare feat for a country to make a successful transition to democracy with a declining economy' (Adams, 1993) has in fact become self-fulfilling. Nigeria may not be one of those few countries to be successful for quite a few years yet.[14]

To a large extent, a healthier international oil market, higher oil prices and therefore higher oil revenues cannot be the cure for Nigeria's economic woes. Without any real attempt to reform the public sector, the higher oil revenues will merely obscure the issues for a while longer. The analogy of the oil economy forming Nigeria's economic core, and of the country's agriculture, manufacturing and services sectors forming its struggling hinterland, is as true today as it has been since the 1970s (Balls, 1992). The non-oil economy is characterized by poor economic performance, increasing indebtedness, fiscal imbalances, and food crises and the difference between the oil and the non-oil economies has become even more apparent now after more than thirty years of oil production and a consistent failure on the part of the Nigerian government to provide the link between the core and the hinterland. After three decades of policy failure in the non-oil economy, there is the risk today that this basic paralysis in economic and political decision-making will finally extend to the oil industry. Signs of this deteriorating situation are already apparent in the countless delays in the removal of petroleum product subsidies, the implementation of the LNG project, as well as the government's inability to come up with its share of investment costs in production and exploration.

Two future developments which may have a significant impact on the recovery of the economy are the completion of the petrochemicals programme and the realization of the LNG project. These seem to be Nigeria's best remaining opportunity to both diversify government revenue and provide the much needed linkages to other potentially productive sectors of the economy. LNG sales will ensure that the little impetus that the non-oil economy does get from government spending is not completely dependent on the vagaries of the oil market; while petrochemicals will provide the possibility of linkages to the economy as a whole, and the manufacturing base, in particular.

Notes

1. The federal government receives about 60 per cent of total crude oil output from joint venture production (these form the majority of producing ventures in the country), and collects tax revenue from the 20 per cent royalty tax on other companies' shares of production, an 85 per cent Petroleum Profits Tax on company earnings as well as excise duties on refining activities. Revenues from oil, therefore, constitute a significant portion in the federal government budget. It is important to keep in mind, however, that as of 1979 this oil revenue must be allocated in the following manner:

Federal government	55.0%	(pre-1975: 80.0%)
State government	35.0%	
of which:		
direct to States	30.0%	
derivation	2.0%	
development of mineral		
producing areas	1.5%	
ecological problems	1.5%	
Local government	10.0%	

   The revenue distribution system does impact on the extent of the disposable oil income available to the government. This should be taken into account given that a large proportion of government expenditure is then allocated to debt repayments and imports of goods and services (Onoh, 1983, p. 122).

2. Windfall exports are estimated by comparing actual export values, observed in 1973 prices, to counter-factual export values, those that would have emerged in the absence of the export boom given specific growth rates. The difference between these two values is then discounted at a rate of 10 per cent to estimate *the present value* of the windfall. Similar calculations (based on actual and counter-factual values) are done on GDP, consumption, investment and savings to approximate the present value of the windfall income that accrued to the country during this boom period, and to estimate the allocation of this income to consumption and/or savings and investment. (Oyejide, forthcoming, pp. 13–17).

3. Expenditure increases in manufacturing arose mainly from the decision to construct a steel industry. Gelb states that public investments of this sort were 'large and complex and frequently ... highly capital-intensive'. Capital expenditure, therefore, which was mostly tied up in large, mainly show-piece projects such as these, did little to encourage more diversified growth in manufacturing (Gelb, 1986, p. 83).

4. Neary and van Wijnbergen (1986, p. 2) very clearly outline the bases of the Dutch Disease theory. The 'spending effect' which follows a resource, or in Nigeria's case an oil boom, operates in the following way:

   1) oil boom → higher domestic incomes → increased spending on both

tradables and non-tradables → prices of non-tradables increase as a result of excess domestic demand since these are determined domestically → less incentive for production of tradables with lower prices → movement of resources from tradables to non-tradable sector → tradable sector output declines, non-tradable sector output increases
2) oil boom → appreciation of real exchange rate consequent to the oil boom has increased domestic tradable prices relative to international → loss of competitiveness → increased imports

The decline of the tradables sector, in Nigeria's case primarily the agriculture sector, is what is essentially known as the Dutch Disease.

5. Whether capital investment in the oil industry and then growth in this industry could have had a direct return on employment levels in the country is suspect. Cochrane and Struthers in their article 'Nigerian Oil Policies: Some Internal Constraints', (1983) point to the possibility that the return on domestic investment can also be measured in terms of employment creation. Growth in the oil sector whether this is in the upstream or in refineries, petrochemicals or LNG, follows a typically 'enclave' pattern, using foreign capital, management and technology. Labour use is limited and fairly technical, and so growth in the sector has little impact on the level of employment. The oil economy, according to this article, not only inhibits the growth of the non-oil economy, 'it also fails to provide in itself the basis for long-term growth' (p. 316). Although the industry in itself may not have been capable of providing employment and employment growth, oil revenues could well have been directed toward other productive sectors, such as manufacturing and/or agriculture, where employment needs were more diversified.

6. Because Nigeria lacks high grade coal or iron ore, the steel industry at both Ajaokuta and Aladja rely on imported ore and technology. It has been estimated consequently that the 'unit cost of Nigerian steel was more than double the world price of steel because of the high import content' (*The Economist*, 'Nigeria' Survey, 21 August, 1993, p. 7; Forrest, 1993, p. 151).

7. In constant (1985) Naira terms, however, the GDP in 1987 was only 8 per cent lower than that in 1980.

3. Calculations of changes in GDP in constant 1985 Naira prices of course show a different picture. The average annual growth rate of constant GDP over the period 1986–92 was approximately 5.6 per cent per annum. Calculations of private and government consumption and of investment, if based on constant 1985 prices, would be similarly modified.

9. According to most recent reports, the Nigerian federal deficit worsened from 2.8 per cent of GDP in 1990 to 6 per cent in 1991 and finally accounted for about 9 per cent of GDP in 1992 (World Bank, *Trends in Developing Economies*, 1993, p. 367).

10. Bright E. Okugu in his paper 'Africa and Economic Structural Adjustment: Case Studies of Ghana, Nigeria and Zambia', points out that while the production of both staple food and cash crops increased over the period 1987–9, (average per annum growth rates averaged 6–7 per cent), the

share of the agriculture sector in GDP barely changed (pp. 33–4). Having said that, however, the effort of the Babingida administration to promote agriculture after 1986 cannot be minimized. Most cereal imports, for instance, were banned by 1989, while other agricultural imports faced tariffs of up to 30 per cent. Although most of these goods were in fact smuggled into the country, it is noteworthy that the government did not concede to the various interests in the country (the wheat lobby included the US government, the main supplier to the country) calling for an end to such protection (Egg, 1988, p. 190).

11. EIU, November 1990, p. 163.

12. *FT*, 11 January, 1994.

13. There is a view that since the impetus for cleaner and more competent government has yet to come from domestic sources, any change embarked upon as a result of external pressure (whether from the World Bank or other members of the international financial community), will be nothing more than window dressing, and each successive regime will retain state patronage to be able to cater to its own distributive priorities. In connection with the lack of success of the SAP, for instance, Forrest finds it noteworthy that this programme was introduced by a military regime under external pressure and not by 'a domestic class of capital that wished to set limits to the extent of state involvement in the economy and restrict corruption because it held them to be obstacles to corporate and national accumulation' (Forrest, 1993, p. 225).

14. Ironically, Babingida, himself, was seen by many as the main threat to the return of democracy. General Obasanjo, ex-chief of state and relinquisher of power to the Shagari civilian regime in 1979, had cast doubt in recent interviews with the press on the Babingida government's plans to allow a democratic government to take power in August (*FT*, 8/9 May, 1993, p. 3).

9 CONCLUSION

Nigeria is an important oil-exporting country, well endowed in terms of both its human and its energy resources. It boasts a well-developed oil industry with large capital investments and infrastructure in place, and can claim a significant presence of foreign participants and investors in the oil sector. Yet, despite all this, the basic economic and political theme in Nigeria has been one of resource mismanagement. The inefficiencies in the oil industry and the consequent losses to the state are necessarily more significant than those in other sectors given the dependence on oil revenues.

Nigeria has seen too many instances of functioning in a wrong policy framework. The prioritization of 'distributive' concerns for most Nigerian governments has resulted in parochial, regional and even tribal issues taking precedence over those of national economic welfare. Certainly, decisions taken in a framework where the main impetus is state patronage, are unlikely to be efficient or welfare enhancing for the state in the long run. Resource mismanagement, in Nigeria, therefore, is mainly attributable to the government – either as a result of the very structure of its institutions of governance and/or to the content and or implementation of its policies.

The 'losses to the system' mentioned earlier, which derive from this mismanagement have been assessed wherever possible. According to one study on Nigeria, economic losses accruing to the refining and distribution sectors added up to $440 million in 1990. These losses resulted mainly from the under-utilization of capacity, fuel losses in refining and product imports consequent to shortages in the system. Net financial losses which include the cost of smuggling, inappropriate pricing and losses in the distribution sector amounted to $2.8 billion in 1990. Of this total, the cost of smuggling was estimated at $200 million a year and that of inappropriate pricing about $1.9 billion.[1] While smuggling costs do not seem significant relative to those associated with pricing, smuggling has been estimated at between 20–25,000 b/d, or 10 per cent of used capacity. More importantly, the possibility of higher estimates has not been ruled out, given the

201

fact that smuggling via ships and tankers offshore appears to be increasing. In the downstream sector alone therefore, Nigeria's mismanagement amounts to economic and financial losses of about 30 per cent the value of its revenues in 1992. These are ample.[2]

The importance of the oil sector to the Nigerian economy has been discussed at length. In 1992, oil export earnings accounted for about 98 per cent of Nigeria's total export earnings, while oil receipts (export revenue and government take) accounted for 75 per cent of total government revenue. As dependency on the revenue from petroleum operations grows, so do the claims on federal expenditure. Of the approximately $8–9 billion in oil receipts to which the Nigerian government will have access in the next couple of years, $5 billion will be swallowed up by debt service repayments. The rest is unlikely to be adequate for government expenditure, the government's 60 per cent share in joint venture investments, and other long-term investments such as those in LNG, petrochemicals, and the expansion of the product distribution network. It is clear that the resource mismanagement in Nigeria over the past thirty years has left the economy in dire financial straits and has put at risk the very industry on which it depends.

In the upstream sector, the government intends to expand productive capacity to 2.5 mb/d and increase reserves to 20 billion barrels by 1998. This will entail significant levels of investment by the producing companies and therefore by NNPC. In order to come up with its share in this investment as well as other projects, the government has divested some of its share in both the LNG venture as well as specific joint ventures. Furthermore, the government has also embarked upon a new trend in production contracts, the PSCs, on the basis of which six new E&P contracts were signed in the summer of 1993. In production-sharing contracts, the state does not make any upfront capital investment and is therefore relieved of the financial burden inherent in joint-venture contracts. It remains true, however, that a large proportion of Nigerian production still issues from joint-venture concerns. Despite the divestment and the new tendency toward PSCs, the future for exploration and a consistent addition to reserves seems fraught with difficulties.

A further dilemma facing the Nigerian upstream sector is that given the precarious financial situation of the state, significant fiscal incentives will be required to maintain foreign interest in exploration and development. However, signing away substantial rights to foreign companies may also have severe political and economic implications for the future. The signing of the most recent PSCs is a case in point. In these contracts, tax and royalty have been reduced, investment credits improved, and the profit sharing mechanism made very favourable for the contracting company. Incentives as encouraging as these can be politically problematic in the future when the economic situation may not warrant such a signing away of reserves. Economically there are also problems. The trade-off between no capital investment requirements today and lower revenues in the future may not be as clear cut as it seems now. It is obvious that the future is to be in production sharing. The wealth of the deep water/frontier acreage, the extent to which Nigeria needs this oil today and will continue to do so for the foreseeable future, and the ample room for resource mismanagement, demands that careful attention (on the part of Nigerian policy-makers) is paid to this shift in structure of ownership in the Nigerian upstream.

There also appears to be some evidence of mismanagement of the contractual relations between the state and the oil companies, in the sense of the perennial problem of giving either too many incentives or not enough. While this problem arises from being both sovereign and dependent on the expertise of the oil companies, there have been instances in Nigeria's oil history where certain corporate decisions have in fact aggravated the problems of falling production and facilitated the displacement of this production by oil companies to the North Sea. Lifting restrictions imposed in the early 1980s are a case in point.

The issue of pricing is important to any crude oil exporting country, and even more so in the context of a slack market when the amount of crude oil sold is very sensitive to pricing. In Nigeria, there is a further complexity, linking the presence of equity partners (who are also the principal foreign investors) and crude oil lifting to crude pricing which is satisfactory to joint-venture partners. In other words, pricing of crude must be such that the appropriate volumes are shifted, the necessary lifting of equity crude and/or the buy-back of government crude (also known as notice oil) carried out. Any rigidity in this matter will not only have an impact on production levels but may have implications on long-term investment in the sector. Nigerian pricing policies in the early 1980s evidenced this dilemma in trying to find the policy beneficial to both the state (in terms of revenues, future investments, position in OPEC) and the oil companies (in terms of margins and markets). Production declined steeply, and oil companies faced with uncompetitive pricing of Nigerian crude (and untimely restrictions on equity lifting) displaced production to the North Sea.

In the downstream sector, the problems are in a sense more severe, because they have more immediate and direct implications on domestic demand. Consequently, the impact on political stability is also more significant. As in the upstream, the dire financial straits of the government merely aggravate the existing structural and institutional problems. Structural failures in the downstream include problems relating to capacity under-utilization, poor maintenance records of both the refineries and the distribution network. These emerge as part of vicious circles: refinery turnarounds being delayed until the last possible moment resulting in shut-downs for lengthier periods of time than would have been otherwise required; tending in turn to coincide with shutdowns in other refineries. Overstaffing of refineries at lower skill levels along with the lack of skilled labour for operations, maintenance and technical control only serve to worsen operational inefficiency in the refineries and ultimately aggravate the product supply problem. Other problems include the severe lack of capital replacement and high levels of cross-border smuggling. The latter two are largely a result of the massive subsidies on petroleum products. The implications of these subsidies on the Nigerian economy have been two-fold. They have not allowed real downstream costs to be adequately reflected and have thus created a system in which losses occur at every level and stage. Where the state is making such losses, it is unlikely that capital replacement and maintenance turn-arounds are of high priority. Subsidies, amounting to about $1.9 billion per year, have also encouraged widespread smuggling of petroleum product, aggravating in turn the product supply system, already constrained by frequent refinery and/or pipeline breakdowns. Institutional failures, as in other sectors of the Nigerian oil industry, are a result of a combination of corruption and ineffective management. It has been said that greater transparency in government and/or NNPC expenditure may in fact be the only change needed to make the removal of subsidies economically palatable and acceptable to the Nigerian people. Given such a situation, the latest downstream incentives in which the government offers full private ownership of *new* refineries (an offer largely geared toward current equity producers), may go largely unheeded for the time being. Until it becomes evident that real effective efforts are being made to improve the marketing and pricing of products in the Nigerian domestic market, foreign investors will steer clear (particularly since given the level of price increases introduced and the devaluation of the currency, the percentage changes in product prices in foreign exchange terms will continue to be negative).

The Nigerian gas industry has three main structural problems: inadequate physical infrastructure, pipelining and projects; a pricing structure which does not reflect the costs of establishing an efficient gas market; and problems in the organizational layout of the industry which results in delayed and at times incorrect payments to NGC or to the gas producers. The main issue to be addressed in this sector is the under-utilization of the resource which essentially stems from cost issues and the under-development of the domestic market. Nigerian gas reserves, which are ample, are divided equally between associated and non-associated reserves. However, the former accounts for about 85 per cent of gross production and more importantly less than 5 per cent of commercial gas use. In other words, more than 95 per cent of associated gas production is flared. In 1991, this amounted to a little less than the equivalent of 400,000 b/d of oil flared daily. The main reason for the greater waste of associated gas is the economies of scale benefiting non-associated gas production which have been estimated at about ten-fold (ESMAP, 1993, p. 45). To aggravate these basic cost differentials is the Nigerian domestic pricing of gas – which in any case does not reflect costs of production, whether of associated or non-associated gas.

In order to resolve the problem of under-utilization of natural gas, therefore, one must first look at the alternatives to gas flaring, i.e. uses for associated gas, and secondly, the issue of domestic under-pricing of gas. The latter, of course, involves institutional and management changes as well. The two alternatives to gas flaring are the development of a domestic gas market and the development of gas for export. While these have been considered at greater length in Chapter 6, it is important to repeat the idea that any expansion of domestic sector gas use lies mainly in the power generation sector and this is essentially a long-term solution. As far as exports are concerned, while associated gas pipelined to neighbouring countries and the export of LPG have viable potential, all such projects will have to somehow compensate for the inherent cost disadvantage linked to associated gas production. In a more competitive international environment, this may be difficult. On a connected note, where the pricing structure is such that even the costs of non-associated gas are not reflected, let alone cross subsidies possible, it is unlikely that there are any easy, relatively quick solutions to effectively increasing the utilization of Nigerian gas reserves.

From a resource-side perspective, the future of the oil industry does not seem bleak. The country has crude oil reserves, which may not be sufficient given the present state of the economy and the size and growth rate of the population, but which are not negligible and which will always be in demand given their quality. Furthermore, gas reserves are also important and there is good potential for developing them. However, obscuring the resource advantages of the country is the present economic situation. At this stage, therefore, forecasts cannot be optimistic, either for the economy as a whole or for the oil industry. The country, unlike other oil exporters, took no measures to counter the effects of fluctuations in oil export revenues by either investing abroad or setting up an oil stabilization fund. On the other hand, the Nigerian track record has shown that to a large extent, a healthier international oil market, higher oil prices and therefore higher oil revenues cannot be the cure for Nigeria's economic woes. Without any real attempt to reform the public sector, the higher oil revenues merely obscure the issues for a little while longer. The loss in terms of corruption aptly reflects the continuing lack of political and economic responsibility in the country. Capital flight is supposed to have first peaked in the period 1979–83 during the Shagari civilian regime (Forrest, 1993, p. 171). Estimated at $14 billion over the four years, this averaged out at about 3–5 per cent of GDP over this period. In 1992, the gap between official and estimated earnings was approximated at about $2.7 billion, or 10 per cent of GDP. The rhetoric against corruption, the structural problems in the economy, and the mismanagement of public funds appear to have increased at the same rate over the last decade; it seems unlikely that significant progress will be achieved this decade.

Notes

1. The annual subsidy based on a 3-product average calculated by *Petroleum Argus* (see Chapter 6) amounted to about $1.6 billion. The ESMAP estimates include subsidies on kerosene and LPG.
2. The ESMAP estimate of annual product subsidies is also based on a comparison of domestic prices with world parity prices. The former, however, includes subsidies on kerosene and LPG. It is important and interesting to note here that subsidies calculated on the basis of a cost-recovery scenario, amount to about $850 million per year according to this study. In other words the annual subsidy to the domestic market can be reduced by about half the present amount if costs are recovered (ESMAP, 1993, pp. xxi, 37, 40).

APPENDIX 1:
HISTORICAL CHRONOLOGY OF NIGERIA

1908	Unsuccessful exploration by the Nigerian Bitumen Corporation, a German company.
1914 31 December	Amalgamation of British colonial territories into the state of Nigeria Mineral Oils Ordinance (Colonial Mineral Ordinance)
1921	First oil exploration licences granted to D'Arcy Exploration Company and Whitehall Petroleum Company. These licences either lapsed or were relinquished by 1923.
1937	Shell–D'Arcy Exploration Parties established.
1938	Shell–D'Arcy granted an oil exploration licence covering all of Nigeria. Prospecting interrupted in 1941 due to Second World War. Activity resumed in 1946 under the new name of Shell–BP Development Company.
1951	First deep exploration well drilled (dry).
1953	First non-commercial oil find at Akata-1.
1955	Mobil obtains its first OEL in acreage relinquished by Shell–BP in northern Nigeria.
1956	First commercial oil find at Oloibiri.
1958	Beginning of oil production and exports.
1959	Petroleum Profits Tax Ordinance
1960 October	Nigerian Independence; member of Commonwealth; ruled by Governor-General and Prime Minister.
1961	Construction of crude oil port and tanker terminal at Bonny.
1961–2	Oil exploration licences granted to Gulf, Agip and Safrap.

1963 October	Nigeria becomes Republic (period of First Republic under Balewa); President replaced British Crown as symbol of national sovereignty and head of state.
1964	First offshore discovery at Okan made by Gulf (production began April 1965).
1965	Port Harcourt refinery completed; Trans-Niger pipeline completed allowing oil flow from mid-western fields to Bonny.
	Crisis throughout the year in the Western region issuing from 1963 census results and elections.
1966 January	Coup d'état, end of First Republic and Balewa regime, replaced by Ironsi regime.
May	Federal system abolished in favour of unitary state.
June	Second coup, Ironsi regime replaced by Gowon.
1967	Oso Condensate field discovered by Mobil;
	Amendment to 1959 PPT: retroactively valid from January 1966.
March	Ojukwu (governor of the Eastern region) promulgates Revenue Collection Edict No. 11 allowing Biafra to collect all revenues destined for the Federal government.
27 May	Gowon abolishes four-region system in favour of twelve states.
30 May	Eastern region secedes as Biafra, led by Ojukwu.
6 July	War declared by Federal government, beginning of civil war; severe curtailment of oil production particularly from Shell–BP and Safrap concessions; Port Harcourt damaged.
1968	OPEC Resolution No. XVI.90 calling for government acquisition of equity stakes in

respective oil industries.

October	Companies' Decree requiring incorporation of petroleum companies in Nigeria.
1969 27 November	Petroleum Decree No. 51 vesting all control and ownership of petroleum with state or its agencies.
1970 January	Surrender of Biafra, end of civil war; Port Harcourt repaired; Texaco/Amoseas produces from Pennington; production exceeds 1 mb/d.
1971 April	Nigerian government acquires 35 per cent participation in Safrap.
14 April	Creation of NNOC.
July	Membership of OPEC, as its eleventh member.
August	Nigerian government acquires 33.33 per cent participation in Agip/Phillips OMLs.
1972 February	Nigerian enterprises Promotion Decree (first indigenization decree).
May	Government participation in Port Harcourt increases from 50 per cent to 60 per cent.
1973 June	NNOC takes a 35 per cent equity stake in Shell–BP, Gulf and Mobil operations; first production-sharing contract signed between NNOC and Ashland;
October	OPEC raises oil prices fourfold; crude oil production exceeds 2 mb/d.
1974 April	Government participation increased to 55 per cent in Elf, Agip/Phillips, Shell–BP, Gulf and Mobil.
October	Gowon delays return to civilian rule.
1975 January	Nigerian government imposes some output restrictions on Shell–BP and Gulf.
July	Third coup d'état; Murtala Mohammad replaces Gowon.

1976 February	Fourth coup (failed); Mohammad assassinated, replaced by Obasanjo regime; official approval of Shell–BP's LNG and NGL scheme at Bonny.
April	Twelve states replaced by nineteen.
September	First Nigerian tanker 'Oloibiri', 270,000 dwt, launched.
1977 January	Second indigenization decree.
April	NNPC replaces and extends powers of NNOC.
July	'Buhari' incentives for exploration offered to oil companies.
1978 September	Warri refinery commissioned.
1979	Production peaks at 2.3 mb/d (annual average); Associated Gas Re-injection Act.
July	Elections to the Senate, House of Representatives, State Houses of Assembly, and state governors.
August	Nationalization of BP; production restrictions on other companies; government equity participation increased to 60 per cent; presidential elections.
September	New concessions offered on service contract terms: Elf signs.
October	Military withdraws: Shagari elected as President.
1980 January	Installation of Second Republic, civilian regime of Shagari.
June	Irikefe Commission's Report
October	Kaduna refinery commissioned.
December	Religious violence in Kano.
1981	Peak level of oil and condensate discoveries in one year; 1.3 billion barrels.
	Irikefe committee findings base equity

division of crude production on actual production rates rather than allowable production rates; company offtake, therefore, limited by government liftings/ sales.

July	Religious riots in Kano.
August	Nigeria cuts oil prices as sales fall.
September	Phillips Petroleum officially retreats from Bonny LNG project.
1982 February	Official liquidation of Bonny LNG project.
July	Government increases production cost allowance for oil companies from $1.10/b to $1.80/b while official profit margins on the company share of production are increased from $0.80/b to $1.60/b.
	Elf creates 'Elf Marketing Nigeria', a NNPC/Elf joint venture responsible for the distribution of petroleum products and lubricants in Nigeria.
December	Nigeria and Venezuela sign a crude exchange contract.
1983 February	Government raises production cost allowances and official profit margins again; both have been raised to $2.00/b.
August	Elections – Shagari re-elected.
December	NNPC chooses Shell as partner in new LNG project.
31 December	Military coup; end of second republic; Buhari takes over.
1984	Reversion to pre-1981 equity lifting rules; oil companies could sustain liftings even when NNPC was unable to.
	New LNG export project launched.
February	1979 legislation to curb associated gas flaring effective 1984 delayed even further to 1985.

October	Nigeria refuses to participate in production cuts agreed to by OPEC; price of Nigerian crude falls by $2.00/b.
November	Compromises found by government and oil companies on issues related to gas flaring legislation (field exemptions, fines, and so on).
1985	Associated Gas Re-Injection (Amendment) Decree.
March	Contract signed with Spie-Batignolles regarding construction of new 150,000 b/d refinery at Port Harcourt.
May	Official participation agreements signed between NNPC and main producing companies.
August	Military coup; Babingida overthrows Buhari.
September	Government confirms its intention of stopping counter-trade.
October	Nigeria concludes some crude oil sales agreements on a netback basis.
December	Failed coup attempt against Babingida; agreement between the state and oil companies regarding the profit margin on concession oil ($2.00/b) and that on NNPC share of equity oil ($1.00/b); further negotiations will be undertaken if the oil price stays below $23.00/b for more than 45 days.
1986	1986 Memorandum of Understanding
January	Babingida announces return to civilian rule by 1990 later changed to 1992.
June	Structural Adjustment Programme announced.
October	Construction begins on fourth refinery.
1987	Revised fiscal terms: protection of equity margins in times of falling prices.

September	Creation of two additional states, bringing federal total to twenty-one.
1988	OPEC legislation on gas condensate: defined as being outside quota restrictions.
1989 June	NNPC sells 20 per cent of its share (now 60 per cent) in the Shell venture to Shell (now 30 per cent) and to Elf (5 per cent) and Agip (5 per cent).
1990 June	NNPC and Mobil agree to develop the Oso Condensate field.
August	Iraq invades Kuwait; quotas abandoned; Nigeria quickly reaches productive capacity of 1.9 mb/d.
1991	Revised Memorandum of Understanding for 1990–95; changes backdated to 1990; changes in production costs and profit margins based on level of capital expenditure of oil company on development;
	Open Bidding Round for upstream acreage: attempt to diversify foreign participation and increase domestic private sector participation in oil industry.
1992	Reform in Federal structure increasing number of states from twenty-one to thirty.
June	Proposals to the government to reduce the royalty tax and the PPT to 50 per cent.
Summer	Election rigging; delay in transfer of power to civilian government till August 1993.
December	Oso Condensate field comes onstream. LNG project delayed further at least six months, probably one year.
1993 January	Formation of transitional council, headed by E.Shonekan, expected to manage the country, economically, for the seven months before the civilian government installed in August 1993.

April	New production-sharing agreements signed; much improved terms.
May	Share reshuffle in LNG project, with NNPC divesting further 11 per cent.
June	Annulled presidential elections.
July	Government expresses intention of reducing its participation in some joint ventures to 50 per cent, in order to raise its own investment capital.
August	Babingida steps down; replaced by interim government headed by Shonekan; unclear whether new elections to be held, or June results to be upheld.
September	Reports of NNPC stake in Shell venture to be reduced to 51 per cent, with Elf taking 5 per cent, and either Shell or some other company taking 4 per cent.
17 November	Military coup. Interim government replaced by General S. Abacha.
December	Reports of cuts of up to 40 per cent of 1993 spending to be enforced on 1994 joint venture budgets.

Sources:

Bienen, H, *Oil Revenues and Policy Choice in Nigeria* (1983), World Bank Staff Working Papers No. 592.

Nelson, H. D. (ed.) (1982), *Nigeria, A Country Study* (Area Handbook Series). Washington, D.C.: American University.

'Nigéria: Activités Pétrolières', Comité Profesionnel du Pétrole (CDDP), Supplement au bulletin analytique petrolière, 22 Decembre, 1986.

'Twenty-five Years of Nigerian Oil', *PE*, October, 1985, p. 357.

Wright, Stephen (1986), *Nigeria: The Dilemmas Ahead: A Political Risk Analysis*, Special Report No. 1072, EIU, November, 1986.

Barrows, *Basic Oil Laws & Concession Contracts South and Central Africa*, various issues.

Platts Oilgram News, PIW, Argus, Energy Compass, Oil and Gas Journal, various issues.

APPENDIX 2
NIGERIAN OILFIELDS

Name of Field, Discovery Date	Number of Wells Producing	Total	Production 1990 Avg.b/d	Cumulative to 31 December 1990. Bbls.	°API Gravity
AGIP					
*Abgara, 1981	16	16	25,774	13,547,028	36.2
Agwe, 1975	1	2	408	2,307,927	44.0
Akri, 1967	6	11	8,814	64,407,651	40.8
Akri W., 1972		2		482,258	
Ashaka, 1968	1	1	1,011	3,344,898	37.4
Azuzuama, 1975	2	2	1,268	463,258	34.1
*Beniboye, 1978	9	9	6,433	16,668,435	28.6
Beniku, 1974	1	2	129	3,407,816	14.8
Clough Creek, 1976	9	9	9,318	28,799,764	25.5
Ebegoro, 1975	6	9	6,197	66,771,341	37.1
Ebocha, 1965	10	18	8,838	116,662,592	36.3
Idu, 1973		10		23,862,581	
Kwale, 1967	6	8	8,370	13,274,523	37.1
Mbede, 1966	10	16	12,589	172,997,990	43.1
Obama, 1973	6	8	14,877	108,476,448	30.7
Obiafu, 1967	16	20	19,249	98,996,243	41.6
Obrikom, 1967	8	14	6,981	59,765,580	43.4
Odugri, 1972	1	2	1,710	10,946,737	45.9
Ogbogene, 1972		2		3,302,763	
Ogbogene W., 1982		1		353,136	
Okpai, 1968	6	8	4,597	22,272,119	42.8
Omoku, W., 1974	1	1	945	5,227,184	40.0
Oshi, 1972	10	11	13,137	75,660,065	35.2
Taylor Creek, 1985	1	1	3,197	1,692,976	37.3
Tebidaba, 1972	7	10	15,901	130,095,927	30.4
Umuora, 1977	2	4	2,356	7,053,937	40.3
Total	135	197	172,099	1,050,841,177	
ELF					
Aghigo, 1972	18	21	6,674	25,900,000	24.8
Erema, 1972	3	5	6,240	13,200,000	24.6
Obagi, 1964	55	74	55,384	386,600,000	24.6
Obodo-Jatumi, 1966	16	17	16,471	75,000,000	24.8
Okpoko, 1967	16	17	6,750	34,600,000	24.8
Upomami, 1965	11	14	4,604	18,400,000	24.8
Total	119	148	96,123	553,700,000	
GULF NIGERIA					
Abiteye, 1970	12	19	6,788	68,620,694	39.7
*Delta, 1965	22	27	18,348	183,849,519	37.3

Name of Field, Discovery Date	Number of Wells		Production		°API Gravity
	Producing	Total	1990 Avg.b/d	Cumulative to 31 December 1990. Bbls.	
GULF NIGERIA					
*Delta S., 1965	20	33	33,748	294,165,950	38.4
*Isan, 1970	6	11	1,946	44,227,300	40.4
Jisike, 1975	3	5	1,041	7,268,105	41.1
Makaraba, 1973	23	26	24,294	109,307,897	27.7
*Malu, 1969	13	18	15,595	114,239,427	40.4
*Mefa, 1965	4	5	6,891	26,261,992	38.1
*Meji, 1965	20	22	18,317	164,923,785	31.9
*Meren, 1965	37	58	58,427	536,009,957	31.9
*Mina, 1965	3	3	4,730	3,975,460	40.3
*Okan, 1964	55	70	42,108	471,062,427	38.1
*Parabe/Eko, 1968	17	28	10,115	110,709,677	40.4
Robertkiri, 1964	11	13	20,878	27,301,921	40.2
*Tapa, 1978	8	10	9,840	34,846,887	39.5
Utonana, 1971	3	5	629	8,599,272	20.4
*W.Isan, 1971	5	9	2,389	36,136,036	40.4
Yorla S., 1974		2		822,618	41.0
Total	262	364	276,084	2,242,328,924	
TEXACO-CHEVRON-NNPC					
*Funiwa, 1978	20	25	19,386	57,447,072	35.5
*Middleton, 1972	3	7	2,137	17,407,040	36.3
*North Apoi, 1973	25	28	34,706	189,057,507	35.5
*Pennington, 1965	2	9	2,348	28,733,949	38.5
*Sengana, 1987		2		666,102	46.7
Total	50	71	58,577	293,311,670	
MOBIL					
*Adua, 1967	7	11	10,664	55,007,899	34.8
*Asabo, 1966	9	27	16,492	173,832,194	34.6
*Asabo D, 1979	1	2	1,199	3,186,472	34.6
*Ata, 1964		5		433	
*Edop, 1988	1	9	38,905	33,368,719	37.4
*Ekpe, 1966	10	22	14,222	198,798,729	34.9
*Ekpe-WW, 1977	2	6	6,036	40,310,161	31.9
*Eku, 1966	3	14	2,487	18,375,442	30.4
*Enang, 1968	18	38	17,261	144,339,212	37.4
*Etim, 1968	7	16	17,972	125,688,898	37.1
*Idoho, 1966	3	7	826	29,559,880	30.5
*Inim, 1966	7	14	13,432	154,868,705	37.5
*Isobo, 1968	3	7	14,841	14,358,750	30.4
*Iyak, SE., 1979	6	7	18,077	54,999,641	38.6
*Mfem, 1968	2	5	4,876	26,886,881	36.1
*Ubit, 1968	30	55	39,586	210,098,065	36.1
*Unam, 1967	7	15	10,762	52,159,220	33.3

Name of Field, Discovery Date	Number of Wells Producing	Total	Production 1990 Avg.b/d	Cumulative to 31 December 1990. Bbls.	°API Gravity
MOBIL					
*Usari, 1965		4		6,885	
*Utue, 1966	5	14	10,901	77,619,051	38.6
Total	121	278	238,539	1,413,465,237	
PANOCEAN					
Ogharefe, 1973	7	18	1,158	29,669,008	46.6
DUBRIL					
Gilli-Gilli, 1967	3	7	906	1,137,667	47.1
ASHLAND					
*Adanga, 1980	7	19	11,376	24,560,874	32.1
*Akam, 1980	5	13	5,735	21,644,440	35.6
*Bogi, 1989	2	4	2.002	1,294,064	23.2
*Ebughu, 1984	3	4	906	911,781	28.0
*Izombe, 1974	8	32	10,196	57,595,735	37.8
*Mimbo, 1984	2	5	5,586	2,593,080	30.7
Ossu, 1974	7	9	843	5,570,639	40.7
*Ukpam, 1989	1	2	1,695	1,564,018	40.6
Total	35	123	38,339	115,734,631	
TENNECO					
Abura, 1979	2	5	1,875	17,932,465	44.7
SHELL					
Adibawa, 1966		27	12,052	86,987,584	26.4
Adibawa NE, 1972	3	4	3,968	18,574,667	25.3
Afam, 1956	8	22	2,287	61,356,325	45.6
Afam Umu, 1957		4		2,378,685	
Afisere, 1966	29	35	11,844	125,204,182	19.6
Afremo, 1972	10	15	15,908	18,077,037	36.8
Agbada, 1960	29	53	19,694	196,223,121	23.9
Ahia, 1965	5	13	4,099	88,370,285	38.2
Ajokpuri, 1967	1	5	527	5,848,952	39.3
Ajuju, 1970	1	5	971	10,304,503	34.7
Akaso, 1979	2	3	1,432	4,293,092	37.1
Akpor, 1965		3		1,833,108	
Akuba, 1967	1	1	254	4,486,154	22.7
Alakiri, 1959	12	26	7,430	70,945,576	44.5
Amukpe, 1970	2	3	1,198	13,591,666	41.7
Apara, 1960	3	10	3,799	29,300,026	38.4
Assa, 1961	2	4	1,060	5,949,721	20.6
Bodo East, 1962	9	12	4,216	83,991,568	27.1
Batan, 1968	9	10	7,777	60,320,288	21.7

Name of Field, Discovery Date	Number of Wells Producing	Total	Production 1990 Avg.b/d	Cumulative to 31 December 1990. Bbls.	°API Gravity
SHELL					
Benisede, 1973	15	22	34,325	127,045,999	21.9
Bomu, 1958	6	49	6,146	359,457,322	37.3
Bonny, 1959	7	23	4,303	93,146,273	32.6
Buguma Crk, 1960	4	10	2,184	14,109,744	37.6
Cawthorne Ch, 1963	21	40	47,581	314,445,240	36.9
Diebu Creek, 1966	7	15	9,753	112,470,475	40.3
Ebubu, 1958	3	10	206	18,883,643	21.2
Egwa, 1967	18	29	16,944	146,784,895	34.1
Egbema, 1960	6	8	3,120	56,520,126	33.1
Egbema W., 1965	6	19	5,146	83,710,410	41.2
Ekulama, 1958	21	33	44,882	231,433,712	31.6
Elelenwa, 1960	6	18	3,716	35,119,812	35.8
Enwhe, 1965		6		2,611,679	
Etelebou, 1971	8	11	14,529	132,206,501	31.3
Eriemu, 1961	13	18	5,372	47,657,877	20.6
Escravos B., 1969	9	14	12,344	66,420,461	31.2
Evrweni, 1967	7	11	4,018	39,342,474	25.6
Forcados Y., 1968	56	124	53,562	590,642,984	24.4
Ibigwe, 1965	3		437,017		
Imo River, 1959	37	57	47,017	498,674,807	30.3
Isimiri, 1964	1	8	391	38,370,370	29.3
Isoku, 1960	4	6	2,368	7,099,065	29.8
Jones Creek, 1967	29	38	37,541	423,977,565	29.7
Kalaekule, 1972	5	12	13,325	13,796,014	40.5
Kolo Creek, 1971	17	38	20,691	144,265,152	39.1
Kokori, 1961	25	32	19,387	322,186,233	39.9
Korokoro, 1959	6	9	3,391	85,541,415	35.8
Krakama, 1958	3	13	1,982	18,773,262	22.9
Nembe Creek, 1973	39	49	96,778	285,191,169	31.0
Nkali, 1963	4	12	3,610	31,860,205	39.2
Nun River, 1960	4	12	2,244	33,569,371	32.7
Oben, 1972	17	28	16,533	134,469,258	37.6
Obeakpu, 1975	2	5	2,983	19,318,618	26.3
Obele, 1964		5		4,721,597	
Obigbo				396,727	
Obigbo N., 1963	28	47	12,142	183,246,416	23.16
Odeama Crk, 1981	5	6	21,632	35,066,963	35.5
Odidi, 1967	34	44	46,405	239,265,369	36.2
Ogini, 1964	8	25	3,977	24,841,774	18.2
Oguta, 1965	13	28	10,622	136,391,060	43.2
Olomoro, 1963	20	33	16,609	292,362,402	21.5
Onne, 1965	3	3	928	10,146,086	35.3
Opuama, 1972	2	7	2,498	27,407,327	43.7
Opobo S., 1974	3	10	4,092	21,762,134	43.7

Name of Field, Discovery Date	Number of Wells Producing	Total	Production 1990 Avg.b/d	Cumulative to 31 December 1990. Bbls.	°API Gravity
SHELL					
Opokushi, 1962	12	18	25,222	133,578,606	28.3
Opokushi N., 1977	1	4	89	2,823,783	35.6
Oloibiri, 1956		18		20,061,673	
Oroni, 1964	6	8	2,495	27,623,535	22.6
Orubiri, 1971	1	11	3,586	19,429,768	38.2
Osioka, 1967	2	4	869	7,820,325	26.2
Otamini, 1973	3	6	1,246	15,021,319	21.0
Otumara, 1969	26	32	46,204	188,341,053	24.9
Oweh, 1964	9	11	5,944	98,666,011	25.8
Oza	9		5,944	1,006,373	25.8
Rapele, 1965	1	6	484	23,188,706	44.0
Ramuekpe, 1961	2	4	1,978	2,551,316	29.3
Saghara, 1970	5	8	7,152	37,421,364	31.8
Sapele, 1969	6	23	10,725	122,119,031	42.9
Soku, 1958	16	25	9,563	118,849,660	27.7
Tai, 1965	2	3	799	5,179,269	38.3
Ubie, 1961	5	10	5,078	34,889,280	27.6
Ughada, 1966	1	2	80	1,094,622	37.7
Ughelli East, 1959	8	14	2,803	91,534,764	38.9
Ughelli West, 1960	9	14	7,260	37,854,301	20.5
Umuchem, 1959	8	23	4,510	151,464,846	37.2
Utapate S., 1974	8	12	9,005	42,591,450	38.5
Utorogu, 1964	17	30	8,454	136,284,367	26.8
Uzere East, 1960	10	15	6,119	92,598,622	28.6
Uzere West, 1963	11	11	5,803	103,685,793	25.4
Warri River, 1961	2	5	1,234	15,816,865	29.8
Yorla, 1960	10	16	6,629	64,229,584	39.2
Yorla South, 1979		2		822,674	39.2
Total	832	1577	1,364,141	7,989,295,496	
Total Nigeria	1,574	2,754	1,810,913	13,708,230,639	

Source and Notes: *O&GJ Special*, 31 December, 1991, p. 294.
* Offshore fields; Company Totals may not add up to Nigeria Total due to missing data.

APPENDIX 3

Appendix 3: Production and Consumption of Refined Products in Nigeria, By Type of Product. In Thousand Barrels/Day. 1971–1991.

	Total Refined Products '000 b/d		Gasoline '000 b/d		Kerosene '000 b/d		Distillate Fuels '000 b/d		Residual Fuels '000 b/d		Other Products '000 b/d	
	Prod.	Cons.	Prod.	Cons.	Prod.	Cons.	Prod.	Cons.	Prod.	Cons.	Prod.	Cons.
1971	40.8	34.3	10.3	12.1	5.8	6.1	11.9	8.7	12.8	5.0	0.0	2.4
1972	43.6	39.8	12.0	14.1	6.5	7.1	11.2	10.0	13.6	5.3	0.3	3.3
1973	56.7	48.9	16.7	16.7	8.9	7.8	13.1	12.1	16.8	7.4	1.2	4.9
1974	53.8	54.4	14.5	20.6	8.0	8.7	13.1	13.0	17.8	7.7	0.4	4.4
1975	46.7	68.1	12.5	27.5	6.9	13.1	11.3	14.8	15.7	8.1	0.3	4.6
1976	55.5	110.2	14.4	47.4	8.2	18.4	14.1	24.2	18.2	14.0	0.6	6.2
1977	48.2	111.9	16.9	43.5	6.6	17.2	13.4	28.6	10.1	9.7	1.2	12.9
1978	60.2	134.0	21.1	48.0	8.3	18.1	16.7	31.9	12.6	11.8	1.5	24.2
1979	89.0	154.3	23.0	56.9	13.0	21.5	24.0	33.6	28.0	12.0	1.0	30.3
1980	90.5	171.0	23.4	69.8	13.2	34.2	24.4	40.7	28.5	14.7	1.0	11.6
1981	151.9	235.8	50.0	96.2	22.2	47.2	45.4	56.1	32.2	20.3	2.1	16.0
1982	162.1	236.3	56.9	104.7	22.2	34.5	49.3	58.5	29.9	26.2	3.8	12.4
1983	151.2	225.9	49.6	95.4	22.8	38.0	42.6	59.3	32.3	25.3	3.9	7.9
1984	160.2	203.3	54.2	93.2	25.8	40.9	44.9	46.4	30.0	15.8	5.3	7.0
1985	135.2	214.0	41.7	96.9	21.6	37.5	33.5	38.9	33.6	24.8	4.8	15.9
1986	136.0	196.3	43.5	85.1	23.6	41.1	33.0	36.5	33.0	27.1	2.9	6.5
1987	135.2	218.6	35.6	90.6	22.0	46.1	31.2	37.6	33.8	30.2	12.6	14.2
1988	154.8	231.8	46.0	106.1	26.5	46.9	36.0	40.9	37.9	28.8	8.4	9.0

Appendix 3: Continued.

	Total Refined Products '000 b/d		Gasoline '000 b/d		Kerosene '000 b/d		Distillate Fuels '000 b/d		Residual Fuels '000 b/d		Other Products '000 b/d	
	Prod.	Cons.	Prod.	Cons.	Prod.	Cons.	Prod.	Cons.	Prod.	Cons.	Prod.	Cons.
1989	214.2	247.9	69.1	113.4	32.7	50.1	47.4	43.8	41.7	30.8	23.3	9.7
1990	270.3	254.9	87.2	116.6	41.3	51.5	59.8	45.0	52.6	31.7	29.4	9.9
1991	242.8	234.7	83.7	110.9	40.4	47.5	60.0	50.2	49.4	14.5	9.3	11.5
1992	245.7	241.7	n.a	114.2	n.a	48.9	n.a	51.7	n.a	14.9	n.a	11.8

Average per Annum Growth Rates of Production and Consumption of Refined Products, by Type. Percentage.

	Total Refined Products		Gasoline		Kerosene		Distillate Fuels		Residual Fuels	
	Prod.	Cons.	Prod.	Cons.	Prod.	Cons.	Prod.	Cons.	Prod.	Cons.
1971–1991	9.3	10.1	11.0	11.7	10.2	10.8	8.4	9.2	7.0	5.5
1971–1981	14.1	21.3	17.1	23.0	14.4	22.7	14.3	20.5	9.7	15.0
1981–1991	4.8	-0.1	5.3	1.4	6.2	0.1	2.8	-1.1	4.4	-3.3
1987–1991	15.8	1.8	23.8	5.2	16.4	0.8	17.8	7.5	10.0	-16.8

Source: *OPEC Annual Statistical Bulletin*, various issues.
Note: Data for 1992 is incomplete and therefore not used in compiling growth rates.

BIBLIOGRAPHY

Abba A. et al. (1985), *The Nigerian Economic Crisis: Causes and Solutions*, Zaria: Academic Staff Union of Universities of Nigeria.

Abdelkader, S.A. (1990), *Development and Resource-Based Industry: The Case of Petroleum Economies*, Pamphlet Series 28, Vienna: OPEC Fund for International Development,

Abdulai, Y.S. (1990), *Africa's External Debt: An Obstacle to Economic Recovery*, Pamphlet Series 27, Vienna: OPEC Fund for International Development.

Aboyade, O. (1991), *Selective Closure in African Economic Relations*, Lecture Series No. 69, Lagos: Nigerian Institute for International Affairs.

Adams, P., (1993) 'A Critical Naira adds to Lagos Transition Woes', *FT*, 19 March.

Afolabi, J.A. and Bladen-Hovell, R. (1988), *The Effect of a Fall in the Price of Oil on an Oil-Exporting Country: The Case of Nigeria*, Discussion Paper No. 52, Department of Economics, University of Manchester.

Alazard, N. (1990), *Aspects stratégiques du pétrole marin: L'offshore africain*, Paris: Institut Français du Pétrole.

Alkasum, Abba et al. (1985), *The Nigerian Economic Crisis: Causes and Solutions*, Zaria, Academic Staff Union of Universities of Nigeria.

Amu, L.A.O. (1982), *Oil Glut and the Nigerian Economy*, NNPC.

Ayoade, J.A.A. (1988) *Federalism in Nigeria: The Problem with the Solution*, Ibadan: Faculty of the Social Sciences, University of Ibadan.

Ayodele, S.A. (ed.) (1987), *Energy Development and Utilization in Nigeria*, Ibadan: Nigerian Institute of Social and Economic Research.

Bach, D.C., J. Egg, and J. Philippe (eds) (1988), *Nigéria, un pouvoir en puissance*, Paris: Editions Karthala.

Balls, E., (1992), 'Ambitious Program of Investment', *FT*, 16 March.

—— (1993) 'Nigeria may need Debt Relief to Secure Democracy', *FT*, 1 March.

Bienen, H. (1983), 'Oil Revenues and Policy Choice in Nigeria', *World Bank Staff Working Papers, No. 52*, Washington: The World Bank, 1983.

—— (1988) 'Nigeria: From Windfall Gains to Welfare Losses?' in Gelb et al, *Oil Windfalls: Blessing or Curse*, For the World Bank, Oxford: Oxford University Press.

Biersteker, T. J. (1987), *Multinationals, the State, and Control of the Nigerian Economy*, Princeton: Princeton University Press.

—— (1989), *Reaching Agreement with the IMF: The Nigerian Negotiations, April 1983–November 1986*, Los Angeles: School of International Relations, University of South California.

British Petroleum Company (1977), *Our Industry: Petroleum*, British Petroleum.

Brown, G. (ed.) (1990), *OPEC and the World Energy Market*, Essex: Longman.

Chukwu, P.O. and Ikoku, C.U. (1991), *A Comparative Evaluation of Evolving Nigerian Petroleum Development Policies*, SPE 22029, Society of Petroleum Engineers.

Cochrane, S. and J. Struthers (1983), 'Nigerian Oil Policies: Some Internal

Constraints,' *The Journal of Energy and Development*, vol.VIII, no. 2.
Compilation of Papers Presented at the Public Relations Seminar Organised by the Public Affairs Department, Lagos: 5–7 February, 1987, NNPC.

Desai, A. (ed.) (1990), *Energy in Africa*, Canada and Japan: International Development Research Center and United Nations University.

Economist Intelligence Unit (EIU) (1986), *Nigeria: The Dilemmas Ahead. A Political Risk Analyis*, Special Report No. 1072 (by Stephen Wright).

—— (1989), *Nigeria to 1993: Will Liberalisation Work?* Special Report No. 1134 (by Richard Synge).

—— (1990), Regional Reference Series, *West Africa: Economic Structure and Analysis.*

—— Country Profile, *Nigeria 1991-92.*

Egg, J. (1988), 'L'Agriculture nigériane dans le marché mondial' in Bach, Egg and Philippe, (eds.), *Nigéria: un pouvoir en puissance*, Paris: Editions Karthala.

Ejedawe, J.E., V.O. Abiola and A.S Young. 'Exploration Maturity and Reserves Discovery Relations in the Niger Delta,' *Energy Exploration & Exploitation*, vol. 2, no.1.

Eleazu, U. (ed.), *Nigeria, The First 25 Years*. Lagos: Infodata Limited.

Energy Sector Management Assistance Programme (ESMAP) with the World Bank (1993), *Nigeria: Issues and Options in the Energy Sector*, Report No.11672-UNI.

Facts about NNPC 1977-82 (1982), NNPC.

Focus on Pipelines and Products Marketing Division, NNPC, 1985.

Forrest, T. (1988), 'L'Economie politique du régime civil et la nigériène' in Bach et al (eds), *Nigéria – un pouvoir en puissance*, Paris: Editions Karthala.

—— (1993), Politics and Economic Development in Nigeria, Oxford: Westview Press.

Gelb, A. (1986), 'Adjustment to Windfall Gains: A Comparative Analysis of Oil-Exporting Countries' in J. P. Neary and S. van Wijnbergen (eds), *Natural Resources and the Macroeconomy*, Oxford: Basil Blackwell.

Gregoire, L. (1988), 'Structure du commerce extérieur' in Bach et al, (eds), *Nigéria, un pouvoir en puissance*, Paris: Editions Karthala.

Hartshorn, J.E. (1978), *Objectives of the Petroleum Exporting Countries*, Nicosia: Middle East Petroleum and Economic Publications.

Horsnell, P. and Mabro, R. (1993), *Oil Markets and Prices: The Brent Market and the Formation of World Oil Prices*, Oxford: Oxford University Press.

Ihonvbere, J. and T. M. Shaw (1988), *Towards a Political Economy of Nigeria*, Vermont: Gower Publishing Company.

Ikeh, G. (1991), *The Nigerian Oil Industry*, Lagos: Starledger Communications Limited.

Ikein, A. A. (1990), *The Impact of Oil on a Developing Country: The Case of Nigeria*, New York: Praeger Publishers.

International Maritime Bureau (1989), *Nigerian Oil Frauds*, Special Report.

Iwayemi, A. (1984), 'Nigeria's Internal Petroleum Problems: Perspectives and Choices,' *The Energy Journal*, vol.5, no. 4.

—— (1988), 'Le Nigéria dans le système pétrolier international' in Bach et al (eds), *Nigéria – un pouvoir en puissance*, Paris: Editions Karthala.

—— (1993), 'Energy Development and Sub-Saharan African Economies in a Global Perspective', *OPEC Review*. vol. XVII, no.1.

Jimoh, I.O. (1987), *Exploration Development in Nigeria*, Lagos: NNPC.

Mabro, R. (1986), 'OPEC's Future Pricing Role May be at Stake' in R. Mabro (ed.), *OPEC and the World Oil Market: The Genesis of the 1986 Price Crisis*, Oxford: Oxford Institute for Energy Studies.

—— (1989), *OPEC's Production Policies*, Oxford: Oxford Institute for Energy Studies,

Marinho, F.R.A. (1984), *Oil Politics and National Development*, Kuru-Jos: NNPC.

—— (1985), *Nigeria: A Regenerative Economy or Vegetative Existence?*, NNPC.

Neary, J.P. and S. van Wijnbergen (eds) (1986), *Natural Resources and the Macroeconomy*. Oxford: Basil Blackwell Ltd.

Nelson, H. D. (ed.) (1982), *Nigeria, a Country Study*, (Area Handbook Series), Washington, D.C.: American University

Nnaji, G. I. (1987), 'Oil in the Economic Development of Nigeria (Optimum Utilisation of Oil Revenues in Economic Growth),' Unpublished Ph.D Dissertation, New York University.

Nzelo, P.C.O. (1987), *Future Impact of Petrochemicals in National Economic Development*, Lagos: NNPC.

Obadan, M. (1992), 'Counter Trade Revisited: The Nigerian Experience', *OPEC Review*.

Ofoh, E.P. (1992), *Trends in Production Sharing Contracts in Nigeria*, Society of Petroleum Engineers Paper No. 24242.

Okeke, O. (1992), *Hausa-Fulani Hegemony: The Dominance of the Muslim North in Contemporary Nigerian Politics*, Enugu: Acena Publishers.

Okogu, B. E. (1991), 'The Oil Sector and the Future of the Nigerian Currency: Perspective Planning Against Instability', *OPEC Review*.

—— (1992), *Africa and Economic Structural Adjustment: Case Studies of Ghana, Nigeria and Zambia*, Pamphlet Series 29, Vienna: OPEC Fund for International Development.

Ola, A. (1987), *Role of Refineries in Nigeria: Today and Tomorrow*, Lagos: NNPC.

Olaniyan, R. O. and Nwoke, C.N. (eds) (1990), *Structural Adjustment in Nigeria: The Impact of the SFEM on the Economy*, Lagos: Nigerian Institute of International Affairs.

Olayiwola, P. O. (1987), *Petroleum and Structural Change in a Developing Country: The Case of Nigeria*, New York: Praeger Publishers.

Olorunfemi, M.A. (1985), *Management of the Petroleum Resources in the 5th National Plan 1986–1990*, NNPC.

Onoh, J. K. (1993), *The Nigerian Oil Economy*, Australia: Croom Helm.

Oremade, T. (1986), *Petroleum Operations in Nigeria*, Lagos: West African Book Publishers.

Orife, J. (1987), *Role of Joint Ventures as the Coordinator of Oil Industry Activity*, NNPC.

Oyedije, T.A. (forthcoming),, 'Trade Shock, Oil Boom and the Nigerian Economy 1973–83,' *The Journal of African Economies*.

Pearson, S. R. (1970), *Petroleum and the Nigerian Economy*, Stanford: Stanford University Press.

Petroleum Exploration and Development in Nigeria, NNPC, n.d.

Pinto, B. (1987), 'Nigeria During and After the Oil Boom: A Policy Comparison with Indonesia,' *The World Bank Economic Review*, vol. I, no. 3.

Quinlan, M., (1985), 'Tough Policy Boosts Revenues', *Petroleum Economist*, March, p. 81.

Sanusi, H. U. (ed.) (1992), *Public Policy Coordination in Nigeria*, Kuru: National Institute for Policy and Strategic Studies.

Schatzl, L.H. (1969), *Petroleum in Nigeria*, Ibadan: Oxford University Press.

Seymour, I. (1980), *OPEC: Instrument of Change*, London: The Macmillan Press.

Shaw, T. M. and Olajide A. (eds) (1983), *Nigerian Foreign Policy: Alternative Perceptions and Projections*, London: The Macmillan Press.

Skeet, I. (1988), *OPEC: Twenty-Five Years of Prices and Politics*, Cambridge: Cambridge University Press.

Stern, E. (1991), *Adjustment and the Development Process*, Lecture Series No. 70, Lagos: The Nigerian Institute for International Affairs.

Summers, L.H. (1992), *The Challenge of Development: Some Lessons of History for Sub-Saharan Africa*, Lecture Series No. 69, Lagos: The Nigerian Institute for International Affairs.

Tiratsoo, E. N. (1984), *Oilfields of the World*, England: Scientific Press (Third Edition).

US Department of Energy (1979), *Report on the Petroleum Resources of the Federal Republic of Nigeria*, Foreign Energy Supply Assessment Program Series.

World Bank (1986), *Nigeria: Trade Policy and Export Development Loan*, Report and Recommendation of the President of the IBRD, 19 September.

—— (1983), *Nigeria: Macroeconomic Policies for Structural Change*, Report No.4506-UNI.

Journals, Annuals, and Periodicals

American Association of Petroleum Geologists Bulletin
Barrows: *IPI Data Service, Africa*
Barrows: *Offshore Petroleum Industry*
Barrows: *Petroleum Taxation and Legislation Report*
Barrows: *Basic Oil Laws & Concession Contracts, South & Central Africa*
BP Statistical Review of World Energy
BP Review of World Gas
Cedigaz News Report
Journal of Energy and Development
The Economist
Energy Compass

Energy Economics
Energy Economist
Energy Exploration and Exploitation
The Energy Journal (EJ)
Energy Policy
Financial Times (FT)
IEA: *Quarterly Oil Statistics & Energy Balances*
IMF: *International Financial Statistics*
IMF: *Balance of Payments Statistics*
International Gas Report (IGR)
International Petroleum Encyclopedia (IPE)
Lloyds Maritime Directory
Middle East Economic Survey (MEES)
Oil Daily Energy Compass
Oil & Gas Journal (O&GJ)
Oil and Gas Journal Databook
OPEC Annual Statistical Bulletin
OPEC Bulletin
OPEC Review
OPECNA News Service
Platts Oilgram News (Platts)
Platts Oil Price Handbook & Oilmanac
Petroconsultants, *World Petroleum Trends*
Petroleum Economist (PE)
Petroleum Review
Petroleum Intelligence Weekly (PIW)
Shell World
Statoil Magazine
United Nations: *Energy Statistics Yearbook*
Weekly Petroleum Argus (Argus)
World Bank, Africa Technical Unit, *Petroleum Industry Data Sheets: Sub-Saharan
    Africa*
World Bank, *Trends in Developing Economies*
World Debt Tables
World Gas Report
World Gas Intelligence

INDEX

Abacha government, 113, 130, 175
Aboyade commission, 105
Aburi agreement, 10
Addax, 136, 142
African Petroleum Producers'
    Association (APPA), 30
Agip, 19, 22, 44, 67–8, 71, 79, 86,
    91–2, 117, 148, 158, 162, 168,
    170–1, 176
agriculture, 183–4, 186–9
Alaska, 51
Algeria, 30, 173, 176
Amoco, 90
Angola, 30
Argentina, 118
Ashland Oil, 67–8, 74–5, 86, 117
Atlantic Basin, 1, 29, 51, 101
Attock, 140
Austria, 30

Babingida government, 7, 12–13, 30,
    104, 129, 163
Bechtel, 143, 175–6
Benin basin, 20
Benin, 31, 127
Benue basin, 20
Biafra war, 5, 9–11, 22, 46, 50, 69
BP, 9, 15, 19–20, 22–3, 46, 67, 70–
    2, 74–5, 90, 120, 138, 170
Brazil, 30, 118
British Gas, 20, 67–8
British National Oil Company
    (BNOC), 29, 102–3
Buhari government, 12, 23
'Buhari Incentives', 46, 51

Calabar refinery, 132, 143, 145
Cameroon, 31, 127, 146
Chad basin, 39
Chevron, 67–8, 72, 86–7, 90, 117,
    120, 136, 140, 142–3, 158, 168,
    177
Citibank, 172
Columbia Gas, 172

concessions, 19–22, 67–94
Conoco, 90
Consolidated Oil, 67
contracts,
    joint-venture, 67–73, 93
    production-sharing, 12, 16, 49,
    67–8, 74–8, 93–4, 202–3
    risk-service, 16, 68, 79
corruption, 7–8, 196
counter-trade, 12, 29–30, 54, 104–5,
    107
Crédit Lyonnais, 172
crude oil packages, 106
crude types, 56–9, 101
Curaçao, 140

debt burden, 2, 92, 104, 147, 184,
    192–6
Delta Steel Company, 165
Department of Petroleum Resources,
    25
Distrigas, 172–3
Dubri, 67, 86
Du Pont, 67, 90, 148
Dutch Disease, 183, 186

Eastern Nigerian Development
    Corporation, 164
economic recession, 52, 102, 118,
    121
economy (Nigerian), 183–97
Egypt, 31
Electricity Corporation of Nigeria,
    164
Elf, 67–8, 74–5, 79, 90–1, 117, 162,
    170–1, 176
Enagas, 172–3
Enel, 172–3
ERTOIL, 150
ethnic groups, 7
exports, 2, 117–23
exploration and development, 43–9
Exxon, 74–5

fiscal incentives, 2, 15, 17, 43–4, 46, 48, 73, 79–86, 93, 149
France, 30, 104, 120
fuel riots, 129, 142, 196
fuel shortages, 15, 127, 142, 144, 146, 150, 196

Gabon, 31
gas fields, 148, 159
  Bomu, 172
  Ibewa, 172
  Idu, 172
  Obagwi, 172
  Oshi, 172
  Soku, 172
  Ubeta, 172
Gaz de France, 172–3
global warming, 163–4
government expenditure, 185–9
government–oil company relations, 9, 92–4
Gowon, Colonel, 10
Gulf crisis 1990, 1, 11, 55–6, 109–10, 123, 192–3
Gulf Oil, 9, 19, 44, 50, 53, 70, 162, 168

Hong Kong Shanghai Banking Corporation, 172

IMF, 92, 128, 194, 196
Import-Export Bank, 174
industry, 189
investment, 1, 5, 13, 26, 86–92, 94, 177
Iran, 128
Iranian revolution, 11, 51, 72
Iraq, 103
Irikefe Commission, 24, 52–3
Ironsi, General, 10
Italy, 30, 120, 176
Ivory Coast, 31

Kaduna refinery, 104, 132–3, 138–40, 144

law, 15–19

Associated Gas Reinjection Decree (1979), 160, 163
Colonial Mineral Ordinance (1914), 16
Companies Decree (1968), 18
Mineral Oil Ordinance (1959), 17
Petroleum Decree (1969), 16, 18, 22, 68
Petroleum Profits Tax Ordinance (1959), 15–16
Petroleum Profits Tax (Amendment) Decree (1967), 17
Revenue Collection Edict (1967), 10
Liberia, 196
Libya, 17, 31
licences, 18–19
Lonrho, 143
LNG projects, 14, 91, 169–77, 197
Lukman, R., 30–1

Maraven, 140
Marc Rich, 142
Mexico, 51, 102
Middle East, 1, 16
Middle Eastern crudes, 11, 51
Ministry of Petroleum, 23
Mobil, 19–20, 46–8, 53, 67, 70–2, 74–5, 86–7, 91, 117, 142, 158, 162, 169
Mohammad, Murtala, 6

Napoil, 150
National Fertilizer Corporation of Nigeria (NAFCON), 165, 178
National Petroleum Investment Management Services (NAPIMS), 26
nationalization, 12, 18, 20, 22, 24, 68, 70–1
natural gas, 157–78, 205–6
  consumption, 165
  flaring, 157, 159–64, 177–8
  pipelines, 162, 165–7
  production, 159, 161
  projects, 167–9
  reserves, 157–8

utilization, 159–65, 176–8
    see also gas fields
Netherlands, 120
Niger, 127
Niger Delta, 20, 39–40, 85, 157–8
Nigermed, 150
Nigerian Electric Power Authority
    (NEPA), 164, 178
Nigerian Gas Corporation (NGC),
    26, 178
Nigerian LNG Project Co. (NLNG),
    172, 175
Nigerian National Oil Corporation
    (NNOC), 18
Nigerian National Petroleum
    Corporation (NNPC), 18, 20,
    47, 52–3, 67–94 passim, 104,
    109–23 passim, 129, 150, 158,
    168, 171, 175–6, 178, 202
    financial difficulties, 71, 94, 158
    structure, 22–8
    subsidiaries, 24, 26, 28
Nigerian Petroleum Development
    Company (NPDC), 20, 24, 26,
    59, 67
Nigus Petroleum, 79
North Sea crudes, 1, 12, 29, 51–2,
    56, 103
    production, 53, 118, 120 1
Norway, 29, 101, 103

Obasanjo government, 12
oil boom, 183
oil price shocks, 183, 190
oil production, 2, 11–15, 28, 49–56,
    85–6, 88–9, 102, 204
oil reserves, 40, 42–3, 46–9, 202
oil revenues, 8, 10, 30, 52, 91, 104,
    183–6
oilfields, 39–43, 49, 55
    Afam, 39, 159
    Afia, 90, 117
    Bomu, 39–40
    Delta South, 40
    Edikan, 90, 117
    Edop, 40, 87
    Ekpe, 40
    Ekiko, 48

Etoro-1, 47
Ewan, 140
Forcados Yorki, 40
Gbaran, 47
Ime, 90, 117
Imo River, 39
Iyak, 87
Koro Koro, 39
Meren, 40
Nembe Creek, 40
Odudu, 90, 117
Okan, 40, 50
Oloibiri, 39, 159
Omon-1, 48
Oredo, 59
Ubit, 87
Umuechem, 39
Yoho-1, 48
Ojukwu, Colonel, 10
OPEC, 1, 15–18, 22, 24, 28–31, 54,
    102–4
    production quotas, 12, 30, 52,
    54–6, 103, 106
Oso condensate project, 57, 62, 87,
    91, 169

Pan Ocean, 67–8, 70–1, 92
Petrobras, 104–5
petrochemical industry, 147 9
Petroleum Inspectorate, 23–5
petroleum products, 127–51, 177
    consumption, 131–2, 135
    pricing, 127–30, 178
    smuggling, 127–8, 132, 135,
    144, 150, 201–2
    subsidies, 127–30, 150, 178, 204
    supply and demand, 130–6
Petromed, 150
Phibro, 115
Phillips Oil, 20, 67–8, 86, 90, 117,
    148, 168, 170–1
pipelines, 50, 60–2, 143–6
Pipelines and Products Marketing
    Co. (PPMC), 143
political instability, 5–6, 11, 14
Port Harcourt refinery, 70, 132–3,
    135–8, 140–5,
prices, 29, 43–4, 51–2, 54, 80–4,

prices (*cont.*), 101–23
    see also petroleum products

Qatar, 176

refineries, 104
    problems, 127, 135–44, 149–51,
    204
resource mismanagement, 2, 7–8,
    201–2

Safrap, 9, 19, 22, 44, 69
Saudi Arabia, 17, 31, 106
Shagari government, 7, 24, 186, 206
Shell, 9, 15–16, 19, 22–3, 46–7, 53,
    67–8, 70–2, 74–5, 85–7, 90–2,
    120–1, 138, 158, 162, 168,
    170–3, 175–6
Shonekan interim government, 113,
    142, 151, 196
Sokoto basin, 39
South Africa, 70
Soviet Union, 102
Statoil, 20, 67, 74–5, 90, 103
storage, 60, 62, 121–3, 143–6
structural adjustment programme,
    128, 183–4, 189–93

Sun, 20, 67–8, 120
Sunray, 71

Tam-West, David, 30–1
tankers, 60, 62, 123, 146
taxation, 16–17, 46
Technimont, 148
Technip, 175
Tehran Agreement (1971), 17
Tenneco, 71
terminals, 50, 60, 121–3, 145
Texaco, 19, 67–8, 71, 87, 90, 92,
    117, 158, 162
Total, 104, 136, 142
trade, 101–23

United Kingdom, 101
United States, 51, 109, 117–120, 135

Venezuela, 16–17, 139–40

Warri refinery, 104, 132–3, 138,
    140, 144
Western Europe, 117–20
World Bank, 87, 148, 168, 176, 196